1979

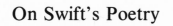

On Swift's Poetry

On Swift's Poetry

JOHN IRWIN FISCHER

A University of Florida Book
The University Presses of Florida
Gainesville / 1978

Library of Congress Cataloging in Publication Data

Fischer, John Irwin, 1940–
   On Swift's poetry.

   "A University of Florida book."
   Includes bibliographical references and index.
   1. Swift, Jonathan, 1667–1745—Poetic works.
   I.   Title.
   PR3728.P58F5   821'.5   77–12705
   ISBN 0–8130–0583–3

The University Presses of Florida is the
scholarly publishing agency for the
State University System of Florida.

TYPOGRAPHY BY CANON GRAPHICS
TALLAHASSEE, FLORIDA
PRINTED BY ROSE PRINTING COMPANY
TALLAHASSEE, FLORIDA

821.5
8977f

Acknowledgments

THIS BOOK has taken longer to write than is usual. In writing it, however, I have incurred more than common obligations. First, I am greatly indebted to the staffs of the following libraries: The University of Florida Library; The University of Miami Library; The Louisiana State University Library; The Ohio State University Library; The Widener, Houghton, Kennedy, and Fine Arts Libraries at Harvard University; The British Museum Library; The University of London Library; The University College English Library (London). Secondly, I am grateful to the Louisiana State University, which, by a variety of grants and favors, has made it possible for me to finish this book. Thirdly, I am grateful to the editors of the *Review of English Studies*, *Tennessee Studies in Literature*, and *Essays in Honor of Esmond Linsworth Marilla* for permission to include essays which they first published in somewhat different form. Finally, I am grateful to the following friends for helpful criticism and warm support: J. David Walker, Clifford Earl Ramsey III, J. Douglas Canfield, Michael J. Conlon, Larry Vonalt, Percy G. Adams, Jim Springer Borck, Nicholai Von Kreisler, James Babin, Roger and Jane Stilling, John J. W. Weaver, Dale Richardson, Herbert Rothschild, Jack Gilbert, and Joan Metcalfe.

Other debts are quite special: to Fred R. Fischer, to Estelle T. Fischer, to Panthea Reid Broughton, to Aubrey L. Williams, and to Judith Lee Sterling. I could not hope to express my obligations to these gifted and dear men and women.

86051

For My Parents

Contents

Introduction
"Je donne au diable . . ." 1
1. "Heaven and Cato both are pleas'd"
   The Early Odes 7
2. "Careful Observers may fortel the Hour"
   Occasional Poems, 1698–1710 55
3. "Left all below at Six and Sev'n"
   Cadenus and Vanessa 110
4. "Believe me *Stella*"
   The Poems to Esther Johnson 121
5. " 'In Princes never put thy Trust' "
   Verses on the Death of Dr. Swift 152
6. "*Caetera desiderantur*"
   On Poetry: A Rapsody 177
Conclusion 198
Index 203

Abbreviated Titles Used in Footnotes

All quotations of Swift's poetry in this book are from *The Poems of Jonathan Swift*, ed. Sir Harold Williams, 2d ed., 3 vols. (Oxford: Clarendon Press, 1958). This edition is regularly abbreviated in the footnotes as *Swift's Poems*. *The Prose Works of Jonathan Swift*, ed. Herbert Davis, 14 vols. (Oxford: Shakespeare Head Press, 1939–68) is abbreviated to *Swift's Prose*. *The Correspondence of Jonathan Swift*, ed. Sir Harold Williams, 5 vols. (Oxford: Clarendon Press, 1965) is abbreviated to *Swift's Correspondence*. *Journal to Stella*, ed. Sir Harold Williams, 2 vols. (Oxford: Clarendon Press, 1948) is noted by title only.

Introduction

"Je donne au diable . . ."

THOUGH HE TELLS IT as badly as he does every anecdote, Patrick Delany's story of a conversation between Swift in old age and his friend Thomas Sheridan is an especially significant and illuminating one. Apparently Swift had been talking violent politics for some time when he noticed that Sheridan was unmoved. Exasperated, he asked his friend "whether the corruption and villainy of men in power, did not eat his flesh, and exhaust his spirits? [Sheridan] answered, that in truth they did not: [Swift] then asked in a fury, why,—why,—how can you help it, how can you avoid it? His friend calmly replied, because I am commanded to the contrary. *Fret not thyself because of the ungodly.* This raised a smile."[1]

Swift's smile, I suspect, was genuine but wry—a wintry smile of self-recognition.[2] For the impasse at which the story points was familiar to him. Possessed of an immensely powerful personality, all his life he burned to judge absolutely of right and wrong among his fellow men—and generally he found them in the wrong. Thus, early in his career as a poet, he threatens to direct such lines against the bulk of mankind as would "stab" and "blast," "like

1. Patrick Delany, *Observations Upon Lord Orrery's Remarks on the Life and Writings of Dr. Jonathan Swift* (London: W. Reeve and A. Linde, 1754), pp. 148–49.

2. In his *Lemuel Gulliver's Mirror for Man* (Berkeley: University of California Press, 1968), W. B. Carnochan thought so, too. I note our agreement in this small detail because I am pleased to think we often agree in our general views about Swift.

1

daggers and like fire" (*Ode to Dr. William Sancroft*, 91).[3] And late
in his career he remarks of Walpole and his crew that, though he
laughs at them, he "would hang them if [he] cou'd" (*Epistle to a
Lady*, 170).

Simultaneously, however, Swift always recognized that individual righteousness gone too far (whether his own or not) became fundamental impiety. And he also knew that the consequences of such impiety were damnable misjudgment on the one
hand, and self-destruction on the other. That is why, in the
Epistle to a Lady, having confessed his readiness to hang men he
immediately ties his willfulness whimsically but directly to the
demonic: "*Deuce* is in you, Mr. *Dean*;/What can all this Passion
mean?" (181–82). And that is why, too, in the story cited above,
it is his own flesh and blood that Swift supposes to be consumed
by his anger.

Because he knew, then, that *saeva indignatio* lacerates first the
heart that supports it, Swift's lifelong task was to temper his
hubristic sense of righteousness with a standard of judgment
larger than himself. Only through such tempering, he knew, could
he transmute what was eccentric and potentially destructive in his
personality into powerful moral vision, and the chief effort of
almost all his works is to effect this tempering. Consequently,
these works have always seemed compellingly dramatic to their
readers. Comprising a series of apparently incompatible positions
finally harmonized, they achieve the status of mental and spiritual
events and thus defy any simple moralistic interpretation. Their
morality is in the tempering they achieve—it can be found no-
where else.

———

In maturity, Swift himself was acutely aware of the radically
dramatic character of his work and of those elements in him
which shaped that drama. He certainly knew his response to the
world was both singular and powerful, and he was proud of its
striking eccentricity. Thus, in *Verses on the Death of Dr. Swift*,
he boasts that he "To steal a hint was never known, / But what
he writ was all his own" (317–18). At the same time, however, he
understood the need to subscribe to a public vision of things, and
that is why he stole his boast to be original almost word for word

3. Parenthetical references after poetry quotations are line numbers.

from John Denham's elegy for Abraham Cowley, *On Mr. Abraham Cowley, his Death and Burial Among the Ancient Poets*. By this theft, of course, Swift does not really undercut his boast of originality. Instead, he makes of his boast itself a sort of mental drama, capturing in the tension between its varied truths the essential—and original—character of his work and thought.

As we have said, however, Swift was not born possessed of the dramatic originality he exhibits in these lines and claims for his works in general. Rather, his natural impulse was towards the eccentricity of a highly individualized righteousness. Necessarily, then, Swift's struggle to attain a poised tension between self and larger-than-self was one of extraordinary difficulty early in his career. And though he eventually came to master the achievement of moral vision through dramatic tension, the basic character of his task made its outcome always something less than certain.

Both the nature of Swift's early struggles and the character of his mature power to effect insight through drama can be seen with special clarity in his poetry; for in his poetry Swift consistently exhibits a greater willingness to expose the grounds of his own art than he does in his prose. Of course, in his earliest poems there is hardly any art to be exposed. Scarcely conscious of the elements of his own mind, Swift in his first odes is more often the victim of than an orchestrator to the nearly preconscious oppugnancy of those elements. Yet even in these early poems we can distinguish his efforts—primitive at first, then increasingly sophisticated—to bring out of the conflict between his own active will and his concurrent sense of human limitation a consciously dramatic statement that is the consequence of both. Thus, moving from the haphazard inconsistencies of the *Ode to the King* to that nicely balanced conflict between himself and his muse which is the real subject of the ode *Occasioned by Sir William Temple's Late Illness and Recovery*, we witness nothing less than the first and most basic formulation of Swift's art.

That this art, once formed, is capable of a wide variety of applications is what we discover—even as Swift did—in the astonishingly varied occasional poems which he wrote between 1698 and 1710. In their subjects these poems reflect much of the scope and excitement of Swift's life during the years he composed them: they range from the minutiae of Dublin domesticity to the sweeping significance of London itself. In their method, however, the poems exhibit a consistent though developing pattern; for in most of them Swift provocatively contrives his verse so that its subjects at once suffer and escape the force of his judgment on them. Of course, the particulars of this method vary to some extent from poem to poem so that no one of them can really stand for all. However, an especially happy example of the effect Swift achieves through this method can be instanced. In *The Humble Petition of Frances Harris*, Frances is clearly fashioned to stand as an example of the folly of cupidity; after all, she not only loses her petty fortune because she insists on counting it over and over again but she also apparently fails to recover it precisely because she is too anxious to do so. Nevertheless, though Frances's motives and actions all call abundantly for condemnation, the vitality with which Swift has endowed her finally prevents both him and us from making so harsh a judgment on her. Instead, faced with her verve, we grant Frances a sort of laughing sympathy—and this sympathy (against all expectation) she converts into a tiny theodicy. Turning judgment itself back on its ultimate source, she comically but significantly questions God's ways with man.

Of course, not all the occasional verse that Swift wrote between 1698 and 1710 turned out so well as Frances's petition. Often enough Swift found nothing to balance against the horror or anger some subject inspired in him. When this happened the effect on his verse was regularly dismal. For example, because it is unenlivened by any recognition of the limits of his own judgment, Swift's dark attack on Lord Cutts in *A Description of a Salamander* is both unjust and mechanically dull. Dull, too, I think, and mechanical in various ways are the first version of *Vanbrug's House*, the second version of *Baucis and Philemon*, and *The Virtues of Sid Hamet the Magician's Rod*. In each of these poems we feel Swift's lash but we miss his smile, and the results, while unpleasant, are neither powerful nor illuminating.

Unhappily, much the same can be said of all of Swift's poems which in any way deal with sexual love. To be sure, Swift did see well enough that the propensity to turn women into goddesses and love into religion must necessarily end in the degradation of women, love, and religion. What Swift did not see, however, and could not see, is that the propensity to effect this transformation arises from precisely that inability to value sexual love which he himself exhibits. Unable to trust physical passion and unwilling to grant its ability to enrich human life, Swift consistently failed to dramatize the possibility that sex, like every other human desire, may eventuate in either base or virtuous conduct. Instead, all his life Swift advised men to found their passions on sense and wit, thus absurdly admonishing them to recreate physical love in reason's name. At his best, in *Cadenus and Vanessa* and a few other poems, he clearly sensed that something was wrong with this advice. Unfortunately, he never discovered what it was.

On almost any other topic, however, Swift does infinitely better. For despite his inability to posit sexuality as a good in itself, he possessed a remarkable gift for seeing possibilities in far less attractive subjects. Thus, though doomed by his own vision always to see the world darkly, he was yet able to draw light from that darkness in most of his mature poetry. For example, in his poems to Stella he teaches his dearest friend that in the very corruption of her flesh there is not only much moral instruction but also a strong hope for immortality. Again, in his verses on his own death he instructs all of us how he and we may transform our shared inclination for evil into virtuous conduct. Finally, in *The Legion Club*, he bravely exploits for our edification his own incipient degeneration.

Of course, none of these poems is in any way Pollyanna-like. For along with their power to educe good out of ill, each of these poems exhibits the same acerbity of spirit that is explicit in Swift's epistolary remark to Gay that "The world is wider to a Poet than to any other Man, and new follyes and Vices will never be wanting any more than new fashions."[4] This acerbity seasons Swift's verse throughout, and permits us, after him, to see anew the possibility for value in the topics he treats.

Finally, however, perhaps the chief value of Swift's poetry is not what it tells us about its subject at all, but rather what it shows us about its author. For other poetry, far less powerful than Swift's, can convince us that death has its uses and that even vice may be spun into so fine a thing as verse. But no other canon I know demonstrates so strikingly the ability of a human spirit actually to transform its very character through art and thus to transcend itself. Tempted constantly by man's folly and vice first to judge the world and then despair, Swift instead makes of

4. *Swift's Correspondence*, 3:360.

his verse successive occasions to judge and laugh, judge and hope, judge and trust, and in brief, to judge himself. Thus in his poetry Swift really achieves that feat which, in his letter to Gay, he claims to be capable of achieving. He does give to the devil—who is its source—that which he recognizes as demonic in himself. "Je donne au diable the wrong notion that *Matter* is exhausted." And because he does reject despair, he finds in himself and for us that special liberty which he claims only God and poets know—"an infinity of space to work in."[5]

5. Ibid.

1

"Heaven and Cato both are pleas'd—"

The Early Odes

ANYONE WHO HAS EXERCISED himself in an attempt to understand those six involuted encomiastic odes which apparently are the earliest of Swift's surviving literary productions[1] will immediately grant the justice of Swift's own judgment on their style: "Igad, I cannot write anything easy to be understood thô it were but in praise of an old shooo."[2] Still, though no one who has read these poems either has or could have claimed that they are elegant, neither has any good reader found them wholly worthless. At worst, readers have come away from the odes impressed with their considerable energy. At best, sensitive readers have found in the poems primitive but prophetic beginnings to Swift's literary career.[3]

1. For references to possible earlier but now lost satiric verse see Herbert Davis, *Jonathan Swift: Essays on His Satire and Other Studies* (New York: Oxford University Press, 1964), pp. 171–72. For arguments that the anonymous poem "A Description of Mother Ludwell's Cave" ought to be considered part of Swift's early canon see John Middleton Murry, *Jonathan Swift: A Critical Biography* (London: J. Cape, 1954), pp. 45–48, and also Joseph Horrell, *Collected Poems of Jonathan Swift*, 2 vols. (Cambridge: Harvard University Press, 1958), 1:381.

2. *Swift's Correspondence*, 1:10.

3. See, for example, Irvin Ehrenpreis, *Swift: The Man, his Works, and the Age* (London: Methuen, 1962–), 1:109–41; Ronald Paulson, "Swift, Stella, and Permanence," *ELH* 27 (December 1960):298–314; Kathryn Harris, " 'Occasions so few': Satire as a Strategy of Praise in Swift's Early Odes," *MLQ* 31 (March 1970):22–37; and Robert W. Uphaus, "From Panegyric to Satire: Swift's Early Odes and *A Tale of a Tub*," *TSLL* 13 (Spring 1971):55–70.

The response to these poems suggested in this chapter can be stated simply enough: I believe that, seen as a group, they exhibit Swift's progress out of a proud and solipsistic idealism towards a mental stance which can variously be called dramatic or existential, skeptical or Christian, but which, however it is called, recognizes in human uncertainty the only possible ground of human wisdom. This progress is not, obviously, a matter of the simple accretion of knowledge; rather, it is a spiritual journey. Neither is this progress one which Swift consciously undertook, or even wished to undertake; rather it is one which he found inevitable. Beginning with an outrageously inflated ideal of human possibility, an ideal founded on and driven by pride, Swift attempted to articulate this ideal within the most exalted short verse form he knew, the Pindaric ode. Because, however, he was finally too proud to lie about either his own experience or the experiences of others, his attempt led him back to that knowledge of human frailty and human need which, had he been minded to do so, he might have discovered earlier than he did in Pindar's verse itself or in Cowley's imitation of it.

That Swift read Cowley's pindarics before he wrote his own is an old story, of course, but he did not read them well. He borrowed from them words, lines, techniques, and even something of a vision. But he borrowed with an ingenuousness so tainted by pride that in the earliest of his odes the sum effect of his borrowing is perfectly caught in the boyish hubris of his remark that though he could not easily please himself yet "when I writt what pleases me I am Cowley to my self and can read it a hundred times over."[4]

If, however, Swift took more from Cowley than he really understood, what he took had life. Engrafted, even crudely, in his own verses, it bore a hybrid fruit there. Thus the questions Swift's odes progressively raise are questions first in Cowley and have their roots in Pindar. To understand the answers Swift finally makes to these questions, it is worthwhile to review their initial contexts and the answers they stimulated there.

Unfortunately, Pindar is difficult for modern readers. To begin with, the heart of his verse is his celebration of athletic prowess, and that in itself is foreign to us. We are accustomed to think of athletic events, no matter how highly publicized, as interruptions

4. *Swift's Correspondence*, 1:9.

in the flow of life, not as its center. This is because we are willing to concede that an activity is part of the serious business of life only if that activity is undertaken for some purpose other than itself. Thus we work in order to make money, make money in order to procure goods, procure goods in order to sustain life, and go on in this way perpetually assigning significance to each activity on the basis of its relationship to the next.

Pindar does not do this; that is why he has something to tell us. Against our penchant for discovering the significance of our activities and of our lives in ends other than themselves, he brings the force of ultimate questions. "What is a man?" Pindar asks. "Creatures of a day," he answers. "What is a man not. A dream of a shadow/Is our mortal being" (Pythian VIII).[5] Obviously, this dream cannot understand the dreamer of whom it is but a projection. Thus of the gods, Pindar insists, we may know that they exist and work their purposes in the affairs of men, but we can neither predict those purposes,

> For no man born of earth has ever yet
> Found a trustworthy sign
> From heaven above, what future days may bring
> > (Olympian XII),

nor judge of them by their effects: "Let me keep utter silence concerning what Zeus does not prefer." In the estimation of Pindar, then, we live in a dumb universe.[6] If the gods are gracious to us, so much the better; if they are not, it is futile to ask why. That is why Pindar never commiserates with the real wretchedness of those who lose in the games; such commiseration would be impertinent. More important, that is also why the games mean everything to Pindar. In a dumb universe, all a man can do is try, knowing that if his struggles produce a victory, the victory must pay itself.

That is not enough. Even Pindar, for all his austerity, knows it is not. If we were gods, it would be enough; our essence would

5. Geoffrey S. Conway, trans., *The Odes of Pindar* (London: J. M. Dent and Sons, Ltd., 1972).
6. The translation of this fragment is by Gilbert Norwood. For a discussion of the fragment and of its relationship to another which is quoted in Plato's *Gorgias* see Norwood's *Pindar* (Berkeley and Los Angeles: University of California Press, 1945), pp. 55–56.

answer perfectly to our existence and we could identify ourselves like Yahweh in Exodus by saying "I Am Who I Am." But we are not gods, and in our imperfection our hearts desire significance for our acts beyond the acts themselves. That is why Pindar celebrates the prowess of a victor in the games, why, in fact, he is paid to do so. Men, he knows, need what he provides—his song answering to their acts—if they are to approach, even momentarily, the wholly perfect significance of the gods.

Finally, then, though the contest, the agon, is all important for Pindar, it is insufficient in itself. Part—and perhaps the richest part—of its significance is in our own remembrance of it, in the new place it wins for us in the hearts and on the lips of men, and in the place it may, just may, bring us in the "Halls of the Blessed." Thus man, in Pindar's verse, is potentially as fragmented a being as he is for any of us. All the questions we usually ask lie in embryo in Pindar: why does one man win in the games and another lose, why is fame so fickle, why do the gods appear so often to give good for ill and ill for good? Pindar, with a patience that sometimes seems wise and sometimes does not, refuses to ask these questions—or even murmur about them. But Cowley, coming to them as Pindar's first serious English imitator since Jonson, does murmur.

More significant than anything else—much more significant than his alteration of Pindar's metrics—Cowley's willingness to murmur against fate and to ask questions of the unknowable gods distinguishes his verse from the verse of his model. Where Pindar was silent, supposing the gods and their reasons to be of a different order entirely from ours, there Cowley aimed the very titles of some of his most characteristic pindarics, writing directly on *Destiny*, *The Resurrection*, *Life*, and *Life and Fame*. Even the footnotes that Cowley supplied for his pindarics (footnotes themselves are an incredible oddity in a Pindaric vision) are stuffed with philosophic lore and bear continuous testimony to his desire to educe answers from what Pindar regarded as the ineffability of things.

Unfortunately, it happened often enough that Cowley's persistent questioning turned up nothing at all, with the result that the worst of his pindarics are patched up out of brave pathos and shrill humility and impress us as being in everything the very reverse of Pindar's majesty. Thus, as the conclusion of his ode *To Dr. Scarborough*—a poem in which he has praised Scarborough's ability to dispose his medical art so as to shore up our frail nature—Cowley turns to consider the sad inevitability of Scarborough's own death in a few lines which Pope might later have included as exemplary of that variety of the bathetic which he called "the Infantine." "Ah, learned *friend*," Cowley remarks,

> it grieves me, when I think
> That *Thou* with all thy *Art* must dy
> As certainly as *I*.[7]   (94–96)

Of course, the trouble with this remark is that the grief which Cowley claims to feel is not conveyed by it. Consequently, Cowley's shocked recognition of the mere fact that both he and his friend are mortal must strike us as being exceedingly simpleminded. Nevertheless, childish as these lines are, they are so precisely because Cowley tried and failed to capture in them an emotional and intellectual response adequate to bestow a decorum of meaning on the sad limitations of our being. The attempt would not have been made by Pindar at all; thus he could not fail at it. Cowley failed at it often, but not always.

Obviously, as a Christian, Cowley possessed a fund of belief not available to Pindar, and in his best odes he found ways to release that belief with sufficient emotional validity to grace the vagaries of human life with significance. To my mind, the most remarkable instance of his ability to do this occurs in that pindaric he entitled, simply, *Brutus*. This poem was written in 1655, under especially difficult circumstances. From 1648 through early 1655 Cowley functioned as an agent of, and sometimes a spy for, England's exiled royalty. Despite his considerable service, however, he was never, temperamentally, a good party man. Rather, he remained too fond of peace, too much committed to the broad ideals of Christian humanism, and too flexible in his response to the world to suit the taste of his less imaginative colleagues. Consequently, by the spring of 1655, the time of his arrest as a Royalist spy in London, he found himself in the painful position

7. Quotations of Cowley's poetry are from *Poems: Abraham Cowley, 1656* (Menston, Yorkshire: The Scolar Press, 1971).

of being distrusted by both sides because he could not, in truth, wholly subscribe to either. In this dilemma, he could neither suffer his imprisonment gladly nor give up that commitment to royalty the renunciation of which would free him. Thus, more than Cromwell's prisoner, he was his own.

How well Cowley the man responded to this dilemma is not, of course, finally knowable. But that Cowley the poet responded to it satisfactorily on at least one occasion is demonstrable: in *Brutus* Cowley transformed that disparity between his broad perception of the world and others' narrow perception of it from an imprisoning dilemma to a liberating recognition. To put it as simply as possible, in *Brutus* Cowley told the best truth he knew, knew as he told it that it would be misunderstood, but knew, too, that the misunderstanding would at once confirm the truth he told and help set him free.

Modern interpretation of *Brutus* perfectly illustrates the problem Cowley had in speaking to his contemporaries. For even now, the poem is usually read (with or without sympathy) as Cowley's sop to his captors. Thus, once readers note the obvious analogy between Rome's virtuous regicide and England's king-killing Cromwell, they immediately transfer Cowley's hearty praise of Brutus to the Protector and register the entire poem as illustrative either of Cowley's political treachery or of his new but "passionate support of Cromwell's government."[8] In fact, however, *Brutus* is not about politics in the usual sense at all. Rather, it is about the limits of human judgment on the one hand, and the human possibilities implicit in suffering on the other.

Of course, as he heaped his praises on Brutus, Cowley could not be unaware how his Puritan captors would read them. And it was to his advantage that those captors weigh his poem as a renunciation of the Royalist party; indeed, the fact that they did so helped to secure his release. For all that, however, *Brutus* is not a dishonest poem. In it Cowley tells his captors as plainly as they can be told that their judgment, like all human judgment, is fallible. He does this by assigning to Brutus (as a surrogate for Cromwell) the keenest mind, soundest heart, and purest motives imaginable and then insisting that with all these gifts and achievements Brutus, in killing Caesar, but cleared the way to

8. James G. Taaffe, *Abraham Cowley* (New York: Twayne Publishing Co., 1972), pp. 68–69.

power for "the false Octavius and the wild Antony." No warning could be more explicit than this. Yet Cowley's contemporaries missed it. We have missed it. And Cowley, long trapped between armed absolutists, almost certainly knew it would be missed.

Indeed, it is Cowley's awareness not only that his warning would be missed but that the best of men almost always fail at what they attempt that is finally the real subject of his poem. It is a subject that Cowley—imprisoned himself and misunderstood —could express with force; thus there is in the opening lines of the final stanza a nearly Pindaric sense of the indifference with which the cosmos meets man's hopes and aspirations. "What joy," Cowley asks,

> can *humane things* to us afford,
> When we see perish thus by odde events,
> *Ill men*, and wretched *Accidents*,
> The best *Cause* and best *Man* that ever drew a *Sword*?
>   (64–67)

If, however, Cowley's question is Pindaric, the answer he makes to it is not. For while Pindar, confronted with such a question, could presumably preserve a sense of human meaning only by insisting that Brutus's virtue must pay itself, Cowley, drawing on both his sense of tragedy and his sense of Christianity, can afford to let virtue go.

> What can we say but thine own *Tragick Word*,
> That *Virtue*, which had worship been by thee
> As the most solid *Good*, and greatest *Deitie*,
> By this fatal Proof became
> An *Idol* only, and a *Name*.   (71–75)

Cowley can afford to do this, not because he does not care for virtue, and certainly not because he is willing to abandon the possibility of human meaning altogether, but because, moving beyond Pindar, he is able to recognize in defeat itself—Pindar's nemesis—the chief source of human meaning. Thus, the final lines of *Brutus* are celebratory, but they celebrate a defeat rather than a victory. For it is in defeat, Cowley asserts, that Brutus found himself and learned, through suffering, who he was. And, Cowley concludes, had Brutus, so educated, lived but a little longer he would have understood that drama at the Cross where God taught man not only that his own salvation is inextricably bound with suffering but that even God Himself, come among men, must endure pain to become Who He is.

> A few Years more, so soon hadst thou not dy'ed,
> Would have confounded *Humane Virtues* pride,
> And shew'd thee a *God crucified*.   (84–86)

These last lines, I think, are a high point in Cowley's Pindaric art. They are also a piece of significant bravery. For had Cromwell read and understood them, he would have found in them no compliment. Indeed, insisting as they do on the ultimate inefficacy of the sword, they must surely have stung him. They might also have freed him, however; for the knowledge they impart is liberating. But engaged in refounding by force Christ's Kingdom among men, Cromwell doubtless had no time to be reminded of what he must certainly have known: that the Kingdom he sought was always within him, available if but accepted, but available no other way.

There is a grand irony here, of course. But it is an irony neither Cromwell and his party nor the king and his were in any position to appreciate. For they had absorbed all the right between them and staked the meaning of their lives on the victorious outcome of their causes. Rather, it was Cowley who could see the irony. Because he was lost between Royalist and Puritan, distrusted by both, and so battered by events that he often doubted the meaning of life itself, he came sometimes to grasp that freedom which is implicit in Christ's crucifixion: not a freedom from suffering but a freedom to discover possibility and meaning in suffering. At such moments, aware that yearning to be understood and being misunderstood are ubiquitous in the human condition, Cowley could wield his wisdom with something very near gaiety. Thus, in *Brutus* Cowley renders unto Cromwell the truth that Cromwell needs, that he will either neglect or mistake, and that yet may set a poet free.

———

Swift, coming to Cowley's pindarics as a young man, imbibed from them almost all that was in them, both good and bad, and of

course, his indiscriminate readiness to do this is a mark of his
own poetic immaturity. It hardly needs to be said that both the
self-indulgent and uneasy posturing of Cowley's *Destiny* and
the lamentable bathos of the ode *To Dr. Scarborough* have their
counterparts in Swift's early verse, for in large part it is for these
unhappy qualities that his odes have met with, at best, interested
disapprobation. But what does need to be said is that the profound wisdom that Cowley brilliantly realized in *Brutus* and
more conventionally achieved in poems such as *Life* and *The
Plagues of Egypt* is sometimes visible in Swift's early odes as
well. Indeed, what makes Swift's early odes interesting is his
struggle to realize this wisdom in them, and the special cast that
his peculiar difficulties bestow upon that struggle.

From almost the first line of his first ode, Swift's early verse is
embattled, caught between two competing visions of the world
and able to realize neither of them fully. On the one hand, Swift
conceives of the world in his odes in much the same way that
Pindar did before him, as a flat empty ground on which such
meaning as there is must be both of our own manufacture and for
our own consumption. But on the other hand, Swift also senses
and suggests that our lives signify beyond themselves and that if it
is true that we are no more than dreams and shadows, the limits
of our certainty and of our being are nevertheless meaningful and
may be made to yield up richness.

In Swift's first ode, *Ode to the King*, these two visions are
particularly distinct. In fact, the *Ode to the King* cannot finally be
read as one poem at all; rather, it is two partially completed and
very different poems, continuously intertwined and with a common subject. That subject, of course, is King William of Orange,
and in one way only do Swift's two treatments of him present him
similarly: neither is an attempt to make him actually alive for us.
Rather, in both treatments of him Swift attempts to tell us what
William means—which is why, in fact, he never really does.

The split in Swift's poem, as well as its excessive talkiness, is
apparent in even its opening lines:

> *Sure* there's some Wondrous Joy in *Doing Good*;
>   Immortal Joy, that suffers no Allay from Fears,
>   Nor dreads the Tyranny of Years,
> By none but its Possessors to be understood:
>   Else where's the Gain in being *Great*?

On the one hand, these lines point backwards towards a traditional and easy distinction. Generations of moralists have urged that goodness is to be preferred before greatness since goodness is more likely to produce both public and private happiness. But on the other hand, these lines press the conventional moralists' distinction well beyond its usual limits. Insisting that greatness is essentially worthless and that the delight of doing good is self-dependent and eternal, these lines actually transmute the moralists' traditional preference for doing God's will rather than man's into an argument which offers the possibility of a real human autonomy. Under cover, then, of presenting a traditional vision of man, these lines suggest a far more radical one.

It is easy enough to see which of these two visions Swift himself preferred; all the enthusiasm of his ode is focused in its portrait of William as an independently meaningful being. Consequently, as his poem develops, Swift generates a frightening problem in it. Elevating active goodness above the approbation or disapprobation of those for whom the good is done, he obscures the distinction between the will to do good and pure will alone. Thus by the third stanza, without any apparent sense of the violence he is doing, he parallels the achievements of King William, his model of active goodness, with the achievements of mighty Tamburlaine, a prime Renaissance model of absolute willfulness. And through the remainder of his poem, he continues to perpetrate, in a variety of ways, this fundamental confusion of virtue with power.

If, however, Swift is distressingly willing to sacrifice the meaning of goodness at the altar of human autonomy, he is not willing finally to sacrifice the meaning of meaning itself. He does come dangerously close to doing this, though. For seeking to find or build in William's character a self-dependence so total that William can carry his meaning wholly in himself, Swift creates in his king a being whom generations of readers have rightly found to be wholly nonreferential and hence incomprehensible. Stuffed full of meaning as an egg is of meat, Swift's William, like an egg, is also a perfectly blank oval when viewed from outside.

Happily, however, from the outset of his poem, Swift recognizes this problem. The meaning of a perfect being, he knows, like the joy of such a being, can be understood by "none but its Possessors." Of course, knowing this, Swift nevertheless wants to understand William. After all, to understand and meaningfully to praise him is the point of Swift's ode. That is why the question Swift asks in the first stanza of his poem,

> What can the Poet's humble Praise?
> What can the Poet's humble Bays?
> . . . .
> Add to the Victor's Happiness?   (7–8, 11),

is much more than simply a rhetorical compliment. Indeed, at the heart of this question is the most serious of human inquiries: how may men reach out to, touch, praise, hold, and finally possess that which is perfectly meaningful?

Of course, the answer is that they cannot, and they must make their meaning out of that. But, apparently, Swift was not ready to know this answer as he composed the *Ode to the King*. For faced by the dilemma that William's incomprehensible autonomy raises, Swift covertly compromises that autonomy. Thus the *Ode to the King* exhibits a sort of doublethink—it is two simultaneous but very different poems. The subject of the first is a king who is beyond death, fear, and even time itself, but who is unknowable. The subject of the second is a king whose deeds and character are significant precisely because they are referable to a providential design that is not only beyond his control but beyond his very understanding.

Indeed, it is probably more accurate to say that the subject of Swift's second poem is not William at all, but rather the existence of Providence as demonstrated by William's victories. For in the second poem, William's successes are not really his: in his battlefield victories he is protected and guided, though without his knowledge, by a particular providence in the form of a destroying angel; in his political successes he but profits from a general providence which destroys his foes, not because they are his foes, but because they are evil. Thus, the King William of Swift's second poem is no force, no Tamburlaine, no controller of death, but only a man whose force is wholly dependent on divine aid. As such he is enormously significant; his goodness and his success taken together illustrate the existence of a providence benevolently concerned in the affairs of men. But as such he is also terribly frail, for there is no guarantee on earth that his virtue must continue to invite divine aid, and that heaven must always work in ways that are humanly comprehensible.

That, of course, is just the dilemma Swift did not want to face in the *Ode to the King* and, to avoid it, he absurdly sought to make William's goodness at once self-dependent and significant. But the dilemma cannot be avoided, at least by any man who thinks at all. Because Swift sought to avoid it in this poem, we properly condemn his work. As we dismiss the poem, however, we ought to remember that it is not easy for any man to face the truth that he is not his own destiny. Further, to the degree that a man is sensitive to those lacunae in experience which suggest the world may be as meaningless and empty as evil itself, he will feel his helplessness as pain. Swift was especially sensitive to such lacunae, as evidenced by the almost physical rage he directed against those apparent traces of the world's meaninglessness which he found in the prosperity of its Scottish hypocrites, in the perverse hopelessness of wretched Ireland, and in the power of such kings as Louis XIV. Pressed by such rage, it is small wonder that Swift found it difficult to acquiesce in the ways of a providence so evidently, frighteningly, infuriatingly beyond him. Such acquiescence must cost the whole force of his personality and thus could be motivated only by the necessity of preserving that personality itself. That is why Swift's acquiescence, when it comes, is such a profound and revelatory act. It is painful, for it at once exposes the human condition as it really is, and dissolves in scorn all the tinsel and trappings with which we usually hide ourselves from ourselves. But it is also transfigurative, for it teaches a way, not Tamburlaine's, to achieve the self-dependence Tamburlaine sought.

Even in this first poem, in which Swift struggles hard not to admit that human frailty which must be admitted, he catches a hint, I think, of that better way. This happens in the third stanza of the ode, as Swift is drawing his comparison between William and Tamburlaine. The comparison rests on William's remarkable control of death, a control that Swift compares to Tamburlaine's conquest of his archenemy, Bajazet:

> The Tyrant Death lay crouching down,
> Waiting for Orders at his Feet,
>   Spoil'd of his Leaden Crown;

He trampled on this Haughty Bajazet,
Made him his Footstool in the War,
And a Grim Slave to wait on his Triumphal Car.   (39–44)

Of course, as we have already noted, this comparison obscures a proper distinction between human willfulness and human goodness. But in the nobly militant language of the comparison we may hear, perhaps, something more than Swift's pride and confusion. For among the echoes in these lines I think there may be an echo of a famous and prophetic passage from Luke: "Till I make thy enemies thy footstool" (Luke 20:43). If so, then this fragmentary memory of the Ascension points the lines finally towards the history of a Man greater far than Tamburlaine or William, a Man who conquered death by dying.

This last suggestion may be premature, however. In his fourth ode, *To Dr. William Sancroft*, Swift clearly felt and could state something of the paradox in "the way that leads to Christ." There is, however, no firm statement of such a paradox in the *Ode to the King*, only perhaps the hint of one. The development of that so faint hint into the full-blown drama of the *Ode to Sancroft* occurs in Swift's two intermediary poems, the *Ode to the Athenian Society*, and the *Ode to Sir William Temple*. Primarily, this development occurs because in these two poems Swift, though grudgingly, proves willing to accept the finitude of his subjects. However, his response to that finitude differs sharply in the two poems, and that difference makes it necessary that we notice each poem separately.

Unfortunately, once one has read Samuel Johnson's *Life of Swift*, it is almost impossible to read the *Ode to the Athenian Society* without remembering that according to Johnson it was this poem that elicited from Dryden the observation "Cousin Swift, you will never be a poet." This remark is certainly apocryphal, however, and funny as it is, it is almost a pity that Johnson chose to preserve it and thus to make the task of reading Swift's ode more difficult than it needs to be. That task is already hard enough, since there is a good deal in the ode that is distracting, silly, or downright perverse.

To begin with, Swift's subject is hopelessly overburdened with his praise of it, for the Athenian Society never amounted to much more than an ambitious Grub Street venture. In March of 1691, John Dunton, hack and printer, began to publish *The Athenian Mercury*, a periodical remembered today only because it happened to be one of *The Tatler*'s immediate precursors and because it included, as part of its original format, a section devoted to answering questions from its readers. Partly because of its salacious possibilities, this section proved to be the most popular in the *Mercury*; and Dunton, alive to the main chance, first expanded the section and then sought out men able and willing to answer anonymously the more serious and complex questions he received. One of these occasional contributors was Swift's patron, Sir William Temple, and thus Swift, anxious enough to see himself in print, found himself composing a poem of praise for a society that was not only more heterogeneous than Athenian but finally no society at all.

Further, if Swift's choice of subject was bad, his treatment is worse. Judging by his extraordinary use of personae, he does not seem to know even who he is. Thus in the first line of the ode, having supposed England's continental war to be comparable with Noah's Flood, he imagines himself a "dovemuse" seeking for poetic subjects amidst a watery waste. Obviously, this characterization is not happily imagined. In the third stanza, however, Swift adds two worse inventions. First, anxious to call attention to the fact that he has already composed an ode to King William, he nominates himself, with more paradox than sense, "an (almost) Virgin Muse." Next, struck with the disparity between himself and his subject, he supposes himself a fly, buzzing about the Athenians' wit. By the end of the third stanza, then, Swift has passed through a series of unlikely transformations only to end pure fool at last.

Yet bad as all this is, there is something here. Swift's choice of subject is unfortunate, but what he makes of it is interesting. Similarly, though his manipulation of personae is awkward, it is at the same time revealing. Thus if we can put aside our prejudice against what is badly written, we can learn something in this poem about the development of Swift's mind.

To begin with, it is clear enough that Swift's impulse in this poem was to make of the Athenians what he had already made of King William, a model of human autonomy. Thus he makes great play with the paradox of the Athenians' famous anonymity, styling them, again and again, "Ye Great Unknown," and insisting, as he had done before, "That all the Praises [men] can give,"

> By which some fondly boast they shall for ever live,
> Won't pay th' *Impertinence* of being known.   (150–53)

But though Swift wants to reaffirm in this poem the same consolatory fiction of human independence that patterns the *Ode to the King*, he is also much more aware than he has been of the uncomfortable limits of that fiction. Will he, nil he, he must admit at the conclusion of his poem that the works of the Athenians, like all mortal things, are finally subject to what he calls "the long and gloomy Night" (282). More significantly still, he also recognizes that insofar as he can successfully pretend that the Athenians are self-dependent and that they have escaped what Wordsworth later called "the burden of the mystery . . . of all this unintelligible world," precisely so far the Athenians become unintelligible to him.

In fact, it is Swift's recognition that the self-dependent Athenians of his imagination are unintelligible to him that is at the center of the great muddle he makes of his personae at the beginning of the poem. This is not to say that the protean shape-shifting that carries Swift from "dovemuse" to "(almost) Virgin Muse," to fly "buzzing about Wit" represents a controlled artistic reaction to the human dilemma that what is perfect in itself is necessarily blank to us. It is only to say that the whirl of personae at the beginning of the poem is Swift's rather desperate attempt to define an identity for himself with respect to the Athenians, an attempt which leads him back to the discovery that (to put it in his terms) his dove-muse cannot quite hear the Athenians' "heavenly Song," or that (to put it in Shakespearean terms) compared to the gods "we are as flies."

As we have already remarked, this is a painful discovery. Further, it is a difficult discovery because it is possible to believe comfortably that one has made it and yet not understand it at all. Thus, even as Swift composed the *Ode to the King* he presumably thought himself a Christian and would have professed belief in Providence and trust in its ways. As we have seen, however, his belief did not prevent him from attempting to transform King

William into a sort of Baal figure, independent as God, yet also ours. So, similarly, in the *Ode to the Athenian Society*, Swift makes a belief in Providence the chief virtue of the Athenians, and he extols their heroic struggle against those "Wondrous *Refiners* of Philosophy, / Of Morals and Divinity" who

> By the new *Modish System* of reducing all to sense,
>   Against all Logick and concluding Laws,
>   Do own th' Effects of Providence,
>   And yet deny the Cause.   (105–10)

But even as Swift renders this praise to the Athenians he is himself—in his very elevation of them, in his bathetic mourning for their inevitable passing, and in his obtrusive ire against most of mankind—engaged in a desperate struggle against the incomprehensible way of the world. Continually insisting that he is "content" to "believe in much he ne're can hope to see" (134), hinting, even, that he may believe in some form of a doctrine of election, he simultaneously expresses—with no apparent sense of contradiction—his overwhelming outrage at everything in the world he cannot understand.

This is absurd, of course, but we must be careful to locate its absurdity properly or we shall simply duplicate it. If we laugh lightly at Swift's outrage at human folly, or shrug at his mourning for the inevitable mortality of human good, we miss the point. For Swift is not wrong in his outrage or in his sorrow; he is wrong in his understanding of what a trust in Providence means and in the kind of "contentment" such a trust brings. In this ode, he is still seeking simple peace; he wants men either to be good-natured flies (as he claims he is) or alternatively to be wholly as the gods are. But men are neither flies nor gods; they are rather creatures with but being enough to know they are not Being itself. That is the truth which, against his will and through repeated contradictions, Swift's pen keeps scratching out about himself. And like all men, until he accepts that truth and acquiesces in the inconclusive struggle that is his birthright, he can neither trust the God that made him so nor be contented.

In the *Ode to Sir William Temple*, Swift makes a marked advance in his understanding of the terms on which human contentment is possible. Of course, we cannot say exactly how this advance occurred, since the way in which a mind comes to know itself is a mystery of a kind with the ancient problem of the chicken and the egg. About the best we can do is to remark that by choosing for the first time a subject whose life is intimately known to him, Swift both indicates some awareness that the meaning of a life must be sought in it, and makes possible the sort of search which terminates in that awareness.

For all its considerable achievement, however, the *Ode to Temple* begins with a treatment of man's fall from Eden which is startling in its naïveté. It is a little hard to provide a satisfactory account of this treatment, because Swift himself is not entirely open in it, but the following summary is not unfair, I think, to its basic thrust. According to Swift, before the Fall man possessed the greatest of kingdoms, which was "Virtue" itself. Because of Adam's rebellion, however, man was deposed and his kingdom shattered. Consequently, none of Adam's progeny ever has possessed more than a shred of his original inheritance. But this unhappy consequence is not a necessary effect of the Fall. Rather, men might yet rule their proper empire. They need only renounce a number of unhappy delusions regarding knowledge. What these delusions are, however, Swift never tells us with any exactness. Instead, he simply argues that if men would but conduct themselves with "common Breeding, common Sense," and disabuse themselves of the satanic heresy "that Knowledge forfeits all Humanity," then all would go well enough.

It is difficult to imagine a more unsatisfactory account than this of the significance inherent in the story of the Fall. But though Swift's version is fundamentally naïve, it does possess a certain perverse ingenuity. Therefore, in order to see what Swift was about in producing it, it is useful to remind ourselves with what simplicity and to what effect the story of the Fall is narrated in Genesis. To begin with, we ought to remember that in the Genesis narration there is no attempt at all to account for the grounds of man's fall; it is merely assumed that man had free will and chose wrongly. Then, too, there is no attempt to explain why the fruit of the Fall—man's new knowledge of good and evil—had as its immediate consequence his own pained awareness that he was naked. Finally, there is no attempt to explain the justice of God's punishment for the Fall in labor and pain.

In sum, then, the story of the Fall as it is narrated in Genesis is only primitively a theodicy; essentially it assumes the rightness of God's dispensation to man. Of course, to say this is not to negate the significance of the story; it is only to recognize that its significance is of the kind that stories have. From it we may not learn why God is as He is; we may, however, rediscover our own nature. As Adam and Eve ate of the apple and saw their nakedness, so, in some way, has each of us done. In them, therefore, we find the truth that though the ability to discriminate between good and evil inevitably entails the pained recognition of our own imperfection, nevertheless we continuously choose that ability and continuously suffer that recognition.

Of course, we have seen Swift demonstrate in a variety of ways that he passionately wished to avoid this truth. But like most men, he was not willing to relinquish the fruit of the Fall and renounce that divine consciousness which unhappily displays to us our own nakedness. Thus, in order to avert the necessity, he refashioned the story of the Fall, making in it, as we may now specify, two radical changes. First, he assumed that Adam's pre-lapsarian virtue was perfect rather than simply capable of perfect obedience. Thus, in fact, he confounded Adam's perfect innocence with perfection itself. Secondly, with an oddly "modern" flourish, he submerged the result of the Fall within the context of an eighteenth-century debate about useful and useless knowledges. Thus, he obliterated the uniquely self-reflexive character of the Fall.

Having made these two changes, Swift can, in fact, seem legitimately to proclaim the Fall to be harmless. For if, with Swift, we suppose Adam to be perfect, then that knowledge of good and evil which in Genesis caused him to know his nakedness and cover himself before Eve could have elicited from him no shame at all. Or, alternatively, if we suppose the knowledge of good and evil to be a knowledge of things only, then Adam's nakedness could never even have occurred to him. But, of course, though these changes effect Swift's end, each of them involves a palpable absurdity. Thus if we suppose Adam to have been perfect before the Fall, then, evidently enough, the Fall could not have occurred. Or, alternatively, if we suppose the knowledge which is the fruit of the Fall to be unreflexive, then that knowledge is not a knowledge of good and evil. In fact, then, Swift's changes add up only to a three-stanza-long *reductio ad absurdum*: if there were no Fall, Swift tells us, there would be no Fall.

Swift's changes, then, are foolish enough. But it is not just because these changes are logically untenable that his account of the Fall is so unsatisfactory. Rather, it is because the account has lost all the elements of story, and with them all human significance of any kind, logical or not. Adam and Eve, the apple and the serpent, the temptation and its consequences have all disappeared, and what is left is mere theory, which is deader than stone, as meaningless as a vacuum. Of course, from this theory Swift can erect a tribute to Sir William Temple which is overwhelming, yet finally insignificant, in exactly the same way as was his praise of King William. And that is what, beginning in the fourth stanza, Swift settles down to do. Proclaiming Sir William the first man since Adam to escape those universal misapprehensions of self and knowledge that have deluded man, Swift once again sets the terms for an encomium which must be meaningless to us.

But he does not write it. For in this poem, Swift knew the man he was praising, and that makes all the difference. No very lengthy biography of Temple need be given here, I think. All that needs to be said is that, though Temple's was essentially a good life, its story can no more be told deprived of complexities, defeats, and failures than can any other man's. Thus, because Swift knew Temple well, his choice of subject automatically involved him in those problems of human limitation which he had so anxiously avoided in his two previous poems. To be sure, he came very near avoiding them in this poem, too; through the first seven stanzas all that we hear of Temple tells us of his miraculous control over circumstances. And when, in the eighth stanza, Swift finally tells us something of Temple's experience with distress and defeat, he chooses to instance the most public and honorable failure of Temple's career: his inability to see for several years that his reputation for integrity in international negotiations was being manipulated by his own court to effect ends which were unknown to him and of which he would have disapproved. But though Swift's instincts, then, were to meliorate the terms of Temple's defeat and to treat it, so far as was possible, as a proof of his subject's radical innocence, he was finally unable to treat it either as less than a defeat or as a defeat wholly incidental to

Temple's essential character. He could not do this because Temple himself had not done it; rather, at his discovery that he had been duped, Temple retired forever from active politics to the estate at Moor Park where Swift probably penned most of this ode.

Following the story of Temple's life, then, Swift, despite all his laundering of the Fall at the beginning of his poem, is inexorably led to the admission that lurking in the affairs of men, in their "palaces and courts," there is a serpent which even Temple "tho' he oft renew'd the Fight,/And almost got priority of Sight" (129–30) could not quite defeat. Of course, we should recall that Swift has made something like this admission before, but in this poem he comes to it in a much more fruitful way than in the *Ode to the Athenian Society*. In the ode to the Athenians, Swift was forced to admit the ultimate limitation of his subject, but he was unable to see in the admission itself a possible ground for human significance. In the *Ode to Temple*, however, the drama of his subject's very life—its persistent vitality even after defeat—points the way for Swift, and Swift, for the first time as a poet, sees the way: "You strove to cultivate a barren Court in vain," he tells Temple,

> Your Garden's better worth your noble Pain,
> Hence Mankind fell, and here must rise again.   (175–77)

Had the *Ode to Temple* ended at this point, then, at the conclusion of its tenth stanza rather than its twelfth, we could properly say it represents a considerable advance, in a number of related ways, over anything that Swift had previously written. First, and most significantly, Swift exhibits in it a new willingness to seek the meaning of his subject in the drama of his subject's life rather than imposing that meaning from without. Consequently, as several readers have noted, this ode enjoys a degree of narrative clarity considerably greater than that of either of its predecessors. Consequently, too, this ode possesses what neither of Swift's first two odes had in any degree at all: the power to move us. Thus, when Swift enjoins Temple to exert all his "noble Pain" to diswork the Fall whose consequence was pain, we note the paradox and respond to it, because we are human, out of our own pain and exertions.

Still, good as this is, we must not overrate it, for even in his
final injunctions to Temple, Swift partly obscures the radical
significance of what he is saying by couching it in language that
threatens to betray it into easy optimism. Drawing on a too
simple version of the retirement motif, Swift so surrounds Temple
with visions of "happy scenes," "luxuriant muses," and "innocent emblems" that the real Moor Park, that significant ground
on which Temple can find content, threatens to collapse into a
fairy Eden, insignificant as it is tempting. It does not quite do so,
however, because in the last two stanzas of his ode, Swift sud-
denly, indeed violently, rejects the comfortable danger and grasps
whole all that he has learned through his first three odes.

Looked at one way, these last two stanzas are an outrageous
disruption. In them, Swift turns almost entirely away from the
praise of Temple which has concerned him for ten stanzas, and
focuses with uncomfortable intensity on his own sense of painful
futility. Regarded thematically, though, these stanzas are not dis-
ruptive at all, for the sense of futility that Swift so intensely
details in them is not his alone, but Temple's, too, and every
man's since the Fall. Of course, Swift feels his unhappiness
singularly, for every man believes every other man to be free of
it, or at least less tainted by it. Thus, comparing himself to
Temple, Swift asks,

> Shall I believe a Spirit so divine
> Was cast in the same Mold with Mine?   (178–79)

But Swift feels his futility this way precisely because its root *is*
alienation. Uncertain of our place among men and in God's order,
certain only of our own inadequacy, we struggle, as Swift perfectly describes, in circumstances we did not choose towards a
goal we cannot reach. Thus, Swift complains, he has been bound
to the muse's galley in which he pulls and tugs an oar, but "When
I almost reach the Shore / Strait the Muse turns the Helm, and I
launch out again" (194–95). From this desperate circumstance, he
recognizes, there is no escape, no Utopia, no Eden, no magic
self-dependence. But as he also finally learns here, the circumstance itself, faced and understood, is radically transformable.
For, if nothing else, the struggle for meaning is itself a meaning; it
can at least define us, and so defined we may reach out, as Swift

does at the end of this poem, to close with need and frailty the
gap between ourselves and others.

> Then (Sir,) accept this worthless Verse,
>   The Tribute of an humble Muse,
> 'Tis all the Portion of my niggard Stars;
>
> . . . .
>
> Whate'er I plant (like Corn on Barren Earth)
>   By an equivocal Birth
> Seeds and runs up to Poetry.   (199–201, 210–12)

In offering to Temple his own "worthless Verse" because, after
all, it is all that he has, Swift captures at a stroke the mute
incomprehensibility of our existence and its potential for rich
meaning. Thus, as a dramatic action, the eleventh and twelfth
stanzas of the *Ode to Temple* can hardly be improved upon; they
tell and they are virtually as much as we know of the paradox of
our situation. If, however, it is not possible to go beyond the
drama of these stanzas it is possible to confront that drama more
broadly, to seek in the perilous uncertainty of our relationships
with other men and with God for what we may know and be.
That is what Swift does in the *Ode to Dr. William Sancroft*.

As fully, perhaps, as any man in his age, Sancroft grasped, and
the close of his life illustrates, the paradoxical terms on which the
meaning of human life can be perceived and enacted. Acutely
aware that man was not God and therefore could not generate his
meaning out of himself, Sancroft resisted any action which
seemed to him to spring from a mistaken sense of human autonomy. As a result, throughout the last five years of his tenure
as Archbishop of Canterbury, he was embroiled in bitter con-
troversy. First, because he resolutely opposed James II's tyranni-
cal assumption that the divine right of kings was tantamount to
the right of kings to govern as if they were gods, he became the
focus of Anglican resistance to James's ecclesiastical meddling.
Consequently, he, along with six of his bishops, was committed
for a time to the Tower of London. Then, because he was equally
opposed to the assumption implicit in the Glorious Revolution
that kings were merely expressions of their subjects' power and
could be made and unmade at their will, he refused to sign the

oath of allegiance to William and Mary required of all Anglican clergy. As a result of this refusal, he was suspended from and then formally deprived of his office. Finally, because he would not seem voluntarily to abandon his episcopal station, he suffered a last indignity and was ejected from Lambeth Palace on June 23, 1691.[9]

Of course, to many of his contemporaries, the history of Sancroft's political stances seemed almost madly contradictory. Blinded by the advantages of William and Mary's solid Protestantism even some of the most ardent admirers of Sancroft's brave resistance to James II failed to grasp that, for Sancroft, the tyranny of James II and the democracy of the Glorious Revolution were but alternative versions of the same autonomous pride. Admittedly, however, even in cooler times than those of the Glorious Revolution, the essence of Sancroft's vision is hard to grasp. To see events as Sancroft saw them, one must consistently affirm with him that, as individuals and as communities, we are able to achieve the ordered, meaningful integrity for which we long only by disavowing that self-dependent power which seems to be its necessary antecedent. Logic must gape at such a paradox. And that is why finally drama alone, in life or in art, can teach its experiential wisdom.

As Swift recognized, the last few years of Sancroft's life themselves illustrate the truth of those principles which earlier informed his political decisions. Deprived, isolated, sometimes even scorned, Sancroft nevertheless achieved in his final years an aura of integrity and a moral stature which few of even his most bitter detractors could wholly deny him. Mysteriously, though cut off from power, he seemed more significant; though deprived of his titles, more identifiable; though isolated from most of his contemporaries, still somehow part of a larger community which included them, too. But this remarkable accretion of meaning, though readily apparent to Swift in the drama of Sancroft's everyday life and crucially important to him, requires, if it is to be successfully conveyed in poetry, both a more sophisticated vocabulary and a more settled understanding than Swift possessed when he wrote the *Ode to Sancroft*. To illustrate Sancroft's significance, the dramatic outburst with which Swift had closed his *Ode to Temple*

9. See *DNB*, ed. Sir Leslie Stephen and Sir Sidney Lee, 22 vols. (1908–9; rpt. Oxford: Oxford University Press, 1949–50).

needed to be translated into a fully conscious dramatic art, and, as Swift recognized, in *Sancroft* he was but partly successful at this task. Thus, in May of 1692, he wrote with some exasperation, "I have had an ode in hand these 5 months inscribed to my late L^d of Canterbury, Dr Sancroft, a gentleman I admire at a degree more than I can express . . . but I say, I cannot finish it for my life, and I have done nine stanzas and do not like half of them. . . ."[10] Still, though Swift never completed the poem—he broke it off at its twelfth stanza—and though it is not wholly successful in any of its parts, it is a very important work. For in his struggle to portray Sancroft's significance, Swift assumed more clearly than ever before the language and the range of a potentially major poet.

Perhaps Swift's most apparent advance in the *Ode to Sancroft* consists in the new breadth and control with which he manages its satiric attack on the willfulness of Sancroft's detractors. This advance represents more than a technical achievement; it evidences intellectual and emotional growth as well. After all, in his three earlier odes Swift attempted to pillory the pride of a variety of men, but in those odes, he blunted and obscured his satiric points by succumbing to the temptation to equate human willfulness with human virtue. In the Sancroft poem, however, whatever its other confusions, Swift steadfastly recognizes in the willfulness of Sancroft's detractors a primary source of human error and a traditional target for satire. And having achieved this recognition, he becomes impressively rich in illustrative, parallel examples of the vanity of human contumacy. Physicians blind to symptoms, religious zealots deaf to sense, disputing pharisees untouched by spirit all rush into his lines to illuminate the character and consequences of that willfulness which so misjudged Sancroft's virtue. Thus, for the first time in his career, Swift is able to build up a picture of a world of men all run individually mad while he still retains a firm grip on the pride which links all their follies together.

Better still, just because Swift does possess so firm a grip on the truth that in the multiplicity of folly there is a ubiquity of pride he is able to make that truth dramatically alive for us through his ode's most general and compelling motif. Beginning with the first stanza of the ode, in which heaven and earth are

10. *Swift's Correspondence*, 1:8–9.

described as separated by the "giddy circumstances" of time and place, Swift repeatedly portrays the human situation in cosmological terms. These terms afforded Swift a perspective in which to display his insight into the general nature of human error. Schooled by Copernicus, Swift recognized that the complex and diverse errors of all prior cosmologists resulted from their failure to realize that they were part of the universe they mapped and that they, like it, were in motion. Thus, in their errors Swift possessed an ideal model, literally universal in scope, with which to illustrate the way men go wrong.[11]

At its best, Swift's utilization of this model is at once deceptively easy and subtly effective. For example, in his fourth stanza, he explains why Sancroft's detractors found his actions contradictory by simply remarking that "holy *Sancroft's* motion quite irregular appears,/Because 'tis opposite to theirs" (81–82). Of course, in a less cosmological context than the *Ode to Sancroft*, this remark might seem to be either enigmatic or ill expressed. In *Sancroft*, however, the remark is perfectly apposite; it defines a perplexing moral error in terms of a more readily perceivable scientific one, and thereby illuminates the significance of both.

The scientific error which Swift draws on in this remark developed out of the attempt by pre-Copernican cosmologists to explain and to formulate the laws of that planetary phenomenon commonly called retrograde. This attempt itself was mistaken because retrograde, which is the little loop or irregularity apparently inscribed by planets in their journey from east to west, is only a trick of perspective, the effect of watching one moving planet from another planet moving at a different pace within the same heliocentric system. Thus, all the mathematics lavished by pre-Copernican cosmologists to formulate the laws of retrograde simply buttressed their mistaken assumption that they themselves were stable observers.

Of course, the assumption that the universe is geocentric is not, on the face of it at least, a moral error. However, by describing the difficulty Sancroft's detractors had in understanding his ac-

11. Of course, Swift was using Ptolemaic cosmology as an emblem for human confusion and was harder on that cosmology than the facts actually warrant. See Thomas S. Kuhn, *The Copernican Revolution* (Cambridge: Harvard University Press, 1957), particularly chap. 1.

tions in terms of the mistaken attempt of pre-Copernican cosmologists to formulate the laws for retrograde, Swift effects a sort of cross-fertilization. The proudly self-induced confusion of Sancroft's detractors is given a palpable weight and shape and thus their ethical eccentricity is made available to us. Simultaneously, the pre-Copernican struggle to formulate the laws for retrograde assumes a moral significance so that the awkward mathematics characteristic of that struggle are made to appear to be the penitential consequences of cosmological pride. In effect, then, the result of Swift's superimposition of one error on the other is the dramatization of both; each is given by the other what it lacked to define its meaning in time and human experience.

Pride, however, is a good deal easier to dramatize in this way than is humility. Thus, though we recognize that it is far more sensible to attribute the geocentricism of Copernicus's precursors not so much to pride as to their failure daringly to imagine what their senses daily assured them was not true, nevertheless, we are willing—in poetry at least—finally to ascribe their failure of imagination itself to some form, vaguely felt, of perverse willfulness. What we are not willing to do, however, no matter how vague the context, is to attribute Copernicus's imaginative triumph to his humility. Now, this unwillingness does not spring, I think, from a general reluctance to attribute power to humility, for most of us have felt the potency of humble men keenly enough so that we cannot doubt their power. Rather, our reluctance to depict humility as a directly causative agent arises from our profound sense that, unlike pride, humility is both a power and the end of that power, the condition for a meaningful life and the meaning that a good life may achieve. Thus humility is dramatic in itself, it is its own significance. Unlike pride, then, which can be readily dramatized by the attribution of some effect to it but which must be dramatized if it is to have any significance at all, humility's creative tension can find no analogue outside the human heart and its dreams. To put all this in a useful paradox, we may say that since it is drama itself, humility cannot be dramatized.

As Swift wrote the *Ode to Sancroft*, he grasped only imperfectly this paradox and the multiple implications that spring from it. Though obviously beyond his first immature confusion of willfulness with virtue, he evidently still ached—even as he had ached when he wrote the *Ode to the King*—to discover some vision of life through which he might establish its significance independent of its pains, joys, and sorrows. Therefore, he sought to transform the power he sensed in Sancroft into the same sort of unmoved mover he had already depicted in his portrait of the impermeable will of King William. To this end, he describes Sancroft, much as he had described William, as a firm, heavenly mind existing above the vicissitudes of worldly fortune, and he arms him with weapons—two powerful swords, submission and humility—which, although the paradox is obvious, seem violently offensive.

Of course, by this depiction, Swift sadly distorts that very humility which he was so anxious to shape into meaningful vision. Aware of a real truth, that humility does achieve its own significance, he betrays that very achievement by removing it from the only ground on which it flourishes. For, just as Sancroft perceived that his community could not achieve unity or integrity when deprived of its traditions and unmindful of the will of God, so Sancroft himself, uprooted from the particulars of his victories and defeats, is without meaning, too. Without his motives, without his joys and sorrows, and without his responses to all of these, Sancroft becomes only a less satisfactory version of the unsatisfactory hero Swift had already portrayed in the *Ode to the King*. Thus, like William, Sancroft so portrayed seems beyond us utterly, but unlike William, whose actions at least have the appearance of significance, Sancroft so portrayed cannot even be "dramatized" because the end of all his powers is only the creation of a truly humble man.

In effect, then, by portraying Sancroft's humility as if it were the equivalent of William's pride, Swift produces a perspective from which it is impossible for him to articulate the significance he senses in Sancroft's life and the worth he believes to inhere in humility. Locked into this position, Swift finds even the Passion itself, surely the most powerful paradigm Christianity offers of the efficacy of humility, essentially unavailable to him. Thus when, in the sixth stanza of his ode, he turns to compare the attacks suffered by Sancroft to the crucifixion endured by Sancroft's "Almighty Master," he is able to discover in Christ's death not an act that transforms human history, stamps it with significance, and makes it whole, but only an instance of stoical calm in the face of an outrageous but all-powerful evil. From this viewpoint then, as Swift himself rightly observes, nothing is left him "but to rail," for *his* poetry, at least, "has lost the art of praise" (110–11).

Of course, as Swift perceived it, his inability to find fit subjects to praise or fit words with which to praise them sprang not from himself but from the "pollution" of his age. Thus, through most of his ode, he himself teeters on the verge of real despair and its inevitable consequence, proud but impotent rage. Beginning with the first stanza of the poem, in which he describes heaven and earth so that they are rendered entirely discrete by the interposition of time and place between them, he again and again portrays the human condition as if it were separated from God and God's truth in just the way that with his whole life's truth Sancroft insisted that it was not. Simultaneously, though contradictorily, he continuously rails at mankind for its failure to appreciate the virtue of humility, a virtue the significance of which he himself is unable to articulate. Finally, equally maddened by the proud about him and by the consequences of pride within him, he achieves in his fifth stanza an almost perfect inversion of the virtue he would teach and calls aloud for the power to manifest humility through lines that will burn like fire and stab like daggers.

Even in this fifth stanza, however, filled with rant as it is, Swift is not wholly benighted. Full himself of that reforming zeal which in but a few years he will loathe as the surest sign of spiritual pride, he still recognizes that there is something wrong in the stance he has assumed. To be sure, he does not see clearly *what* is wrong; thus, at the beginning of his sixth stanza he repents of his outburst in the fifth, but he does so only because he thinks the outburst unworthy of that unfathomable calm which he has attributed to Sancroft and which he would emulate. Nevertheless, though his repentance is based on a false ideal—one raised by his own pride—the repentance itself is a true and illuminating imitation of Sancroft's real virtue. For in repenting of his outburst against a world that has offended him, Swift, at least momentarily, transforms both that world and his own outrage at it from instances of pointless flux and fury to occasions for self-amendment, and that self-amendment, like Sancroft's humility, is good in itself and exemplary to others.

Admittedly, however, Swift has no very firm control over the transformation he effects at the beginning of his sixth stanza. Rather, like the offer he makes of his own "worthless Verse" at the close of his third ode, his repentance here is no more than a fleeting insight into the way in which human existence can become richly significant. But this insight, though always fleeting, does occur over and over again in the *Ode to Sancroft*; thus it forms a series of bright patches through the poem, perfect in themselves and prognostics of a wisdom not yet ripe enough to recognize its own significance.

A surprisingly large number of such patches might be instanced. For example, in the first stanza of his ode, even as he gloomily portrays heaven and earth as eternally divided by the "giddy circumstances" of time and place, Swift draws his dark portrait in language which is generally reminiscent of and occasionally directly borrowed from Milton's glorious invocation to light at the beginning of the third book of *Paradise Lost*. Thus, as a number of Swift's readers have already observed, the second line of Swift's ode, "Bright effluence of th' immortal ray," is apparently formed from the sixth line of Milton's passage. Indeed Milton's line runs, "Bright effluence of bright essence increate,"[12] and Swift not only borrows "bright effluence"—Milton's figure for light—to form one line but employs "bright essence" as a figure for truth to form another: "Since the bright essence fled, where haunts the reverend ghost?" More impressive still, the first line of Swift's ode is apparently intended to recall the first line of Milton's invocation; for like Milton's line, "Hail, holy Light, offspring of Heaven first-born," Swift's line announces its subject with three heavily emphasized words, "Truth is eternal," and connects that subject obliquely to Christ, "and the Son of Heav'n." In effect then, Swift's whole first stanza illustrates, though covertly, Swift's heart in conflict with itself. Gloomy as Dis and far too proudly quick to despair, Swift is nevertheless drawn to that passage in which Milton—bringing prayer out of blindness and accomplished meaning out of prayer—reaches from the darkness of his isolation to both "see and tell/Of things invisible to mortal sight."

Of course, Swift himself can effect no such complete transformation of his own blindness. Stretching towards Milton as Milton

12. Quotations from Milton are from *The Poems of Milton*, ed. John Carey and Alastair Fowler (London: Longmans, 1968).

reaches towards light, or repenting of pride by pride's own standard, Swift is still far from achieving that conscious vision which
will eventually permit him to transform his own human blindness
and pride into significant drama by counterpointing that blindness
against his best wisdom. Nevertheless, because all through his
ode Swift pushes towards that vision, we can see clearly in its last
stanza how far he has come.

The twelfth stanza of the *Ode to Sancroft* is incomplete, of
course, but it breaks off brilliantly a poem certainly too diffuse and
perplexed to achieve a more polished conclusion. Possibly the
stanza was written after Sancroft's death in 1693; at all events,
Swift assumes that death and having nominated Sancroft a
"happy Saint," he begs the "pow'rful blessing" of Sancroft's
prayers. By doing so, Swift solves beautifully, if belatedly, the
most vexing problem of his ode; for he employs a doctrine
through which he can articulate the possibility of creative action
inherent even in the most painful of human circumstances. The
central affirmation of the intercession of the saints is that, by
virtue of the humility and grace with which the saints bore their
own afflictions, they may pray with special efficacy for the relief
of affliction in others. Thus, seen through this doctrine, adversity,
defeat, even physical pain become not so many obstacles for
isolated greatness to overcome in a fragmentary and hostile
world, but rather occasions through which men like Sancroft can
act within a community that finally transcends all times and
places.

From the beginning of the *Ode to Sancroft*, Swift sensed that
this possibility inhered in its subject's virtue. That is why, I
think, he worked into his poem praises for other good men: men
like King William, who deprived Sancroft of his office, and John
Tillotson, who replaced Sancroft as archbishop. But though Swift
sensed, then, that a communion of the virtuous does exist in God
and beyond the causes that divide men from one another, he is
unable to state through most of his ode the nature of this communion. Only in the final stanza of his poem—indeed, only in its
final line—does Swift come into nearly full possession of the truth
he has pursued through four lengthy odes. There, however, having concluded at last the railing which characterizes so much of
this poem, he achieves a statement of almost magical insight and
power:

Let not the outcasts of this outcast age
Provoke the honor of my Muse's rage,
   Nor be thy mighty spirit rais'd,
   Since Heaven and Cato both are pleas'd—

We may assume, I think, that the last line of this passage, that is, the last line of the *Ode to Sancroft*, represents the rejection of a favorite text. After all, the line it echoes is the most famous in Lucan's *De Bello Civilii*: "Victrix causa deis placuit, sed victa Catoni,"[13]

The Side that won the Gods approved most
But Cato better lik'd the side that lost.[14]

And given Swift's proudly desperate predilection for seeking the significance of human life in models of monumental strength, he must have once greatly admired the way this ringing line celebrates Cato's worth by opposing him—as an equal—to the gods themselves. But by the end of the *Ode to Sancroft* Swift knows that Lucan's line—powerful as it is—is wrong and must be changed. For finally, by portraying Cato as a just man who pits his will against the unjust gods, is defeated, and commits suicide, Lucan leads us only to a vision in which the very greatness he extols is lost in a wild and pointless universe.

Of course, Lucan's portrait may be accurate; we cannot know that, nor can Swift, nor could even Lucan himself. But by the last line of this ode Swift does know, at whatever level such knowing is finally accomplished, that for man to mean anything at all the very adversities he faces, struggles with, and is defeated by must mean something, too. That is why Swift alters Lucan's line so that it affirms what Swift cannot know but may only believe. Daringly—because the evidence of Cato's suicide seems to make against it—Swift asserts by faith that Cato by faith was pleased to accept the dispensation of a heaven that both, by faith, believe just. In so doing, Swift at last does successfully express the

13. *The Civil War: Books I–X*, ed. J. D. Duff (London and New York: W. Heinemann, G. P. Putnam's Sons, 1928), p. 12.
14. This ironic but accurate enough translation is by Thomas Hobbes. It appears in the brief introductory essay with which he prefaced his translation of the *Iliad* and the *Odyssey*.

degree of admiration he felt for Sancroft, another great man in defeat. Accepting Cato's struggle, and Sancroft's, and by implication his own, Swift dramatizes in the language of the heart —which is the only language in which it can be dramatized—the power of humility to evoke community and illuminate our dark estate.[15]

The final line of the *Ode to Sancroft* is also nearly the last line in Swift's Pindaric measure that we possess. In that measure, through four successive odes, Swift attempted to praise men in such a way that their worth might stand independent of everything but themselves. Inevitably, the attempt failed. Not inevitably—indeed, actually against his will—Swift recognized this failure and accepted, in the closing lines of the *Ode to Temple* and, again, in the final line of the *Ode to Sancroft*, the burden of poetry to affirm meaning out of uncertainty itself.

To accept this burden, however, even to accept it as artfully and strikingly as Swift does in the last line of the *Ode to Sancroft*, is not necessarily to understand it fully. Attempting to achieve certitude, but driven by the attempt to the brink of meaninglessness, one may leap instantaneously—as Swift does in both the ode to Temple and the ode to Sancroft—to a faith that posits meaning. But only after one makes that leap, and then only if one turns to trace its origin in self, can one assume a fully conscious responsibility for it, and thus for that faith, unprovable beyond the existence of our need of it.

Obviously, for this sort of introspective journey and confrontation with self, the declamatory pindaric with which Swift had been shrilly iterating the praises of great men is an inappropriate form. On the other hand, there was within Swift's easy purview at the close of the seventeenth century no clearly favorite form appropriated to such a purpose, and Swift, who had been moving towards his own self-confrontation only with the greatest reluctance, did not seek one out. Instead, aware perhaps of nothing more than that the exalted tenor of high pindaric had grown

----

15. Too late for me to take notice of it in my own discussion of *Sancroft*, Edward W. Rosenheim, Jr., published his essay "Swift's *Ode to Sancroft*: Another Look," *MP* 73, pt. 2 (May 1976):24–39. This essay offers a view of the poem which is sensitive, scholarly, and antithetical to my own.

burdensome to him, he pitched on the more colloquial and more fashionable heroic couplet in which to compose his last two early odes: *To Mr. Congreve*, and *Occasioned by Sir William Temple's Late Illness and Recovery*. Fortunately, however, though his choice was not an imaginative one, the propensity of the heroic couplet to encourage dialogue, storytelling, and the recognition of ambivalence did at least allow Swift to discover in his last two odes that ground of needs, doubts, and dreams from which we at once shape and find our meaning.

Before Swift composed those last two odes, though, he apparently attempted at least one more Pindaric celebration, this time in praise of poetry itself and entitled, pretentiously enough, *The Poet*. Unhappily, Swift either failed to complete this poem, or having completed it, chose to destroy it. At all events, we know of the poem only because Swift quotes briefly from it towards the close of the ode to Congreve (205–12) and then identifies the quotation—with tantalizing perversity—as being "Out of an Ode I writ, inscribed The Poet. The Rest is lost." Obviously, with such scanty information little can be said with confidence about the poem, but the little we can guess is both fascinating and relevant to the difficulties and triumphs of Swift's last two odes.

To begin with, it is just the right time for Swift to have composed a poem on the topic of his own craft. For it seems almost inevitable that, having been forced, in both the ode to Temple and the ode to Sancroft, to trust that there is a significance in human affairs before he could affirm that significance, he should then feel himself forced to defend his procedure. Thus, in the few lines of *The Poet* preserved to us in the form of advice to Congreve, what comes through most clearly is their quality of assertive self-justification. "*Beat not the dirty paths where vulgar feet have trod,*" Swift exhorts his ironically more successful friend,

> *But give the vigorous fancy room.*
> For when like stupid alchymists you try
>   To fix this nimble god,
>   This volatile mercury,
> The subtil spirit all flies up in fume;
>   Nor shall the bubbl'd virtuoso find
> More than a fade insipid mixture left behind.

Of course, the passionately righteous self-justification of these lines is not simply evident; rather, it is intrusive. Yet, though the lines are badly overwritten, they are not unsubtle and they do repay exploration. For example, it is certainly worth remarking that even insofar as their exhortation is just a simple admonition to Congreve to permit himself a poet's freedom in form, style, and subject, it is a formally skillful one. Its Pindaric measure, falling as it does in the midst of the heroic couplets in which the rest of the ode is cast, exemplifies the very freedom Swift is advising. Thus, as Swift has set these lines in the ode to Congreve, they testify to a prosodic self-consciousness which is a significant milestone in his work.

When Swift originally composed these lines as part of a Pindaric celebration of "the poet," of course, they did not bear the prosodic weight they acquire in the context of the ode *To Mr. Congreve*. However, even in their original setting they were —what they remain in *To Mr. Congreve*—an attempt to define the nature of the poet's work by comparing his imaginative activity with the process of alchemical projection. This is, inherently, an exciting comparison, and to the extent that Swift was willing to convey his own advice in the language of alchemy, that language projects through his lines a startling theory of poetry.

Thus, even the first line of Swift's passage, *"Beat not the dirty paths where vulgar feet have trod,"* though it does not present us with a very happy instance of metonymy, is brightened by a share of alchemical potency. For the word "vulgar," which is clearly the operative one in the line, bore a crucial significance in alchemical writings.[16] Used as an adjective, the word meant "in itself" or, more simply, "ordinary"; it signified, that is, everything the alchemist was not seeking in his work: ordinary gold, stone in itself, simple wealth. Used as a noun, the word meant everyone who sought the simple material transformations the true alchemist did not care for and would not seek. Read alchemically, then, Swift's rather awkward line does not simply call for originality with a slight aristocratic bias; rather, it defines the sort of originality Swift sought as a kind that leads directly away from any usual apprehension of the material world, away, that is, from the world we usually call real.

16. In my discussion both of the vocabulary and the practice of alchemy I am indebted to C. G. Jung's *Psychology and Alchemy*, Bollingen Series, vol. 12, no. 20 (New York: Pantheon, 1953).

Towards what? Swift never answers this question, and that is what is wrong with this passage. But in order to examine the nature of his failure, we should note first that even in evading an answer Swift does continue to borrow his language from alchemical lore. Thus, in text after alchemical text (though in a variety of ways) the novitiate practitioner of the transformative art was first warned that what he sought was *non vulgi*, and then told that his goal could be reached only through the use of an active imagination. Similarly, Swift, having warned the feet of poets from the paths trod by the vulgar, follows his warning by exhorting his presumptive student to *"give the vigorous fancy room."* In fact, then, in the ordonnance of his advice, as well as in its character and vocabulary, Swift follows with some precision the alchemical way.

Yet, as Swift's third line makes clear enough, it is a way that he does not trust. Of course, even this line, though seemingly blustery, is also ambivalent. For by warning poets not to emulate the "stupid alchymists" Swift does teeter, after all, between rejecting all alchemy as stupid and rejecting only those practitioners of it who are stupid. If such trembling grammar can be interpreted in any way, it can only suggest what the whole of this passage suggests: that though Swift is profoundly suspicious of alchemy he nevertheless is loath to relinquish a language he can feel to be a significant way of describing the work of poetry. Here again, then, Swift apparently comes breathtakingly near a great idea which he seems able to sense but which he cannot finally grasp.

In this case, of course, what Swift failed to see, or at least failed to say, is that the true goal of alchemy was never anything but itself. Of course, Swift saw clearly enough that the goal of alchemy could not be found in its retorts and vessels. As he contemptuously remarks, at the end of alchemical experiment all that remains is a "fade insipid mixture left behind." On the other hand, what Swift failed to see is that the goal of alchemy is nevertheless related to the matter alchemists worked upon. Indeed, though in his endless experiments the true alchemist never sought what we might call a knowledge of something, and far less did he seek a product of some kind, he could hardly renounce his experiments in matter since they—the dramatically perceived experience of something—were what he sought. Filtering and distilling at the same time that he fasted and prayed, the true alchemist attempted, through the power of imagination, to enter himself into his own experiment both as an active agent in it and a passive receptor of its agency.

Had Swift grasped the drama of this interaction as the true goal of alchemy he would have gained, at a stroke, a most significant and moving insight into the problem of poetic meaning he was attempting to articulate. For it is a short enough step from understanding the drama of alchemy to grasping that, like alchemy, the writing of poetry need have no other end than itself and need offer no other truth than our endless struggles with our hearts and our world. But, of course, Swift does not quite achieve this vision. He was obviously attracted to the language of an art which, long before Wordsworth, found in the "mighty world/Of eye and ear, both what they half-create,/And what perceive," the sad but significantly powerful "music of humanity." Yet, as the ambivalence of the third line of his passage illustrates, he was simultaneously uncomfortable with the tensions inherent in that language and with an art that, as Jung said, is utterly *non vulgi* since it strives to realize itself neither in mind nor in matter but rather in an intermediate third realm—a dramatic one which can be represented only in symbols.[17] Consequently, in the final lines of his passage, Swift, though he continues to use the language of alchemy, betrays its balance. Admonishing poets not to attempt, as stupid alchemists do, "To fix this nimble god,/This volatile mercury," Swift pushes poetry not simply beyond matter—for every true alchemist knew as well as Swift that what alchemy sought could not be found in matter itself—but beyond that tension which was the steadying center of the alchemical enterprise and the paradoxical ground on which alone its golden self-discovery could be enacted. In fact, then, though Swift seems to exhort poets to a course far more daring than that of the alchemist in that he asks for a total commitment to the life of the imagination, what Swift actually prompts is a view of poetry far more restricted, and hence less daring and less satisfying than the alchemical way implicit in the language he uses. Too enamored still of heroes whose lives might be defined by their powers rather than by their struggles, he transmutes alchemical gold into the familiar leaden dream of human independence through vain imagination.

17. Ibid., pp. 269–71.

Of course, it is a disappointment in these lines to see Swift thus snatch delusion from the very jaws of insight. But we must remember that the lines themselves are part of a process of self-definition; struggling to understand his craft and his relationship to it, Swift, after all, is playing his own alchemist and seeking himself in his work. In choosing out the language of alchemy, then, even though he misapprehends and finally rejects it, Swift does touch momentarily on an image of himself and thus makes what we may see to be a promising step towards fixing the nimble god he seeks. To be sure, advance by such slight steps is painfully slow, but, traditionally, self-knowledge is understood to be a difficult goal.

Viewed symptomatically, self-knowledge is also a peculiar goal in that progress towards it is often marked not by evidences of an increasing wisdom but rather by increasingly obvious instances of prevarication and self-delusion. This is because, as the real tissues of personality begin to surface in a man or in his poems, hypocrisy and semiconscious evasion of the truth become at once very tempting to him and increasingly obvious to his observers or readers. Thus, as Swift risks more and more of himself in his poems, we are likely to discover more improbabilities in what he says and more discrepancies among the range of things he says. For example, as we have already remarked, it is most unlikely that Swift actually lost every version of his poem *The Poet* save the few lines preserved in the ode *To Mr. Congreve*. It is far more likely that he was either unable to complete the poem to his satisfaction or that, having completed it, he chose to suppress most of it. Anxious, however, to press his claims as an author, he seems to have been unable to resist recording in some way a poem he either could not or would not publish. Thus, he stumbles into clumsy prevarication and reveals far more of himself than his lie can conceal.

Of course, until Swift is willing to illustrate his tensions in his poetry, he can produce only an incipient art, revealing in lies what, in art, is realized as truth. Thus, in the ode to Congreve, which is fittingly the penultimate of Swift's early odes, we can discover a great deal of the drama of Swift's personal situation, but we can do so only by recognizing that the poem often wages a sullen war on truth which we are compelled to clarify. The occasion of this war is understandable: the ode *To Mr. Congreve* necessarily exposes some of Swift's most covert tensions in what he must have found to be their most painful and ignominious form. Writing from his own obscurity to a contemporary who had become, almost overnight, an astonishingly successful playwright, Swift is confronted by the harrowing general truth that human beings are not independent creatures, and he is confronted with this truth through the humiliating circumstance that he himself longed for the recognition that Congreve had achieved. Nevertheless, though it is perfectly understandable why his spirit quailed from admitting that even in writing this poem he was attempting to imp his wing on Congreve's more precocious flight, it is only when he grew able to make such admissions consistently that he learned to see into and dramatically articulate the paradoxes and potentialities inherent in our state of being.

Surprisingly, the ode *To Mr. Congreve* begins extremely well. Indeed, it is the delightful dramatic honesty of the poem's opening lines that best exposes the flat mendacity of much of the rest. Swift knows, of course, that he is not at one with himself as he begins this poem, but he is willing for us to know it, too. Thus he creates two separate, bickering characters, each of whom clearly reflects him. That part of himself which longs to affirm the independent significance of both self and poetry he embodies as a muse. Simultaneously, he depicts the part of himself that longs for fame and active power as a pretentious self-ignorant young man. As the poem begins, these two characters are engaged in a quarrel over the appropriateness of writing an ode for Congreve, and the quarrel promptly exposes both of them. The muse correctly perceives that her young man is more worldly and more ambitious than he will admit. But at the same time, by confounding all ambition with corruption and simple courtesy with debauchery, the muse reveals herself to be much of a prude and something of a tyrant. Thus, in the argument between these two, Swift not only exposes the dilemma posed him by his own mixed ambition and idealism, he transcends that dilemma. Making poetry out of his own hesitation to make poetry, he illustrates at once the paralyzing limitation of either worldly ambition or proud idealism by itself and demonstrates that it is from the tension between such absolute opposites that good things, like poetry, can be generated.

If, however, the first twenty-two lines of the ode *To Mr. Congreve* effect a happy transmutation of personal tension into dramatic truth, their achievement can be readily betrayed; for that achievement depends first on Swift's willingness to confront his own ambition with all its risks and implications. Such confrontation requires constant courage since, as we have seen, Swift is always tempted to substitute logic for dramatic truth and simply reason away the evidence not only of his own ambitiousness but of all human dependency. Of course, such reasoning is always obviously specious. Thus when, in the lines that follow those we have just examined, Swift abandons the dialogue form and insists in his own voice that it is no mark of ambition in him to praise Congreve since Congreve's "godlike" worth demands praise, it is apparent that he at once impossibly inflates his subject's value and represses the truth of his own heart. Having done so, he makes it much more difficult for himself through the rest of his ode to express either Congreve's real significance or his own. Indeed, finally he can only protest the purity of his motives again and again, while his real sentiments perpetually undercut his protestations.

Instances of this unhappy process are plentiful throughout this poem, but perhaps the most transparent and the most interesting example occurs in the following lines: "Nor tax the goddess [that is, Swift's muse] of a mean design," Swift warns Congreve,

> To praise your parts by publishing of mine;
> That be my thought when some large bulky writ
> Shows in the front the ambition of my wit;
> There to surmount what bears me up, and sing
> Like the victorious wren perch'd on the eagle's wing;
> This could I do, and proudly o'er him tow'r,
> Were my desires but heighten'd to my pow'r.   (33–40)

Here the mingled emotions that Swift is trying desperately to suppress—his consciousness of being superior to Congreve and his desire to have his own powers acknowledged—burst outrageously through the net in which he has sought to confine them. Thus, having just attempted to demonstrate the purity of his motives in addressing Congreve by comparing such fame as he might achieve in his address to the triumph of a wren, he nevertheless feels compelled by that very desire for fame which he has just dismissed to claim that he possesses the power to be a triumphant wren even though he does not wish to exert it. Nothing could more substantially prove how powerful are the constraints Swift places on his real feelings in these lines than that his feelings must emerge through the lines so grotesquely deformed. That ambition which in the dramatic expressiveness of the first twenty-two lines of the ode to Congreve emerges as but a necessary part of our human identity becomes in this passage at once ludicrous and nearly perverse.

Unhappily, a great deal of the ode to Congreve is similarly deformed. For, compelled by ambition to communicate to the world, but compelled, too, to deny that ambition, Swift is led by a process usually called projection to fix on the world what he fears and thinks weakening in himself. Of course, on the one hand this process does produce some of the most astute satirical analysis that Swift has so far written of the shams with which all of us sometimes attempt to lend meaning to our lives. But on the other hand, and far more crucially, the process absolutely isolates Swift both from the world and from himself. Thus, what emerges from the poem are two distinct pictures: one of Swift at Moor Park, autonomous and perfect; the other of all the world besides, degenerate and hateful. Even Congreve, whose goodness, Swift argues early in the poem, legitimizes praise, is finally classified at the close as part of the "bad world" which cannot understand him and which threatens his values. Put bluntly, then, the central vision of this poem is a mad one. Of course, a skilled satirist might exploit such a vision by carefully juxtaposing against it evidences of his own humanity. But Swift does not, dares not, do this.

He does do something else, though, which if it does not save this poem does preserve our sense of his basic soundness. Virtually unwilling to admit his own humanity, he nevertheless recognizes that he cannot quite remove himself from the world he castigates since, if nothing else, he must confront at least that rage it evokes from him. Thus at one point in the poem he asks, with considerable ingenuousness, "What's that to her [his muse] if mankind be a fool?" (178). And at another point he observes that in lashing fools in whom he expects no reformation he himself is engaged in a task which is, as he sardonically says, just "as curious and as wise/As virtuosos' in dissecting flies'' (93–94). Of course, neither of these remarks brings him near a real examination of his own sentiments. But they do indicate his awareness of his quandary and thus help us to understand two other points, near the end of the poem, at which we can sense how close such an examination must be.

The first of these occasions is given special poignancy because earlier in the poem Swift characterizes the life of Londoners —caught up in rumors, false judgment, and pride—as "a sort of dreams/Rend'ring shades, things, and substances of names" (147–48). But towards the close of his poem he recognizes that to Londoners his own life in Moor Park, with all its hopeful absolutes and significant emblems, must also seem only a dream: "But, ah! you think I dream,/And the bad world may well believe the same" (197–98). Of course, as the qualifying phrase "the bad world" indicates, Swift is not yet ready to say with either the finality or the richness of Prospero that we are all of us simply "such stuff as dreams are made on." But at some level Swift knows that this is so; he knows, that is, that only when we accept the dreamstuff of life itself as our given can we begin to know the truth of ourselves and others. Thus, even before he sat down to write this poem he dabbled, fretfully, in the dark esotericism of alchemy. And thus, too, at the conclusion of this ode he is led virtually against his will to a dream that utterly exposes the vanity of human absolutes.

The dream that Swift recalls at the close of this poem is one that is crucial to the development of Christianity. It is the famous dream, or vision, of St. Peter, which is so fully explored in the tenth and eleventh chapters of the Acts of the Apostles. As Peter's dream begins, two men are, in fact, traveling to him from Caesarea to ask him to return with them and preach the Christian doctrine for the first time to the gentiles. Peter's dream specifically prepares him to receive them. He dreams that he sees heaven open and a vessel descend to him "as it had been a great sheet knit at the four corners, and let down to the earth." In this sheet he discovers "all manner of . . . beasts," and he hears a voice which commands him, "Rise, Peter, kill, and eat." Obedient to Hebraic dietary law, however, he refuses, "Not so, Lord; for I have never eaten anything that is common or unclean.'' Therefore the voice speaks to him again and, significantly admonishing him, tells him, "What God hath cleansed, that call not thou common."

Of course, the immediate implication of this dream is clear enough. Thus, when he is summoned, Peter does go to the gentiles at Caesarea. But the broader implications of the dream are worked out only during Peter's visitation to the Caesareans and they culminate in his deepened recognition that ultimately all truth, value, and significance are not with man but with God, available through faith but not through law. Thus, as Peter explains to the Judeans after his visit among the gentiles, "Forasmuch then as God gave them the like gift as he did unto us, who believed on the Lord Jesus Christ; what was I, that I could withstand God." Or as Peter put it to the gentiles themselves in his famous summary, "Of a truth I perceive that God is no respecter of persons; But in every nation he that feareth him, and worketh righteousness, is accepted with him."

Of course, this is a conclusion that Swift certainly accepted intellectually. As we have seen, however, in the ode to Congreve he is emotionally miles away from it. Indeed, insisting on his own righteousness and the folly of all the world besides, he continuously transforms into mere pharisaism precisely that moral vision which Peter rightly perceived to be an abrogation of all simply human law. Nevertheless, though Swift does remain vigorously committed throughout his ode to arguing for his own separateness, independence, and substantiality, it is apparent that somewhere in his artistic consciousness a recognition of his real dependence on God and community with men remains emotionally alive though severely repressed. In fact, it is almost as if by the conclusion of his poem Swift's repressed sense of dependence had developed that gift for ironic exposure which prisoners under severe confinement often find in themselves. For even as Swift closes his poem by cursing, again, the citified critics of London under the appellation of odious cattle, something impels him, with wild inappropriateness, to incorporate the antithetical dream of St. Peter into the rant of his final lines. Of course, to do so without producing a most apparent instance of self-contradiction, Swift must attempt utterly to reverse the significance of Peter's vision. He attempts to do this in two ways. First, he wholly suppresses the fact that the chief lesson of Peter's visionary experience is to teach men the nature of their community under God. Secondly, he depicts himself, in an act of outrageous impiety, not as a man who receives Peter's vision but instead as the very God who gives it. Thus in his last lines Swift informs Congreve that "In this descending sheet" (by which he means his own poem)

> you'll haply find
> Some short refreshment for your weary mind,
> Nought it contains is common or unclean,
> And once drawn up, is ne'er let down again.

Of course these lines are almost unbelievably proud, and from the height of their pride we must judge, I think, Swift's real fear and hatred of his own dependence. Simultaneously, however, from the almost parodically self-exposing character of the lines we may also gauge, favorably, I believe, the fundamental strength of his understanding. Thus, at the point Swift arrives at in these lines, he has but two real choices; he may either embrace a proud, despairing madness, or he may say of himself what Peter said when the Caesareans knelt at his feet to worship him, "Stand up, I myself also am a man."

To understand the choice Swift makes in his final ode, it is useful to review once more a basic paradox. To be a man is to be dependent. But to know that one is dependent is not to be a man; it is to be an unfallen angel. For men do not really know their dependence except at rare moments; rather, they discover it again and again by struggling to be independent. That struggle for independence is uniquely human. To accept the fact of that struggle and of its inevitable failure is to know oneself. But nothing is harder to do than this.

In the ode *Occasioned by Sir William Temple's Late Illness and Recovery* Swift accepts the fact of his own struggle. He does not attempt to resolve the struggle; instead for the first time in the odes he is content simply to realize it in his art. Because he is content to do so, he achieves a much clearer articulation than in any previous ode both of its nature and of its constituent elements. Thus, in a way—the only way possible, really—he transcends his struggle. Like Jacob, in wrestling, he learns his name.

That name is Legion, not because Swift is more wicked than most men but only because, like most men, he is many characters at once. Thus, though in this ode Swift is represented by only two principal speakers, his muse and himself, the number of actual viewpoints in the poem is far greater than the number of its principals. These viewpoints are rarely in harmony; rather they qualify, modify, and sometimes flatly contradict one another just as the principal speakers themselves do. But though these viewpoints, then, are each something less than and different from the poem itself, taken together they do form a coherent dramatic meaning and represent intelligibly the sum of what Swift feels.

Because most readers have described this poem as if its full significance could be found in its final lines, in exploring the poem's real dramatic intricacy it is perhaps best to begin with those lines. The fascination they have cast over readers is understandable, for in them Swift denounces his muse and renounces poetry with great power and seeming finality. "From this hour" he shouts at his muse,

> I here renounce thy visionary pow'r;
> And since thy essence on my breath depends,
> Thus with a puff the whole delusion ends.   (151–54)

Despite their force, however, these lines are not as absolute a renunciation as they at first seem. This is not to argue that Swift does not mean what he says in them. But it is to argue that what he says is necessarily qualified both by the way he says it and the context in which he places it.

First, it is worth remarking that what Swift renounces in these lines is not quite what a number of readers have suggested he renounces. For several critics the lines have marked at once Swift's rejection of epideictic verse and his acceptance of a moral, satiric, and realistic stance. But this reading reflects only the most general overview of the poem. Admittedly, the reading is initially attractive because the poem, though difficult to unravel, is easy to summarize. It begins with Swift, in a darkly contemplative mood, being visited by his muse. At some length, the muse exhorts him to write the praises of the intimate circle at Moor Park. Since he completes the poem by refusing to do so, it is tempting to assign his refusal to some new and noble motive. But such an assignment cannot be supported. For as the lines immediately preceding his refusal make clear enough, in rejecting his muse Swift is rejecting precisely those moral and literary values which are the satirist's traditional standards.[18] It is the muse, after all, who admonishes Swift just before he rejects her, to "Stoop not to int'rest, flattery, or deceit" (138) and to "Know no base action" (142) in the pursuit of wealth or fame. Thus in renouncing her and denouncing her dictums as madness—"Madness like this no fancy ever seiz'd,/Still to be cheated, never to be pleas'd" (147–48) —Swift is hardly stepping into the satirist's robes. Rather, he is announcing his intention to gratify his desire for fame and wealth by donning the moral motley of easy roguery. Thus, if we are determined to discover the full significance of this poem in a paraphrase of its closing couplets, we must read it as a shocking affirmation of Swift's unprincipled ambition.

Although mostly wrong, such a reading would also be partly right. For it is the chief virtue of this poem that in it Swift says truthfully, if complexly, what he really feels—among other things, that outrage at the uneven distribution of earthly rewards which is foreign, probably, to no man. The trouble is that this outrage is neither all Swift feels nor all we respond to even in the final lines of his poem. For as each of us knows, pure outrage makes no rhymes. Therefore, the writer of a versified renunciation of verse necessarily tells us, quite apart from the paraphrasable content of his lines, that he is in that condition of emotional bafflement which is as old as man but which contemporary psychologists call a double bind. He is damned if he makes verses; but he is damned if he can stop making them, also.

In fact, Swift's final lines illustrate his emotional bafflement in a second way, too. For the controlling fiction of his poem is that it records a dialogue that took place between himself and his muse sometime in the recent past, "late, near yon whispering stream" (13). Thus, though Swift manages that dialogue in the present tense as if it were happening now, nevertheless both the muse's speech to him and his rebuttal of her are qualified by the fact that

18. For example, when the muse advises Swift—"Be this thy sure defense, thy brazen wall/Know no base action, at no guilt turn pale"—she is echoing (though in awkward English) Horace's advice in *Epistle* 1. 1.: "Hic murus aheneus esto/Nil conscire sibi, nullâ pallescere culpâ."

they are being remembered rather than being enacted. Obviously, this qualification is most significant with respect to the poem's final lines. For within the formal fiction of the poem, those lines are really no more than a versified recollection of a previous renunciation of verse. In effect, then, the lines are absolutely self-cancelling.

Finally, however, the situation is even more complicated. For Swift's renunciation of his muse not only breaks off the dialogue between the two of them but it also ends the poem itself. Thus his renunciation escapes, at least in part, the fiction of the poem in which it occurs and acquires a palpable measure of present tense force. That is why ultimately the final lines of Swift's ode are not susceptible of any simple explication or paraphrase. The renunciation they record is just too protean to be so confined. Instead, shimmering between the past and the present and between art itself and a violent renunciation of art, these lines finally discover for us not the persuasion but the struggling ambivalence of the mind and heart that formed them.

Of the two principal speakers in the poem, both of whom, of course, are Swift, it is the muse who best understands and can most consistently articulate that struggle of which she herself is a part. In fact, the muse understands every truth of this poem save one: what it feels like to be human and in doubt. This is because she is that part of Swift which accepts uncertainty with perfect equanimity and absolute faith. Thus she is at once something more and something less than fully human. Undisturbed by all the exigencies of life and death she moves through them with grace and economy to illustrate the moral truths they import. But of the experience of life itself, she understands nothing.

Significantly, the occasion that summons her into this poem is neither the illness nor the recovery of Sir William Temple but rather the combination of his illness with his recovery. For it is the essence of her vision to see human experience as being as transitory and as mutable as Temple's wavering mortality. Thus, as Swift has contrived it, she sees all things as she herself is. Only a synesthetic experience, a visionary sound dependent for her being upon Swift's creative imagination, she insists that all other things are in fact as ephemeral as she and as dependent for their being on the mind of God as she is on Swift's. Indeed, she argues, even the face of earth itself would "turn pale and life decay,/Should heaven suspend to act but for a day'' (63–64). Further, just because she does see all human things as dependent and only relationally significant, all things are for her as infinitely transformable as her own teardrops, which even as Swift watches them, shimmer into a rainbow to show "God's dart is shot, and wrath o'erblown" (28). Thus each human experience, no matter how dire, becomes in her transforming measures an emblem of God's gracious presence; and even age, earthquakes, storms, pain, and death reflect for her that steady faith with which she illuminates them.

That steady faith, however, though it is her character, is Swift's achievement. For she, after all, is but an allegory of faith in him, and her expression of faith without his doubt is not only flat but also impotent to demonstrate its own validity. Thus, to choose a simple example, only as her generous praise of Sir William and of his family, retainers, and estate resonates against Swift's nearly desperate concern for his own welfare, expressed everywhere else in the poem, can we appreciate the real full-heartedness of Swift's praise of them as it is embodied in her. So similarly, though in a much more complex way, it is only against Swift's desire to confirm his own worth through a variety of worldly satisfactions that his muse's insistence that we find ourselves only by giving ourselves away becomes fully meaningful. For precisely because the muse believes absolutely in a providential God who ever brings good out of ill and fills our lives with meaning, her belief is absolutely unconfirmable. Only a creature who must live in the very struggle of uncertainty can ever illustrate, by writing such poems as this one, the validity of the muse's faith.

Finally, however, all this is not to say that in this poem Swift displays his doubts and his desires merely to set off his muse's faith and give it substance. Only when he has grown much more experienced with all the forms of his doubt will he be able to use it in such a way. Here, in this poem, it is clear enough that Swift's rejection of his muse, though not uncomplex, is made in anger and felt with force. Thus, the virtue of the poem is certainly not that it is an especially subtle profession of faith either in God's providence or in poetry's truth. Rather, it is that the poem is so complete a profession of doubt mingled with faith, baffled anger, and fear that it strips away all pretense to human certitude and reveals the grounds of our communal faith in our common doubts and needs. Like the cry "Lord, I disbelieve and am in pain," the poem is at once a renunciation of faith, the way that leads to faith, and in its dramatic honesty an act of faith itself. It marks the distance Swift has come from the insistent, fractured certitude of the *Ode to the King* and points towards that dramatically unified uncertainty which at once vexes and graces his later verse.

2
"Careful Observers may fortel the Hour"
Occasional Poems, 1698–1710

A FIVE-YEAR HIATUS separates Swift's completion of the ode
Occasioned by Sir William Temple's Late Illness and Recovery
from the next poem we possess that is generally conceded to be
his, *Verses Wrote in a Lady's Ivory Table-Book*.[1] This hiatus has
proved mischievous in at least two ways. First, it apparently has
caused Swift's readers to accept his renunciation of verse at the
close of his last ode more absolutely than they might otherwise
have done. Secondly, it also has encouraged critics to underesti-
mate drastically the significance of most of that group of brilliantly suggestive occasional poems Swift wrote between 1698 and
1710. Assuming these later poems to be the product of Swift's
reaction against his early and too idealistic muse, critics have
failed to appreciate a point that it is the burden of this chapter to
demonstrate: that despite their obvious dissimilarity to Swift's
early odes, the remarkably variegated occasional poems produced
in what we might call Swift's second period are in fact a further
development of the same shared concerns, problems and assumptions which we have traced in his pindarics. As in those early
verses, so in these occasional poems, Swift's primary struggle and
his achievement are to articulate a vision of human life that
discovers its meaning and its power through a *dramatic* apprehension of its worth.

1. In fact, the year in which Swift composed *Verses Wrote in a Lady's Ivory
Table-Book* cannot itself be fixed with certainty. See Williams's headnote, *Swift's
Poems*, 1:60.

Of course, to discover fundamental similarities between Swift's early odes and his later occasional verse is not to deny that, prosodically, Swift moves with a great deal more maturity in the occasional verse than he exhibited in any of his earlier work. Indeed, even the earliest of the occasional verse, *Verses Wrote in a Lady's Ivory Table-Book*, displays most of the prosodic elements characteristic of Swift's mature poetic style. For example, that octosyllabic energy generated by a rush of short, choppy, run-on lines which gives so much of Swift's verse a feel of paradoxically mingled stasis and force is there fully established. So, too, is Swift's penchant for beginning his poems with some form of flat challenge and then incorporating within them a remarkable amount of direct address. And so, finally, is Swift's habit of constructing those long chains of meaningfully shocking rhymes which teeter constantly on the brink of linguistic instability and thus remind us how easily words can slide first into bathos and thence to nonsense.

But though the *Verses*, then, represents so considerable an advance in Swift's prosodic skill as to suggest that during the apparent hiatus which separates it from the early odes Swift probably did at least some poetic experimentation,[2] nevertheless, the central problem the poem presents to us is hauntingly familiar. That is why the *Verses* is a particularly fine introduction to the occasional poetry which follows it. For on the one hand, the poem displays much of Swift's mature ability to speak with memorable authority. But on the other hand, in the *Verses*, just as in the ode *Occasioned by Sir William Temple's Late Illness and Recovery*, the central problem of the poem develops out of a conflict between what Swift says in it and what he seems to say.

What Swift seems to say in the *Verses* is easy to summarize, for though the formal narrator of the poem is the lady's table-book itself, the table-book initially appears to speak for Swift.[3] Thus as the poem begins we have every reason to feel that it is

2. George P. Mayhew argues persuasively that Swift wrote at least one poem during this period. See his essay "Jonathan Swift's 'On the Burning of Whitehall in 1697' Reexamined," *HLB* 19 (October 1971):399–411.
3. Of course, the table-book does not speak for Swift. Peter J. Schakel recently noted this fact, but drew different conclusions from mine. See his article, "Swift's 'Verses Wrote in a Lady's Ivory Table-Book,'" *Explicator* 28 (May 1970):83.

Swift who first invites us to peruse the table-book in every part, then scornfully exposes the foolish entries of its owner and the men who keep her company, and finally warns us not to meddle either with its pages or with its owner's heart since wisdom can hold a place in neither the one nor the other. The problem is, however, that finally Swift's practice flatly contradicts the table-book's advice. For as the full title of the poem makes clear enough, Swift does meddle with the pages of the table-book. Further, by seeking to instruct its owner, he also meddles with the lady's heart. Thus, to the table-book's indignantly rhetorical question, "Who that had Wit would place it here" (17), we must answer, "Swift would." In effect then, in the *Verses*, as in the ode *Occasioned by Sir William Temple's Late Illness and Recovery*, the very existence of the poem contradicts its argument.

Of course, there is no reason to suppose that, in the *Verses*, Swift either intended or noted this contradiction. Indeed, his conscious motive for writing the poem probably amounted to no more than a desire to parody an established form of gallant address which he found foolish and saccharine. But the fact that his poem does contradict itself thus points with special vigor to an ambivalence in Swift deeper than conscious motive. This ambivalence, as we examine it more closely in the *Verses*, proves to be about the very worth of human life.

Admittedly, to insist on so significant an ambivalence in the *Verses* may seem initially perverse, since the poem at first appears to be no more than a rueful but comic attack aimed at the silly preoccupations of a lady and her beaux. Thus, when the notes the lady scribbles to herself and her beaux scribble to her are read together, they exhibit only that general carelessness of mind which produces hilarious incongruity.

> Here you may read (*Dear Charming Saint*)
> Beneath (*A new Receit for Paint*)
> Here in Beau-spelling (*tru tel deth*)
> There in her own (*far an el breth*)
> Here (*lovely Nymph pronounce my doom*)
> There (*a safe way to use Perfume*)
> Here, a Page fill'd with Billet Doux;
> On t' other side (*laid out for Shoes*)
> (*Madam, I dye without your Grace*)
> (Item, *for half a Yard of Lace.*)   (7–16)

Read individually however, the entries in this comic passage suggest a failure of self-knowledge which is dark enough in implication. For individually, the lady's notes are really a series of
reminders that even the nicest of us are imperfectly formed, often
smelly, and always aging creatures. So, too, the beaux' exhorta-
tions turn continuously on the ineluctable fact of human mortality:
"tru tel deth," says one; "pronounce my doom," demands a
second; "I dye without your Grace," proclaims the last. Ironically, of course, neither the lady nor any of her beaux understands anything of the implications of their scribblings. Rather,
trapped by cosmetics and by the windy language of courtship,
they foolishly forget that men and women court, love, and marry
not because they are incorruptible but because, being mortal, they
must get issue. Thus at once seeking and claiming a false immortality, they lose a real one.

That Swift's attack in the *Verses* is in fact aimed directly at the
infertility implicit in the stylish courtship of the lady and her
beaux is made clear enough in the openly phallic joke of the
poem's final lines.

> Who e're expects to hold his part
> In such a Book and such a Heart,
> If he be Wealthy and a Fool
> Is in all Points the fittest tool;
> Of whom it may be justly said,
> He's a Gold Pencil tipt with Lead.   (25–30)

The basic meaning of these lines hardly requires explication;
Swift's golden, leaden, phallic pencil intelligibly conveys the
foolish impotence of seeking permanence in matter (as the lady
and her beaux do) rather than through it. However, what does
require examination is the markedly strained and leaden character
of the lines themselves. Of course, we ought to note that the jest
Swift struggles to produce in them is probably learned enough.
Thus it is almost certainly worth remembering as one reads the
lines that, according to Ovid, Cupid was armed with two sorts of
arrows: golden ones which impel love and leaden ones which
discourage it.[4] It may also be worth recollecting that in alchemy,
as in love, one is to produce gold from lead rather than, as here,

4. See, for example, *The Metamorphoses* 1.12.19–20.

producing lead out of gold. Unhappily, however, knowledge of neither of these possible references much alters the basic problem of the lines in which they occur. For finally, that problem is simply that the lines are both so heavily contrived and so jammed with contempt that they cannot yield us much delight. And that is a very serious failure, because it means that at the imaginative level, where poetry matters most, Swift fails to discover for himself a joyous and fertile alternative to the sterile folly he condemns.

We are led back, then, to the contradiction from which we began. For looked at one way, in this poem Swift is close kin to the characters he creates. They, faced with mortality, attempt to powder over their condition with cosmetics and the sort of deifying delusions common to the gallantry of table-book compliments. But he, though he knows that they are wrong, is unable to transmute their folly into gold. Instead, neither quite merry enough nor quite moral enough, he stands back from them in contempt, and in the closing lines of his poem asks through the persona of his table-book, "Who that had Wit would place it here,/For every peeping Fop to Jear" (17–18). Because he does this, his poem fails to gel as a dramatic event in itself.

On the other hand, since despite his ambivalence Swift records his ambivalence, his poem is a dramatic event when viewed from the standpoint of his own development as a poet. For by risking what he significantly calls his "Brains Issue" (19) among those ladies and beaux who are all too likely to "blot it out" (22), he effects a dramatic transmutation of his own doubts into poetry and exhibits that brave fertility he cannot yet quite articulate. Finally, then, though *Verses Wrote in a Lady's Ivory Table-Book* does not discover to us much of the power or worth of human life itself, it does suggest—in much the same way as do the early odes—something of what will ultimately become Swift's special ability to grasp that power and that worth and to convey it in a voice that is among the most believable because it is among the most honest and precise in English literature.

The first poem that fully suggests Swift's mature power to capture the richness of life within his lines is the outrageously titled petition *To Their Excellencies, the Lords Justices of Ireland. The*

*Humble Petition of Frances Harris, Who must Starve, and Die a
Maid if it miscarries.* But though it is, then, in many ways a
prophetic poem, the *Petition* is also something of an anomaly in
Swift's canon. For unlike most of Swift's verse, in which the
narrator is either Swift himself or some more or less transparent
persona, the *Petition* is wholly narrated by a substantial character, one taken from life and transmuted into what John Dryden
called real "playhouse flesh and blood." Of course, no one can
say why Swift chose to do this, for the process of artistic growth
is always ultimately a mystery. But what we can remark is that in
order to capture Frances, Swift was forced to abandon elements
of his own vocabulary, adopt elements from hers, and develop a
four-stress doggerel couplet. Consequently, the *Petition* lacks
most of the urgency and at least some of the moral intensity we
usually associate with Swift's verse. But on the other hand, the
poem possesses a full-blown character through whom Swift can
record not only human follies and limitations, but also the essential vigor of human life itself. Thus in the *Petition*, Swift for the
first time in his poetic career is able to depict that redeeming
energy in life which, in later poems far more characteristic of him,
he will recover again and again.

   To discover what in fact Swift has accomplished in the *Petition*,
it is useful to begin by reading the poem from a relatively simple
ethical standpoint. Read so, the *Petition* demonstrates the perils
of Mammon through the misfortunes of poor Frances Harris. As
the poem opens we learn that Frances, a lady-in-waiting in Lord
Berkeley's Irish household where Swift, too, served, as a chap-
lain, has sustained the loss of the whole of her meagre savings,
"seven Pound, four Shillings and six Pence, besides Farthings, in
Money, and Gold." As she tells her story, it becomes plain
enough that this loss is completely her own fault. A perfect little
worldling, she loses her small hoard because she insists on carry-
ing it on her person wherever she goes and because she tries to
count it over once too often in hurried circumstances and thus
drops it. Since she is later unable to find it again, she assumes it
has been stolen, and after contemplating suicide, she attempts to
recover it. Predictably, however, her attempts at recovery merely
complicate her difficulties. She suspects the thief is one Mrs.
Dukes, the wife of a footman, but she is hilariously unable to
wring a confession from her suspect or to procure any help from

her fellow servants. Thus, in both her loss and her subsequent frustration she embodies a paradox: not only are worldly goods transitory in themselves, but they perversely prove most ephemeral to those who value them most highly.

Comically, however, though Frances embodies this truth, she does not learn it. Instead, goaded by her frustrations, she confirms her ironically inefficacious worldliness by committing two additional errors. First, she completely exasperates her parson-sweetheart (who, hilariously, seems to be Swift himself) by confounding his function with that of a conjuror and asking him to cast a nativity to catch her thief. Then, having received something against her loss from Lord and Lady Berkeley, she takes seriously their whimsical suggestion to petition the Lords Justices of Ireland for the return of her parson. Of that suggestion this poetic petition is the supposed but improbable fruit, and she ends it with typical impertinence by asking for both a share in next Sunday's collection and for a title with which to claim either Swift or some better parson in marriage. Through her whole narration, then, Frances proves to be completely unwilling or unable to see that the cause of all her misfortune is that she loves fortune too much.

Yet despite her perversity, Frances is not simply a morality character, a creature constructed to point a lesson. For though she is unchanging and uneducable, she nevertheless possesses an abundance of attractive verve. Of course, verve is precisely the quality she should not have. Committed with all her heart to pounds and pence in money and gold, she ought be as heavy and lumpish as what she loves. As it is, however, what Swift sees and makes us see is that the worth of Frances's life is greater than the sum of its parts.

How Swift accomplishes this is a thing embarrassingly difficult to define, though the delight of generations of readers testifies that it does happen. In part it happens, I suspect, because Swift contrives the inspired chatter between Frances and Berkeley's lesser servants to point a lesson for us. Peeping out at the great world from their stations below stairs, she and her companions regard the lords and ladies they serve as but accidental backgrounds moving behind the major events of their own lives. Thus, confounding Galway with Collway and rhyming Shrewsbury's great title with gooseberries, these valets and housekeepers and ladies-in-waiting remind us that looked at one way all human lives are lilliputian. So reminded, we are at least encouraged to discover worth in Frances's life and small concerns in order that we may affirm it in our own.

Mostly, however, Swift causes us to discover and acknowledge Frances's significant presence in ways both less logical and less self-interested. Let us take for instance the way he manages her attempt to procure a confession from her prime suspect, Mrs. Dukes. Having dreamt that this suspect holds her money, Frances approaches her warily, "resolv'd," as she puts it, "to bring the Discourse slily about" (36). But all the charm of the following scene develops out of Frances's irrepressible nature, her absolute inability to be anybody but herself.[5] Thus, though she begins well enough by voicing her suspicions obliquely and appealing to an abstract code of honor, nevertheless, her initial appeal is tinctured by her characteristic but incongruous expressiveness.

> Mrs. *Dukes*, said I, here's an ugly Accident has
>   happen'd out;
> 'Tis not that I value the Money three Skips of a Louse;
> But the Thing I stand upon, is the Credit of the House.
>   (37–39)

Now the expression "three Skips of a Louse," particularly as it echoes off "the Credit of the House," quite betrays Frances's attempt at distance and decorum. Better still, as Swift delightedly notes in Faulkner's 1735 edition of his poems, the expression was actually common to Frances and thus its appearance here, trembling between pure inanity and real vigor, perfectly, because simultaneously, portrays her significant liveliness within her obvious limitations. So, too, and in precisely the same way, the clichés that tumble from Frances throughout the scene inexorably undo her little diplomacy; but they undo it with such vivaciousness that even when she arrives at the lie direct it is still hard to say whether her accusation of Mrs. Dukes better illustrates her numbing opacity or her personal verve: "Now, Mrs. *Dukes*, you know, and every Body understands,/That tho' 'tis hard to judge, yet

5. Richard Reynolds makes this point in a brief essay which in some ways parallels my own. See his "Swift's 'Humble Petition' From a Pregnant Frances Harris?" *The Scriblerian* 5 (Autumn 1972):38–39.

Money can't go without Hands" (42–43). At best, what one must say is that a good deal of both folly and life is present throughout this scene.

Of course, the subject of the *Petition* is only Frances Harris, and one must be careful not to claim too much either for her or for it. Nevertheless, the achievement of the poem is considerable. For from his earliest odes straight through to *Verses Wrote in a Lady's Ivory Table-Book*, Swift's consistent problem has been to record simultaneously his awareness of human frailty and his awareness of human worth. In the *Petition*, abandoning didacticism for drama, Swift solves this problem; and the result is that the poem possesses, to my ear at least, that vigorous confidence characteristic of Swift's best poetry.

Further, because in the *Petition* Swift does realize for us the miscibility of human worth and human weakness, he also establishes the necessary groundwork on which to base that providential view of human experience towards which he struggled in his earlier verse. In that verse, we recollect, his attempts to dramatize a divinely ordered world usually broke against his powerful sense of the world's deep shabbiness. Swift remained painfully aware of that shabbiness all his life. Thus, his verse always reflects his unwillingness to see the hand of God too readily in the affairs of men. But because he gradually discovered, first in the *Petition* and then in poems that follow it, a way to capture significant worth even amidst human folly, loss, and pain, he freed himself to mingle carefully the world of flesh with an order of spirit that affirms our potential and our meaning.

Almost invariably in Swift's mature work, this mingling takes place both covertly and in a climate of irony in which it seems at once poignant and ludicrous. To take the present example, not only does one hardly know how to respond to the discovery that the *Petition* is, in fact, a tiny theodicy, but the discovery itself has the sort of shimmering, quicksilvery feel about it that makes one review one's arguments again and again. Nevertheless, though it is evident that she does so wholly unwittingly, Frances does begin her narration by accusing God of being the author of all her misfortunes. "So," she flutters, "when I went to put up my Purse, as *God* would have it, my Smock was unript,/And, instead of putting it into my Pocket, down it slipt" (7–8). Further, she continues to question God's justice towards her throughout the poem, both implicitly and explicitly. *"God* knows," she murmurs on one occasion, "I thought my Money was as safe as my Maidenhead" (11), and *"Lord,"* she queries on another, "what shall I do?" (64). Thus, naïvely funny as is her thoughtless assumption that the first cause of her loss was the Prime Mover working through a rip in her smock and plainly naïve as is her implicit assumption that God owes her virginity some better recompense, both assumptions raise the traditional questions of theodicy: why does God permit loss and suffering at all and why particularly does He permit the virtuous to experience ill?

Of course, the way these questions are raised in the *Petition* is, in part, the poem's answer to them. We laugh at Frances precisely because in naïvely appealing to God out of her tiny troubles she but more sharply illuminates that distinction between the order of the flesh and the order of the spirit which she is too foolish to recognize even in its grossest form. Nevertheless, as Swift manipulates her foolishness to remind us how distant God is from the things that matter most to Frances, he simultaneously blurs that distinction by drawing God intimately into her world. This event occurs near the end of the poem at the point at which, having exhausted all apparent remedies, Frances records that she fell to mere lamentation: "Well; I thought I should have swoon'd; *Lord*, said I, what shall I do?/I have lost my Money, and shall lose my *True-Love* too" (64–65). Obviously, Frances's question represents no change of heart in her, not even a significant awareness that she is indeed dependent on God's benignity. But the question does permit Swift to illustrate for us what Frances herself does not learn. For no sooner does Frances ask the question, than she receives an answer: "Then my *Lord* call'd me" (66), she tells us. To be sure, this apparently divine intervention on Frances's behalf is really no more than the consequence of a simple pun since the "lord" who calls Frances is only Lord Berkeley, as the succeeding lines make perfectly clear: "[Frances], said my *Lord*, don't cry./I'll give you something towards thy Loss; and says my *Lady*, so will I" (66–67). Nevertheless, as a consequence of this pun, Swift casts over Lord Berkeley's kindness towards Frances a sort of providential sheen so that in his timely ministrations to her he seems to stand, momentarily at least, in God's role and to vindicate His ways to Frances Harris.

This is, I think, a supremely Swiftian tactic. Alive with laughter at itself, and more generally at the tradition of too easy verse which sees in every lord of a manor the Lord God of Hosts, it simultaneously participates in what it laughs at. Thus, no loss of distinction happens here. What does happen is that, led by his dramatization of Frances, Swift discovers a means to translate his mixed sense of her being into a theological matrix which preserves our awareness of her folly and yet authenticates her worth. For the first time in his verse, then, Swift fully escapes the dilemma of a moralist unable to affirm the significance of a world he nevertheless wishes to correct. But of course, this escape is not permanent. Rather, Swift must rewin it again and again in poems in which, unlike the *Petition*, the drama of his own doubt and pain itself becomes his only means of escape.

Probably because the feat initially must be done intuitively and all at once, Swift first exhibits his ability to escape doubt through doubt in an apparently whimsical and wholly obscure ballad called *To the Tune of the Cutpurse*. In this ballad, Swift turns his gaze directly on himself as doubter and at once enacts the drama of his own doubt while demonstrating the significance of that doubt within his poem. Despite the ballad's apparent slightness, then, it is the earliest ripe fruit of Swift's struggle to articulate a human meaningfulness which doubt itself cannot destroy. Built on doubt, the ballad is impervious to it, and insists on its own meaning through thick and through thin.

Unfortunately, the occasion that evoked *To the Tune of the Cutpurse* also stunted the development of an earlier and very promising poem, *A Ballad on the Game of Traffick*. Apparently, Swift had completed only six stanzas of the earlier ballad when Lord Berkeley's daughter, Lady Betty, happened to discover it. Obviously, Betty thought the poem only a bit of friendly raillery directed at various members of the Berkeley household. Therefore, she added to it what she clearly conceived to be the poem's final lines. In the context of the poem they end, however, these lines are more pointed than Betty probably knew; and they moved Swift to write *To the Tune of the Cutpurse*. That is why, in order fully to understand the later poem, we must first examine Betty's lines in the context of the earlier poem they cut off.

Almost certainly, Swift initially contrived the *Ballad on Traffick* as a considerably more ambitious poem than Betty guessed. Of course, the unwritten portions of the poem can hardly be constructed, but something at least of the poem's intended length and nature can be surmised on the basis of the work as it stands and from a knowledge of the game, traffick.[6] Traffick (or, to give it what was apparently its far more common name, commerce) is a card game specifically tailored to permit a large number of people to play together at once. Indeed, traffick must play badly with too few people, as Swift, who prided himself on being somewhat of a card buff, surely understood.[7] Therefore, since in his first six stanzas Swift was able to sketch only five members of his imaginary evening at cards, it is reasonable to assume that he originally intended his poem to contain at least several more stanzas than it does.

Further, as it stands the ballad itself seems to call for additional stanzas; for even in its truncated form it possesses an incipient but promising motif in traffick itself. Even more than most card games, traffick reflects a spirit of concordia-discors; thus, for one player to emerge a winner in the game, it is necessary for each player to barter (that is, to "traffick") with opponents. By setting the Berkeley household to play this game, then, Swift establishes a context which initially suggests a potential harmony in human community. And within the five sketches that comprise the ballad so far as he himself wrote it, Swift explores the transformative power of that harmony.

Taken together, the five sketches portray a charming evening *en famille*. Capturing, for an instant, some aspect of the play as it illuminates the individual character of the players, the sketches combine to illustrate a "trafficking" community, one, that is,

6. Knowledge of traffick is hard to get. Neither Charles Cotton in *The Compleat Gamester* nor Richard Seymour in *The Court Gamester* recognizes such a game. However, the *Académie Universelle des Jeux*, 2d ed. (Paris: T. Legras, 1725), pp. 44–49, does describe a game called commerce and that game, I believe, is Swift's traffick. This assumption is based on the following points. First, though Cotton and Seymour do not describe commerce, the game was known in early eighteenth-century England (see *OED* entry under *Commerce*). Secondly, the word *traffic* does, after all, mean commerce. Thirdly, the game described in the *Académie* is a three-card poker variant, which corresponds with the game Swift describes. Dame Herries facetiously claims she would have won with three aces and Dame Floyd is clearly looking for a poker hand.

7. Both Swift's pride in his card sense and his gift for whimsy are apparent in several passages in the *Journal to Stella*. See especially 1:43.

which is cooperating and harmonious. Within this community the individual shortcomings of some of the players are subsumed, as a matter of course, within the requirements of the game. Thus,

> My *Lady* tho' she is no Player
> Some bungling Partner takes,
> And wedg'd in Corner of a Chair
> Takes Snuff, and holds the Stakes.   (9–12)

Similarly, any unseemly hope for gain harbored, perhaps, in the breasts of other players is softened by humor to a merely entertaining eccentricity:

> Quoth *Herries*, fairly putting Cases,
> I'd won it on my Word,
> If I had but a Pair of Aces,
> And could pick up a third.   (17–20)

Finally, then, this process of adjustment and humorous coloration results in a family portrait that is as civilized and as civilizing as the game of traffick itself.

Yet because the charm of this portrait, like that of traffick, is the charm of harmony, the potential for dissonance is never more than half a note away. Of course, such dissonance as appears in this poem is mostly muted. The tiny avarice of Frances Harris, for example, and the miniature penuriousness of Dame Floyd do no more than texture the surface of the Berkeley's harmonious evening. But there is one exception to this pattern of consistently muted strife, one moment when the greater strifes of an outside world jostle, at least, the Berkeley's charmed circle. That moment comes early in the poem when Lord Berkeley, in the process of determining deal, turns up a knave:

> But then his *Honour* cry'd, Godzooks!
> And seem'd to knit his Brow;
> For on a Knave he never looks
> But H' thinks upon *Jack How*.   (5–8)

On the one hand, of course, the tone of this stanza remains clearly humorous. But on the other hand, its subject, John Grubham Howe, was a truly vicious man, a violent Tory, and a

political and personal enemy of Lord Berkeley.[8] Thus his comic
entry into the conviviality of the Berkeley's quiet evening at cards
represents a significant transformation of menace into laughter. It
further suggests that Swift's exploration of that harmony beyond
strife for which he had found so excellent an emblem in the game
of traffick has but just begun in the poem as we have it.

Just why Swift stopped work on his poem at the stage at which
Betty discovered it is what no one can say with certainty.
Perhaps he was only temporarily distracted from completing it by
the pressures of other work and other worries. But in the ballad
To the Tune of the Cutpurse, Swift himself suggests that having
written six stanzas of the *Ballad on Traffick* he found himself run
dry, at a point he calls "dead lift." If, in fact, he did strike this
sort of impasse, then the stanza Lady Betty added to his work
must have seemed especially pointed to him.

At all events, Betty's stanza is almost certainly more pointed
than she herself realized. No poet, she cast her lines clumsily and
even inadvertently reversed the meter of Swift's ballad. But
somehow, within an already sophisticated text, she managed to
construct an extremely sophisticated statement. Intuitively capturing the transformative humor of Swift's poem by which animad-
version is spun into laughter and strife into jest, Betty turned that
humor on Swift himself and added to his poem one final transformation. Thus she wrote:

> "With these is Parson *Swift*,
> "Not knowing how to spend his Time,
> "Does make a wretched Shift,
> "To deafen 'em with Puns and Rhime.   (25–28)

Looked at one way, of course, these lines are an outrageous
impertinence. Through them, Betty drags into Swift's own comic
circle that fear—so much a part of his earlier verse—that neither
his poetry nor his life meant anything at all. But looked at another
way, these lines are nearly an act of grace. For in them Swift's
fear itself is transformed into laughter and thus made to illustrate
that even the worst of things may have its human uses. In effect
then, these lines legitimate the very activity they disparage. And
that is the lesson which, whatever Betty meant by them, Swift

8. *DNB*.

took from her lines and insisted on in the answer he penned to them.

That answer is extraordinarily subtle. In fact, had Swift not appended to the poem's rambling title (*Lady B---- B---- finding in the Authors Room some Verses Unfinished, underwrit a Stanza of her own, with Railery upon him, which gave Occasion to this Ballade*) the very broad hint, *To the Tune of the Cutpurse*, it is doubtful whether Lady Betty or anyone else would have ever understood it. Composed of only three stanzas, which Swift wrote in a counterfeit hand as if a third person had done it, the majority of the poem is a whimsical narration of the miraculous experience and consequent problem of a (presumably medieval) friar. Both the friar's experience and his problem are commonplaces of folk tale. Unable to complete a poem, the friar, we are told, goes "to Bed in a desperate case." The next morning, however, he awakens to find his poem completed: ". . . Behold the next Morning, a wonderful Riddle,/He found it was strangely fill'd in the Middle" (8–9). Though the friar is pleased by this event, he is troubled by it, too, since he does not know the source of his help.

> This put me the Fryar into an Amazement,
>   For he wisely consider'd it must be a Sprite,
>   . . . .
>   Yet he did not know
>   If it were Friend or Foe,
> Or whether it came from Above or Below.   (12–13, 16–18)

The resolution of this problem becomes the crux of the poem.

Of course, Swift's narration of this miraculous experience appears to be so obviously flippant that it seems foolish to take seriously either the friar's problem or Swift's consequent application of the friar's situation to his own:

> Even so Master Doctor had Puzzled his Brains
>   In making a Ballad, but was at a Stand,
> He had mixt little Wit with a great deal of Pains,
>   When he found a new Help from Invisible Hand.   (22–25)

Nevertheless, in one way, at least, Swift does suggest that both the friar's problem and its application to himself have serious

enough implications. For even as he seems to treat as lightly as
had Lady Betty herself both the process and the purpose of his
poetry, he simultaneously connects his frolicsome treatment with
one of the most striking justifications of poetry in English comic
literature: Ben Jonson's *Bartholomew Fayre*.

The "Ballad of the Cutpurse," to the meter of which Swift
pointedly tells us he set his own ballad, functions within its ironic
context in Jonson's *Fayre* as a powerful condensation of both the
play's view of poetry and its morality. Sung by Nightingale, the
Fayre's ballad singer and general knave, the song simultaneously
warns passers-by to beware of cutpurses and admonishes cutpurses
to give over their dangerous professions. But though the matter of
the song is thus blamelessly sound, Nightingale's sole purpose in
singing it is to attract a crowd and divert its attention in order that
his partner, the cutpurse Ezekiel Edgeworth, may be provided
with a fair field full of gulls. Thus the song illustrates and illuminates that double truth which is central to both Jonson's play and
Swift's allusive ballad: that even the best of things may have its
geniture in ill, and that there is nothing so good in itself that it is
not susceptible to human abuse.

To be sure, Swift's story of a friar and a sprite, himself and
Lady Betty, has nothing of the massiveness of *Bartholomew
Fayre* in which, among other such lessons, a too-enthusiastic
judge learns that even justice carried too far may bear injustice, a
bigoted zealot demonstrates the ultimate irreligiousness of a too-
hot zeal, an over-trusting husband begets his own cuckolding, and
Jonson's audience learns, it is to be hoped, that though poetry,
like everything else, can be dangerous when it is abused, it can
also transform so tawdry a thing as Bartholomew Fair itself into a
place of great human instruction. Nevertheless, though Swift's
poem is far more narrow than Jonson's play, it is connected to
that play by more than mere metric imitation. For when Swift's
whimsically told story of a friar and his problem are seen through
the glass of *Bartholomew Fayre* then Swift's poem expands into a
very proper poetry lesson for Lady Betty and, perhaps, for us
too. Seen through that glass, the friar's concern for the source of
his poetry is a comic yet still somehow almost touching restatement of the problem that Jonson illustrated with Nightingale's
song, that Lady Betty herself noted in her stanza on Swift, and
that, perhaps, every poet who has ever lived has faced in one

form or another. For if poets through the ages are to be believed, the seed of poetry is often obscure or hateful. Yet ages of poets have continued to make poems, justifying their verses with something like those words Jonson delivered to his king at the first performance of *Bartholomew Fayre*.

> *Your* Maiesty *is welcome to a Fayre.*
> *Such place, such men, such language & such ware,*
> *You must expect*:
> . . . .
> *These for your sport*,
> . . . .
> *The Maker doth present: and hopes, to night*
> *To give you for a* Fayring, *true delight.*[9]

And it is with a sentiment very much like that which Jonson expressed that Swift, having voiced the friar's problem, goes on to settle it.

> Yet he did not know
> If it were Friend or Foe,
> Or whether it came from Above or Below.
> Howe'er it was civil in Angel or Elf,
> For he ne're could have fill'd it so well of himself.   (16–20)

Thus Swift suggests to Lady Betty, on the basis of the goodness of her own stanza, a point the truth of which this poem itself superbly suggests—that though a poem be generated in ennui and nurtured in whimsy, out of such seeds and such soil may grow much that is valuable.

One final point needs to be made about the narration of this poem and what that narration suggests about Swift himself. For Swift's handling of voice in this poem casts a curious ambivalence over everything in it. Thus, on the one hand, we know that the whole poem was occasioned by Lady Betty's raillery and that, therefore, its miniature justification of poetry must be understood as Swift's response to that raillery. On the other hand, the speaker of this poem is not formally Swift, but rather an anonymous third person who admonishes Swift. Of course, Swift's deci-

---

9. *Ben Jonson*, ed. C. H. Herford, Percy and Evelyn Simpson, 11 vols. (Oxford: Clarendon Press, 1925–52), 6:11.

sions to narrate this poem through an anonymous third person, to
inscribe it in an unfamiliar hand, and to make himself thus at once
its author and its recipient, all follow well enough, by a fanciful
sort of logic, from the piece of incognito versifying by which
Lady Betty had originally occasioned the poem. But though the
narrative fiction of this poem is thus, in part, attributable to the
particular circumstances of its composition, nevertheless, one effect of its narration remains strangely haunting. For, as a result of
the way in which the poem is narrated, it is Swift who is likened
to the friar uncertain of the origin of his verse, Swift who receives
a poetry lesson, and Swift who is exhorted, in the poem's chorus,
to versify despite his doubts and the devil: "Let Censuring
Criticks then think what they list on't/Who would not Write Verses with such an assistant." Thus, taken whole, the ballad *To the
Tune of the Cutpurse* finally suggests not only Swift's faith (which
he shared with Jonson) that out of fancy, friars, fairs, and motley,
poetry can erect something of value, but also the fears which, in
Swift, always flecked that faith and returned it over and over to
those doubts which are its dramatic origin.

One of the most interesting opportunities to explore that tension
between doubt and faith which is the source of Swift's special
power is provided by the very different but related patterns of
revision which we can trace in two of Swift's occasional poems:
Baucis and Philemon, and *Vanbrug's House*. Unfortunately, the
compositional history of neither poem is complete and we apparently lack a number of working drafts between what we call the
first version and the final printed version of each poem. Nevertheless, some basic bibliographical facts about both poems are certain enough.[10] Thus, we do know that the first version of each
was composed around the period of Swift's Irish residency from
1704 through 1707. Further, by Swift's recorded testimony, we
also know that an extensive revision of one of the poems, *Baucis
and Philemon*, was carried out as a joint enterprise between Swift
and Joseph Addison, probably in 1708. Finally, we know that during that same year, and amidst the same general influences, Swift
also revised *Vanbrug's House* but apparently carried out this re-

---

10. For a discussion of these facts see Williams, *Swift's Poems*, 1:78, 88–90.

vision independent of Addison's particular advice. These facts, when they are combined with the observation that the first versions of these poems are much more like each other than are their final versions, suffice to legitimate and guide a comparison of the poems in their divergent development. And in its turn, this comparison can clarify the elements of that complexity which is the heart of Swift's creative impulse.

Happily, the task of comparing the development of *Baucis and Philemon* with the development of *Vanbrug's House* has been made markedly easier by the recent publication of Eric Rothstein's valuable essay "Jonathan Swift as Jupiter: *Baucis and Philemon*."[11] In this essay, Rothstein convincingly demonstrates that under Addison's cool tutelage Swift forms a much more consistent poem in the second version of *Baucis and Philemon* than he had written in the first. Rothstein distinguishes in the first version the same radical dichotomization of purpose that we have already noticed in poem after poem. Thus, on the one hand, Swift tells Ovid's famous story with an obvious and energetic delight in its things and people. But on the other hand, he remolds the story so as to suggest, *contra* Ovid's providential vision, that the world he describes is utterly enmeshed in its own materiality and thus hopelessly irredeemable. As Rothstein notes, then, two distinct but apparently incommensurate world visions are represented in the first version of the poem, neither of them satisfactorily.

What the evidence of the second version demonstrates is that Addison perfectly grasped the conflict in the first. For as Rothstein meticulously illustrates, under Addison's instruction Swift methodically altered line after line of his first version, draining these lines of their original and contravening energy and recasting them to a formal and static precision. The result is a poem which marches all one way and which indisputably is meant to assert against both Ovid and his still more sanguine imitators and explicators the ultimately untransformable and mortal character of the material world. Whether, however, this almost obdurately consistent poem is a good one or not is another question.

Obviously, this question troubled Rothstein, and in the final

11. In *The Augustan Milieu: Essays Presented To Louis A. Landa*, ed. Henry Knight Miller, Eric Rothstein, and G. S. Rousseau (Oxford: Clarendon Press, 1970), pp. 205–24.

paragraphs of his essay he attempts to respond to it. Unfortunately, his response muddies, I think, the results of an otherwise
sensitive study. Aware that the final version of *Baucis and
Philemon* is open to the charge that it flattens human experience
by excluding the sort of divine intervention into worldly affairs
that Ovid's poem insists is possible, Rothstein attempts to defend
the richness of Swift's poem by arguing that Ovid's version
stands constantly behind it and constantly tempers it. This is an
attractive argument, of course, because it seems to offer us the
best of two worlds at once. But the fact is that Swift's poem simply shows no signs of such tempering. Thus the argument is only
a form of begging the question. Worse, though this argument in
no way makes Swift's poem richer, it does obscure a very important point.

As Rothstein claims, and as we too have seen, Swift's vision
normally expresses itself in multiple sets of varied perspectives.
In fact, the final version of *Baucis and Philemon* seems to be one
of the few poems in Swift's canon that is as resolutely single-
minded as readers once thought all his verse to be. Thus, what
the very deliberate development of *Baucis and Philemon* suggests, and the parallel yet different development of *Vanbrug's
House* confirms, is that to a greater degree than we usually admit
the multiple perspectives in Swift's work are an involuntary
phenomenon. Something like the color of our eyes, which is unknowable to us until either we are told it or see it reflected in
some other substance, Swift's proclivity to see the world as
simultaneously significant and meaningless seems to have been
too much a part of him often to fall itself under his gaze. When
this proclivity does grow visible to him (as it does in *Baucis and
Philemon* through the agency of Addison) Swift disburdens himself of it with disconcerting ease and becomes very nearly the
misanthropic dean of popular legend, the contemptuous master of
black comedy. But when, as in his revision of *Vanbrug's House*,
the inherent conflict of his vision remains obscure to him, then he
must work his way through that conflict itself as the given of his
world and struggle to achieve a coherence out of it. It is in this
struggle that Swift becomes, in Rothstein's fine phrase, "the master of metamorphosis."[12]

Whether the final version of *Baucis and Philemon* or of

12. Rothstein, p. 224.

Vanbrug's House is the finer poem is probably an unanswerable question. Fronting itself against both Ovid and his softly pietistic explicators, *Baucis and Philemon* is certainly the bigger poem; it may be, however, that measured by depth and range of vision, *Vanbrug's House* is the richer one. For in the latter poem Swift travels his own road and, apparently aided little by Addison, moves from a conflicted to a complex meaning through a process far less conscious than that employed in *Baucis and Philemon* but eliminating none of the elements of Swift's mingled response to the world.

The process begins with Vanbrugh's house itself and its placement in a densely significant topography. On January 4, 1698, fire consumed all of Whitehall Palace save only Inigo Jones's famous Banqueting House. Though plans were immediately drawn to rebuild the palace, they came to nothing and the great seat of the Tudors and Stuarts was allowed to perish in an England that had learned to crown its kings by convocation. A few years after the fire, Vanbrugh, never a timorous man, asked for and received permission to build his own private residence on the site and from the old materials of Whitehall. The house he built was architecturally bolder, perhaps, than his initial request had been. But boldness is not always a virtue and Swift apparently felt deeply that both the site and the style of the house formed an irreverent comment on the past and a bleak prophecy for the future.

Obviously, however, Swift found his response to Vanbrugh's house difficult to organize, for over at least a five-year period he produced three distinct poems treating it, not counting minor revisions. His first essay at it, entitled *Vanbrug's House: Built from the burnt Ruins of Whitehall*, was not published during his lifetime. This version survives in two manuscripts, one written fair in Swift's hand and then corrected by Swift, the other, which varies slightly from the first, in the hand of Swift's friend, Charles Ford. Both manuscripts display a poem organized around three motifs: the first part of the poem is a narration of the myth of Amphion as a "type" of classical poetry; the second part describes modern poets in terms of insect imagery; the third part is an ironic comparison of piddling restorations such as Vanbrugh's building with the great notion of restoration expressed in the phoenix myth.

Swift's second attempt to define his response to Vanbrugh's art was penned under a fresh impetus. In 1705 Vanbrugh was appointed architect at Blenheim, and Swift, annoyed anew, wrote *The History of Vanbrug's House*. This poem, which in one manuscript version bears the mordantly ironic title *The Architect*, shares nothing with the earlier *Vanbrug's House*. It is the weakest of Swift's poems on Vanbrugh: its mockery is confined to the something less than piercing assertion that Vanbrugh (whose formal training as an architect seems to have been slender) had learned his art by watching children build houses from clay and mud. But though the poem is weak it was a necessary transitional exercise for Swift and it does provide us one piece of significant information about his architectural tastes and values. One might guess it anyway, but it is pleasant to have confirmation that Swift's standard for harmonious architectural excellence was, as it was for most of his contemporaries, the theory of Vitruvius. Thus, Swift comments mockingly on Vanbrugh that he is now "justly reckond/At Court, Vitruvius the second" (37–38).

Swift's final poem on Vanbrugh and his works properly carries essentially the same title as his first (*V——'s House: Built from the Ruins of Whitehall that was burnt*); for though it is highly revised and significantly altered it is no more than a final revision of the early poem. As noted above, Swift apparently wrote this version in 1708; but because it was not published until 1711 it is difficult to guess what stimulated him to make the revision. Quite possibly, though he was not directly involved in this project, Addison did encourage its initiation. Additionally, it may be that sometime around 1708 Swift chanced to see or read Vanbrugh's adaptation of Dancourt's farce, *La Maison de Campagne*, and recognized in it elements which helped unify his own poem. At all events, he retained in his revision almost all of the first and third parts of the early version, making in the almost seventy lines involved only a few truly important alterations. But the second section of the early version, with its motif of insect imagery, is entirely expunged and replaced by seventy new lines. These lines, which describe the miraculous construction of Vanbrugh's house, entirely alter the stance of Swift's original poem. Apparently, with this alteration, the poem finally achieved a form that satisfied him.

Part of the difficulty Swift experienced in defining his response to Vanbrugh probably stemmed from the distinction he almost certainly drew between Vanbrugh the man and Vanbrugh the artist. For as Swift, who saw him frequently, doubtless appreciated, Vanbrugh was apparently a very good-natured man. Such a man is difficult to satirize, no matter how grievously wrong-headed his art may be. Thus, years later Swift was still uncomfortably aware that though his attack was carefully made, it might also be, in some way deeply felt, regrettable.[13]

Regrettable or not, however, Swift's satire on Vanbrugh was also nearly inevitable; for it is the nature of Vanbrugh's art, and of his private residence in particular, implicitly to question those assumptions which, though Swift was paradoxically willing to surrender them to Addison's logic and sometimes to his own doubt, he was simultaneously most tender of. These assumptions are stated clearly enough in the first lines of every version we have of *Vanbrug's House*; because they provide a nearly overt statement of Swift's poetic idealism, I cite them here in full.

> In times of *Old*, when Time was *Young*,
> And Poets their own Verses Sung,
> A Song could draw a Stone or Beam,
> That now would overload a Team;
> Lead 'em a Dance of many a Mile,
> Then rear 'em to a goodly Pile,
> Each Number had it's diff'rent pow'r;
> Heroick Strains could build a Tow'r;
> Sonnets or Elogies to *Chloris*
> Might raise a House about two Storyes;
> A Lyrick Ode would Slate; a Catch
> Would Tile; an Epigram would Thatch.   (1–12)

Commentators have long noted that these lines, which contrast so strikingly to the static transformations described in the final version of *Baucis and Philemon*, derive from their own myth, the story of Amphion. Amphion, a son of Zeus and Antiope, was granted the gift of music by Hermes and practiced it so successfully that the very rocks moved to the magic of his lyre to form

13. The preface to *Miscellanies: The Last Volume* contains this statement: "In regard to two persons only, we wish our Raillery, though ever so tender, or resentment, though ever so just, had not been indulged. We speak of Sir John Vanbrugh, who was a man of wit and honor; and of Mr. Addison . . ." (London: Benjamin Motte, 1733, p. 6).

the massive wall behind which Thebes grew great. Of course, it is obvious that Swift interlines his version of this myth with considerable whimsy and a pointed ironic intention: thus because the story of Amphion traditionally emblemized the divine power not only of music, but of all measured forms to educe harmony and civility out of wasteland,[14] the myth is brilliantly suited to Swift's attack on a man he felt to be an ill dramatist and a worse architect. Nevertheless, significantly subsumed in the whimsy with which Swift protects the myth from rude incredulity and implicit in his ironic intention in telling it is his acceptance of its central insight—that human art, though a gift wholly divine in origin and half divine in practice, can and ought to function harmoniously with the stuff of this world to draw from it the terms on which civilization is possible.

Judged by this view of art, Vanbrugh's architecture in general and his small house at Whitehall in particular are wholly unsatisfactory. To be sure, Vanbrugh was a remarkable architect, but for good or ill his power lay entirely in the vigor with which he attacked that architectural program which best affirmed a reciprocal harmony of man and nature—Palladianism. Of course, Palladianism can be described in a multitude of ways: its inspiration was the one surviving architectural treatise from the age of Augustus Caesar, Vitruvius's *De Architectura*; its models are the works of the sixteenth-century Italian, Andrea di Pieto da Padova; its aesthetic is profoundly baroque; and its effects are unusually solemn. But finally, the essence of Palladianism, as Wittkower pointed out years ago, is its theory of proportion.[15] That theory in full is enormously complicated; but its root assumption is simply that even as the delightful harmony of music is not the effect of chance, but is rather the auditory experience of

14. Edmund Waller, in his congratulatory poem, *Upon his Majesty's Repairing of Paul's*, provides an example of the sort of breadth Stuart writers found in the myth:

> He, [Charles] like Amphion, makes those quarries leap
> Into Fair Figures from a confused heap;
> For in his art of regiment is found
> A power like that of harmony in sound.

Quotation from *The Poems of Edmund Waller*, ed. G. Thorn Drury, 2 vols. (1893; rpt. London and New York: G. Routledge and Sons, E. P. Dutton and Co., 1904), 1:16.

15. Rudolph Wittkower, *Architectural Principles in the Age of Humanism*, 3d ed. (London: Tiranti, 1962). This point is the center of Wittkower's entire study.

mathematically expressible harmonic ratios, so, similarly, all beauty is the function of universally valid mathematical proportions. Thus, Palladianism is ultimately a search for and an architectural deployment of those universally valid proportions which men, because they are part of that great harmony which informs all creation, see as beauty though they know not why.

That Vanbrugh planned his works with great disregard for the classic Palladian proportions favored by his age can be proved merely with a tape measure. More important, that his work projects an utterly different view of the world from the harmonious reciprocity of God, man, and nature that Palladian architects sought to capture is what a clever contemporary, Dr. Abel Evans, immediately sensed and wittily expressed in an epitaph in which Vanbrugh is cast as virtually an anti-Amphion at war with his natural element.

> Under this stone, reader, survey
> Dead Sir John Vanbrugh's house of clay:
> Lie heavy on him, earth! for he
> Has laid many heavy loads on thee.[16]

Of course, in this epitaph Evans was thinking of Vanbrugh's great works and principally, perhaps, of Blenheim, the house too expensive for a queen to build and too great for anyone else to inhabit. But, in fact, all Vanbrugh's work, great and small, is purposively inharmonious with its surroundings and with itself. Built for dramatic effect alone, his strongest works seem almost to emblemize discord among the elements: "Almost any part of the structure," observes one admiring historian of architecture, "is a menace to the others."[17] Thus, though he had no personal school of disciples, Vanbrugh's work was prophetic of a great architectural transition. A few years after Vanbrugh's death, Edmund Burke put in words the statement most of Vanbrugh's building implicitly makes. Utterly disavowing the symbolism implicit in Evans's epitaph, Burke commented, "I know it has been said long since . . . that the proportions of building have been

16. Quoted from W. C. Ward's introduction to his edition of Vanbrugh's works, *Sir John Vanbrugh*, 2 vols. (London: Lawrence and Bullen, 1893), 1:50.
17. Emil Kaufmann, *Architecture in the Age of Reason* (Cambridge: Harvard University Press, 1955), p. 18.

taken from the human body. [But] certainly nothing could be more unaccountably whimsical, than for an architect to model his performance by the human figure, since no two things can have less resemblance or analogy, than a man, and a house or temple."[18] In this statement one may hear both the death knell of Amphion, who called a city into being with his song, and the birth cry of that architecture of purely geometric possibility we call "modern."

It was typical, of course, of Vanbrugh's dissociative genius that he chose to build his bachelor's *pied à terre* on the recent site of England's most famous palace. To be sure, it is difficult to say how deeply Vanbrugh's choice of site may, in itself, have disturbed Swift's sense of harmonious propriety, for at one point in his life at least Swift possibly regarded the destruction of Whitehall as an act of providential purgation. Nevertheless, there is a difference between acknowledging an act of divine justice and condoning a piece of human impertinence and Swift certainly could always make that distinction. Further, because Vanbrugh built his residence at Whitehall for himself rather than for a patron, it was the most radically individualistic of his works, "distinguished by dissonances both on the surfaces and in the masses, by emphasis on cubes and by [a] disproportionate height and scale of rustication."[19] To an eye accustomed to seeking in architecture the symbolic representation of a binding universal harmony the house must have seemed an incredible combination of lunettes and half-columns, the devil and all. Swift, at all events, saw in Vanbrugh's house nothing less than an antitype of art; and just as the myth of Amphion in some sort expressed his belief in art's harmonic powers, so the spectacle of Vanbrugh's "dissonant" house quickened his always present fear that his belief was foolishly illusory. Thus, having narrated the tale of Amphion's powers, Swift closes that narration in the earliest version of *Vanbrug's House* with the grimly comic remark "Now Poets find [his] Art is lost,/Both to their own and Landlord's Cost" (13–14); and it is the hopeless irony of this couplet which controls the whole first version of his poem.

18. Edmund Burke, *A Philosophical Enquiry into the Origins of our Ideas of the Sublime and the Beautiful*, ed. J. T. Boulton (New York: Columbia University Press, 1958), p. 100.

19. Kaufmann, p. 16.

Perhaps, however, "controls" is too absolute an expression to use in describing this poem. For the fact is that, like the first version of *Baucis and Philemon*, the first version of *Vanbrug's House* is a poem divided against itself. Thus, on the one hand, it depicts a universe in which sense and substance have been rendered utterly discrete by divine decree since the time of Amphion:

> For Jove consider'd well the Case,
> That Poets were a numerous Race,
> And if they all had Power to build,
> The Earth would very soon be filld:
> Materials would be quickly spent,
> And Houses would not give a Rent.
> The God of Wealth was therefore made
> Sole Patron of the building Trade,
> Leaving to Wits the spatious Air,
> With License to build Castles there;
> And 'tis conceiv'd, their old Pretence
> To lodge in Garrats comes from thence.   (17–28)

But on the other hand, it violently attacks the incongruous art of one particular man as if a harmony of sense and substance were possible:

> After hard Throws of many a Day
> Van was deliver'd of a Play,
> Which in due time brought forth a House;
> Just as the Mountain did the Mouse;
> One Story high, one postern Door,
> And one small Chamber on a Floor.
> Born like a Phoenix from the Flame,
> But neither Bulk nor Shape the same.   (73–80)

The result is that the 1703 version of *Vanbrug's House* ends a prey to the very disharmony it would satirize; making two inharmonious points it ends by making none at all, and Vanbrugh emerges from it less a target of satire than a victim, along with Swift himself, of the dissonance of a post-Amphionic age.

Of course, to remark the fundamental incongruity of this poem is not to deny the power or logic of several of its individual passages. For example, the comparison of poets to silk worms which comprises the entire second section of the poem is both a carefully worked out and a striking example of what was almost an eighteenth-century genre in itself, the deprecatory likening of human activity to that of the insects whose ambiguous generation, frailty, and brief life span seemed almost to exclude from participatory significance in the great harmony of the universe. Working all the possibilities in this analogy, Swift tells us that, like the silk worm, the poet, "unprovided where to dwell," spins his house out of himself only to lose it to others' tawdry uses while he is metamorphosed into a creature which, being a proper denizen of neither air nor earth, "flutters when he Thinks he flyes,/ Then sheds about his Spaun, and dyes" (37–38). Clearly, this passage is well done; its only flaw is that it states too absolutely the uselessness of verse and versifiers. Good in itself, it nevertheless renders inexplicable Swift's attack on the particular emptiness of Vanbrugh's drama and architecture.

To reform the individual passages of *Vanbrug's House* into a coherent whole Swift logically might have followed either one of two opposed procedures: he might have further generalized his attack on Vanbrugh's art to include all human art since Amphion's time, or he might have particularized that attack. Either course would have yielded him a thematically consistent poem; but either course, too, involves a penalty which is the necessary consequence of the consistency it permits. Thus if, on the one hand, Swift had generalized his attack on Vanbrugh's art so as to imply no special and corrigible error in that art, the resultant poem, though internally consistent, could only have suggested an utterly fragmented world view, one in which matter and meaning are irrevocably parted. If, on the other hand, Swift had particularized his attack on Vanbrugh's art so as to produce a poem both internally consistent and offering a holistic world view, then, for reasons we shall presently see, the resultant poem must necessarily have lacked both power and point. In effect, then, in his attempt to revise the first version of *Vanbrug's House* so that its damaging self-contradictoriness yields to coherency, Swift seems to struggle with an insurmountable problem. But as the final version of *Vanbrug's House* demonstrates, this problem itself is also an answer.

Apparently, Swift never even attempted to revise *Vanbrug's House* by generalizing its attack, though to have followed that procedure would have been his simplest course for at least two reasons. First, though the earliest version of the poem teeters between general despair and particular attack, it does exhibit a distinct bias towards despair. Thus, to have drained away the contravening energy of the poem's particular attack would have been a relatively easy thing to do. Secondly, to refocus the poem in this way would have been especially easy because this procedure imitates almost exactly the method Swift and Addison, working together, were simultaneously developing in the final version of *Baucis and Philemon*. Nevertheless, despite the several inducements to revise *Vanbrug's House* towards a gloomy consistency, Swift, working alone, significantly works towards a more holistic goal.

Swift's movement towards that goal hardly forms a steady track, however. Rather, his movement exhibits a process of discovery, carried on in the work itself as well as evidenced by it and carried on, too, at a level perhaps never wholly conscious. In *The History of Vanbrug's House* we can catch a fascinating glimpse of this process. As we have already noted, the *History*—which is really little more than a squib—has nothing in common with either major version of *Vanbrug's House*. But the *History* does chronicle a significant step in Swift's struggle with the elements of his larger poem. This step can be described tactically by simply remarking that, in the *History*, Swift manages to contain the force of his dislike for Vanbrugh's art within his attack on that art itself. To say only this much, however, is to risk missing the heart of Swift's achievement. For, because the scope of the *History* is confined to simple raillery, the poem itself is not especially impressive. What is impressive is the perceptual shift implicit in the poem's tactics. This shift occurred before the actual composition of the *History*, and consequently, its very existence is apparent only when the *History* is viewed from the perspective of the first version of *Vanbrug's House*. So viewed, however, the vigorous self-assurance of the *History* testifies that before its composition Swift had effected, probably unconsciously, a real metamorphosis of his own vision in which he not only pushed himself past his own despair but forced the very cause of that despair, Vanbrugh's house, to yield him up a comic vision of Vanbrugh's ineptitude. In the *History*, that is, Swift demonstrates his recovery of a coherent world vision: the fact of Vanbrugh's house no longer threatens to separate matter from meaning or heaven from earth.

The trouble is, however, that in the *History* Swift recovers this coherent world vision all too completely. Ironically, by first transforming Vanbrugh's blundering art from a real threat to an object of simple scorn, Swift renders his subsequent attack on it pointless. That is why, unless we place the *History* against the first version of *Vanbrug's House* and thus experience it as a processive achievement, we necessarily feel the poem to be inconsequential. For, finally, nothing is "doing" in the *History*, and the only thing attacked by it is, according to Swift's own admission, inconsequential.

Encouragingly, though, by the close of the *History* Swift himself seemed to grow aware that his poem did not sum up to much, and in its final lines he attempts to point its significance. First he notes that, despite his ineptitude, Vanbrugh is thought at court to be another Vitruvius; thus he suggests that a serious corruption of artistic values exists at the center of his society. Secondly, to point the danger inherent in such corruption, he concludes his poem by officiously laying aside his raillery and drawing a moral of sorts from Marlborough's inappropriate employment of Vanbrugh as his chief architect at Blenheim. "But Raillery, for once, apart," he warns,

> If this Rule [of rewarding ineptitude] holds in ev'ry
>   art,
> Or if his Grace were no more skilld in
> The Art of battring Walls, than building,
> We might expect to find next Year
> A Mousetrap-man chief Engineer.   (43–48)

This warning, however, is not very effective. Caught—despite Swift's disclaimer—between raillery and earnest, it has too little humor to pass for jest but comes too near confounding the art of building walls with the act of battering them to be taken seriously, either. Thus, rather than bolstering Swift's attack on Vanbrugh's art, the last lines of the *History* merely emphasize the weakness of that attack.

Finally, however, despite Swift's failure to instill into its concluding lines the degree of gravity necessary to give the *History*

force, those lines, like the body of his poem, indicate real progress in his thought about Vanbrugh's house. Thus, just as the aggressively contemptuous body of the poem demonstrates Swift's
a priori mastery of that despair which mars the first version
of *Vanbrug's House*, so his final lines indicate his awareness
of the difficulties implicit in that mastery. In fact, then, though
not a good poem itself, the *History* does demonstrate at its completion nearly all the elements necessary to the creation of a
good poem which, without sacrificing the complexity of Swift's
response to Vanbrugh's art, moves beyond the blind contradicto-
riness of the first version of *Vanbrug's House* towards a new
consistency, dramatically apprehended and portrayed.

Strikingly enough, in the final lines of the first version of
Vanbrug's House Swift had already begun to move, though grop-
ingly, towards such a consistency. Obviously already a little troubled by the disparity between the general pessimism of his poem
on the one hand and its particular attack on the other, he attempted to effect a resolution of this disparity through a clever
but still quibbling play on "modern." This play depends upon the
fact that, as a consequence of the famous battle of the Ancients
and Moderns, "modern" carried for Swift and for his audience at
once a general and a particular meaning. Thus, in the context of
the first version of *Vanbrug's House*, the phrase "modern rhymers" could refer either to the generations of hopelessly blighted
post-Amphionic writers postulated by the poem, or it could refer
to just those writers, contemporary with Swift, who subscribed to
the Modern side. In his final lines, Swift availed himself of this
ambivalence and permitted the phrase "modern rhymers" to float
between its two possible meanings. Consequently, in those final
lines, the general despair and the particular attack of his poem do
seem to cohere in a last synthesized outburst.

> So, Modern Rhymers strive to blast
> The Poetry of Ages past,
> Which having wisely overthrown,
> They from it's Ruins build their own.   (89–92)

In fact, of course, considered from the perspective of the entire
poem, the synthetic effect of these lines is purely illusory. The
lines work simply because they encourage us to forget that the
"moderns" who have been attacked throughout the poem are not

at all Swift's contemporary Moderns who purposively reject the past, but are rather those generations of poets disestablished by Jove. Forgetting this distinction, we may indeed temporarily feel that in his final lines Swift has escaped the crippling dichotomy of his poem and found a meaningful target for his anger. But so soon as we recover the distinction, the dichotomy reappears.

Nevertheless, though Swift's play with "modern" obscures rather than resolves the basic dichotomy of his poem, it is vitally important for us to recognize the significance of this play, considered simply by itself and in itself. For whatever else this play is—successful or unsuccessful, hoax or not—it is itself neither despair nor particular attack but rather a mental activity which goes beyond either previous state. Thus, though in the final lines of the first version of *Vanbrug's House* Swift does not (indeed, cannot) efface the dichotomous nature of the whole preceding poem, he does overcome the cause; that is, he overcomes that contradiction of despair and attack into which Vanbrugh's work had initially pitched him. In effect, then, in seeking to mend his broken poem Swift does something infinitely better; he mends himself and thereby becomes, through his own procedure, that which he seeks: a dramatic middle term between Vanbrugh's disharmonious architecture and his own idealism.

Of course, Swift was seeking this middle term not in himself but in the world. Therefore, and understandably, the nature of his achievement was not initially clear to him. His genius, however, consists in part in the fact that, caught between his desire to discover the marks of a harmonious world and his fear that no such marks are to be found, he was usually willing to abide the consequent tension long enough to see in his very ambivalence the marks for which he sought. Thus, at some point beyond his composition of the sterile *History of Vanbrug's House*, Swift saw again (at whatever level such seeing occurs) that truth which, like most of us, he needed to discover over and over throughout his life—that the world's meaning consists precisely in that ambivalence through which it presents itself to us, an ambivalence rich with the potential for metamorphosis. To put all this another way, Swift saw, as he wrote his final version of *Vanbrug's House*, that for the story of Amphion to be meaningful it is not merely sufficient but absolutely necessary that we ourselves become Amphion-like.

In the final version of *Vanbrug's House* Swift does indeed become Amphion-like, transforming dichotomy into ambivalence and ambivalence into meaning. Thus, though the opening lines of the final version of the poem duplicate almost exactly the opening lines of its earlier version, Swift effects two slight changes in the lines which magically alter their entire stance. One of these changes occurs in Jove's interdiction of further poet builders like Amphion. In the early version of the poem, we recall, Jove's justification for this interdiction is couched in the harsh terms of brutal material necessity: "Materials would be quickly spent," he claims, "And Houses would not give a Rent" (21–22). In the 1708 version, however, Jove's decision is softened by an explanation which places it humorously within the convention of service to the highest good.

> For, *Jove* consider'd well the Case,
> Observ'd they [poets] grew a num'rous race.
> And should they *Build* as fast as *Write*,
> 'Twould ruin Undertakers quite.
> This Evil, therefore to prevent,
> He wisely chang'd their Element.   (17–22)

Of course, by softening Jove's prohibition, Swift does not absolutely alter the effect of it; presumably poets are still prevented from working the stuff of this world. But because the terms of this prohibition are milder, Swift is able to discover just enough room in them to make a second change in his opening lines, and this change does substantially modify the consequence of Jove's fiat. Thus, in the original version of the poem, Swift summed the effect of that fiat in the following, rigid lines: "Now Poets find [Amphion's] Art is lost,/Both to their own and Landlord's Cost" (13–14). But in his final version, Swift alters these lines so that they instead read, "But, to their own, or Landlord's Cost,/Now Poets feel this Art is lost" (13–14). For this alteration no convincing explanation can be offered, I think, except that Swift, apparently, chose to rework his opening lines so that they reflect a purposive ambivalence. Changing the phrase "Now Poets find" to "Now Poets feel this art is lost," Swift presents us with a world in which this art is and is not lost; banished by divine action it remains still somehow contingent on poetic sensibility.

This is, of course, a much more perplexing world than the cut-and-dried unmagical one of Swift's first version. But if uncertain, it is also a world of human possibilty.

Obviously, such a world accords badly with the certain despair of the original second section of *Vanbrug's House*. Understandably, then, in his final version of the poem, Swift expunges this section entirely and replaces its bitter portrayal of all poets as fated insects (which but "flutter" when they think they fly) with a quite lengthy narration which carefully details the miraculous construction of Vanbrugh's blighted estate. Now, like so much else in the final version of the poem, the first hint for this narration also exists in its original version. Indeed, the hint was scarcely avoidable there since if Swift's poem was to make thematic sense at all he was compelled to account for the actual existence of Vanbrugh's house within the poem's mythical framework. Logically, however, in the first version of the poem this necessity could only embarrass Swift; for having insisted that Amphion's power was absolutely lost to subsequent poets, he really had no way to absorb the actual existence of Vanbrugh's house into the framework of his poem. Consequently, he was forced to scuttle past the miraculous construction of the house as best he could, clambering over rather than exploiting the evident paradox that for Vanbrugh alone Jove has waived an eternal fiat and permitted a poet to build a house as ancient poets built them.

In the final version of the poem, however, having re-rendered his account of Amphion's power so as to make that power ambiguously available to contemporary poets, Swift is able to utilize brilliantly the paradoxical existence of Vanbrugh's house in order to illustrate not only a potential reciprocity between man, the stuff of this world, and the God Whose world this is, but also to depict the terms on which this reciprocity is possible. Thus, on the one hand, by imagining Vanbrugh to have prayed for and received Jove's permission "to build by Verse as heretofor," Swift affirms his faith in the enduring capacity of human art to participate in that harmony which Amphion knew. But on the other hand, by imagining Vanbrugh to have abused and thereby forfeited the gift of significant creativity he received, Swift forcefully delineates the grounds on which that gift exists.

This process of simultaneous affirmation and qualification is initially apparent in the very terms of Vanbrugh's prayer to Jove;

for, as Swift manages it, this prayer is an instructively riven one. On the face of it, it is apparently an act of bold faith: it assumes the existence of a Jove to pray to and affirms that poets have previously built palaces in conjunction with him. Thus far, then, the prayer is recognizably sound, for as we have seen, both of these assumptions are absolutely necessary if one hopes to build palaces as Amphion built them. As we have also seen, however, neither of these assumptions is demonstrable; both must rest upon radical faith or upon nothing at all. And in the instance of Vanbrugh's prayer, they are made to rest upon nothing at all.

Indeed, under examination, the whole force of Vanbrugh's prayer operates to exhibit both the meaning and the consequences of a lifeless faith, a form without the substance. For even as Vanbrugh invokes great Jove's aid in building, Swift continuously chooses his words so as to betray the fundamental solipsism of his heart. For example, by claiming he will construct a "Pile . . . Fit to Invade or prop the Skies" (49–50), Vanbrugh only succeeds in imagining himself the builder of what is obviously a Babel. Thus, like every successive builder of that crazy edifice, he reveals himself as a man who (despite his prayer) finally trusts nothing to be substantial except his own words and his own acts. That is why, though Jove consents to his project and promises to flesh his words in stone, that consent does him not good but ill. For under compulsion, now, to write, and believing in nothing really but himself, he discovers the comic fact that he has literally nothing to write about. Even farce, which is his own choice of forms, is utterly beyond him; for every form of drama requires the creation of some sort of life existing apart from its author, and that is just what the proud spirit that Swift ascribes to Vanbrugh cannot produce. All such pride can do is what Swift finally described Vanbrugh's attempting to do: it can steal another man's work and try to pass it off as its own.

Finally, then, by making Vanbrugh's prayer at once apparently successful and yet disastrously solipsistic, Swift presses home that truth for which he himself had to struggle as he composed *Vanbrug's House*: that belief itself is the necessary ground of the meaningful reciprocity that belief affirms. To put the matter negatively, in Vanbrugh's comic dilemma Swift shows us that without belief even Jove's consent to our very wishes must be useless to us, for we neither receive what we do not believe exists, nor can we create what is capable of standing apart from us. That is why, as Swift perceived, it really does not matter whether Vanbrugh attempts to build a highly original house or simply to steal another man's play. For these two activities, apparently so different, are from the solipsistic point of view merely equal manifestations of self. Thus, what may seem at first either odd or unjustly malicious—that in the final denouement of Vanbrugh's project Swift insists on linking the bold singularity of Vanbrugh's architecture to Vanbrugh's character as a literary plagiary—is, in fact, neither odd nor unjust. Rather, by imagining that through the agency of Jove, Vanbrugh's most individualized building literally grew as a perfect image of a stolen farce, Swift asks us to recognize that it is neither an irrelevance nor an accident but rather a confirmation of Vanbrugh's solipsism that he really was both a highly eccentric architect and an often derivative dramatist. Achieving this recognition himself, Swift completes the long journey back from that inarticulate despair into which Vanbrugh's house had originally cast him. For having discovered the meaning of that house's meaninglessness, he, echoing the Jove he imagined, could afford to see the matter as a jest and laugh the good, full, laughter of the gods.

Yet even as Swift laughed this affirming laughter, one problem still remained for him and it remains still for us. As we have seen, Swift continued to worry for years whether the last version of *Vanbrug's House* was finally a fair poem, whether, that is, it rightly presented Vanbrugh and his work as both of them really were. Of course, this sort of question is a dangerous one because, when it is clumsily asked, it tends to reduce satire to simple representation and thus obscures the fact that, like every other form of art, satire evolves its truth out of a system of fictions whose interrelationship, in each individual work, produces the satire's world view. Mindful of this danger, however, we need also to be mindful of the necessity to validate, at some point, the world view so produced, lest satire itself grow wholly introverted and its truth ossify to falsehood or rarefy to cliché. Further, as Swift himself was aware, in the instance of *Vanbrug's House* it is especially necessary to validate the poem's attack by comparing it to what we can know of its subject. For a proud assumption of self-sufficiency is exactly what Swift accuses Vanbrugh of. If, then, Swift's attack itself is in some perverse way prejudiced, that circumstance must throw into doubt not only the soundness of its aesthetic assumptions but the sum of its moral judgment as well.

Uncomfortably enough, there is some reason to entertain such doubts about *Vanbrug's House*; for at least three effects of Vanbrugh's art—Blenheim, *The Provoked Wife*, and *The Relapse*—have proved to be of lasting value. Thus, because Swift's attack, though directed at Vanbrugh's house in particular, strikes at the very basis of Vanbrugh's art, the real worth of these artifacts at first seems to gainsay Swift's judgment. Finally, however, even these three best achievements do not explode that judgment, I think; rather, they simply exhibit its character. For example, because he never possessed an eye for monumental glory, it is almost certain that Swift failed to appreciate the virtually militant power with which Blenheim dominates its landscape. This failure constitutes an aesthetic disability and certainly we must remark it as such. At the same time, however, we must note that this failure does not utterly impugn Swift's judgment. For if we regard Blenheim through Swift's eyes we discover a valid and disturbing point which we might easily have missed on our own: that the monumental power of Marlborough's great estate celebrates nothing if it does not celebrate the ultimate solipsism of force of arms. Thus, in architecture at least, Swift's judgment of Vanbrugh's work is useful if not perfectly sound: it misses some real virtues, but the faults it illuminates are confirmed even in Vanbrugh's best building.

So, too, and in much the same way, Swift's judgment of Vanbrugh's dramatic skills is also useful and is confirmed by Vanbrugh's best plays. Of course, what we value about these plays is that, in plot at least, each is informed by a keen sense of moral justice. In fact, even that "stolen" play which is probably Swift's target in *Vanbrug's House*, Vanbrugh's adaptation of Dancourt's *La Maison de Campagne*, participates in this virtue.[20] Because it does so, Swift's attack suggests that he may not have

20. Swift does not name the play he imagines to have called Vanbrugh's house into existence; but it is almost certainly this one. For though *The Country House* has only two acts rather than the five described by Swift's poem, it does fit the rest of Swift's specifications. Not only is it Vanbrugh's single wholly borrowed French farce, it also illustrates that bent of mind for which Swift satirized Vanbrugh. A collection of jokes at the expense of a penurious and perhaps dishonest lawyer, the play does suggest that the lawyer's misfortunes are the result of his avarice, but it offers no workable alternative to his country misery, no vision of either a proper country life or a harmonious country estate.

recognized as fully as we do the general moral framework of Vanbrugh's drama. If he did not, his omission certainly flaws his response to Vanbrugh's work. Again, however, this omission is not a fatal one; for in *Vanbrug's House* Swift's attack is not really aimed at the moral content of Vanbrugh's plays at all. Rather, it is aimed at Vanbrugh's failure to create a living drama. This failure is real, and it mars even Vanbrugh's best work. Thus, for example, *The Relapse* is peopled with static characters who, though they do evoke our sympathy, prove to be utterly incapable of significant change. Inevitably, these characters militate against the moral force of the very dramas they populate; for their general inflexibility suggests that though a moral order does exist in the world of Vanbrugh's plays it is unavailable to all but a small elect of Vanbrugh's characters. In effect, then, Vanbrugh's drama creates a result that is the mirror image of that created by Blenheim. For as Blenheim celebrates the violent power of the human will in war, so the dramas exhibit a moral order to which that will can aspire but scarcely ever attain. In neither art, then, does Vanbrugh capture an order which, because it is both transcendent and immanent, can meaningfully inform our lives. And that is why, despite its brilliance, his work in either art finally appears hollow and brittle when compared to the best that has been built and said.

Happily, such a comparison is exactly the business of the final section of Swift's poem. In that section, Swift pens the following comic paean of praise to Vanbrugh and to his house, now imagined to be complete:

> THRICE happy Poet, who may trail
> Thy House about thee like a Snail;
> Or Harness'd to a Nag, at ease
> Take Journies in it like a chaise;
> Or in a Boat when e're thou wilt
> Canst make it serve thee for a Tilt.
> Capacious House! 'tis own'd by all
> Thou'rt well contriv'd, tho' thou art small.   (109–16)

That this praise is ludicrous is, of course, evident enough. What is not so evident, perhaps, is the way in which it is ludicrous, for Swift is not simply laughing at Vanbrugh's house because it is small. Rather, he is laughing because like all Vanbrugh's art, large and small, the house partially embodies a noble ideal, but embodies it badly. With Vanbrugh's house the ideal is self-expression, and aiming at it Vanbrugh aims only at what a variety of seventeenth-century estate poems affirm again and again is the proper end of architectural endeavor. Such poems insist, however, that self-expression is not the same thing as self-aggrandizement, and in the passage cited above Swift sharpens this truth by applying to Vanbrugh's domicile the sort of praise that a Jonson or a Marvell reserved for a Penshurst or a Nun Appleton House.

The result of this application is extremely subtle; for on the face of it the traditional praises Swift employs seem to fit Vanbrugh's house very well. Thus, just as Marvell could favorably compare the unostentatious comfort of Nun Appleton House to that perfect harmony of dwelling and dweller exhibited by "the low roof'd tortoises [which] do dwell/In cases fit of tortoise-shell" (13–14),[21] so Swift, by merely substituting a snail for a tortoise, can make the same comparison to Vanbrugh's house. Or again, just as Ben Jonson could praise the modest proportions and materials of Penshurst by suggesting that its modesty displayed a true capaciousness:

> . . . though thy walls be of the Countrey stone
> They'are rear'd with no mans ruine, no mans grone:
> There's none, that dwell about them, wish them downe,
> But all come in, the farmer, and the clowne[22]   (45–48),

so Swift can offer the same praise for capacious smallness to the subject of his poem: "For ev'ry Wit in *Britain's* Isle/May lodge within the Spacious Pile" (117–18).

Of course, finally the congruence of Swift's praise with that of Marvell and Jonson only works to parody Vanbrugh's house, for it, though pretentious, is *merely* small. Nevertheless, the parody so produced is not itself simple. Rather, it reminds us that for all Vanbrugh's radical originality, the impetus of his art was the

---

21. *Poems of Andrew Marvell*, introduction by C. V. Wedgwood (London: The Folio Society, 1964), p. 81.
22. *Ben Jonson*, 8:94.

same desire for self-expression that impelled the builders of Appleton House or Penshurst. And it reminds us, too, that looked at one way and ironically, Vanbrugh is as successful as those builders were in expressing through his art not only himself but also all the rest of us. For after all, the truth is that man is small, often barbaric, and usually ridiculous. All art, good and bad, inevitably tells us these things and so does Vanbrugh's. But bad art can tell us nothing more. Stuck with a self it half rejects and half dotes upon, it can only vacillate weakly between pride and despair, illustrating the smallness of self by its own failures. Good art, on the other hand, can move beyond both pride and despair because it sees beyond self. The difference between the two is perfectly mirrored in the parodic collapse into blame of Swift's praise of Vanbrugh's house. For while Vanbrugh's house is *only* small, the modesty of Penshurst exists within the context of a life that is larger than itself and informs its modesty with meaning. Thus, reaching beyond itself, a Penshurst or an Appleton House can achieve, both as architectural edifice and as human estate, the perfected domesticity emblemized by the tortoise. But failing so to reach, a Vanbrugh, whether he builds large or small, can only image the traditionally mean concentricity of the snail.

This last point leads us back to the place from which we began. For like Vanbrugh, Swift himself was a man too apt to reduce all things to the size of his own gaze and the shape of his judgment. Unlike Vanbrugh, however, left undisturbed, Swift had the ability to work his way through the pride and despair that were the consequence of his introversion and to rediscover, in the ambiguity of his experience, a belief in meaning beyond himself. Thus, though often enough an easy prey to the sort of despair Vanbrugh's house initially engendered in him, he usually could effect a recovery from it. Only rarely (as in the case of the final version of *Baucis and Philemon*) did his despair flesh itself so firmly in him that he became one of that species of poets the description of which marks the beginning of his recovery in the development of *Vanbrug's House*.

> So, Modern Rhymers strive to blast
> The Poetry of Ages past,
> Which having wisely overthrown,
> They from it's Ruins build their own.   (89–92)

Far more frequently (as in *Vanbrug's House* itself and even more strikingly in *Description of a City Shower*), having been given ruins to work with, Swift labors mightily to rescue meaning from them.

Swift's *A Description of a City Shower* is formed by the same techniques and informed by the same concerns as are many of the poems already discussed in this chapter. Like its predecessors, the *Shower* is composed of details mundane in themselves but significantly disposed. And, again like its predecessors, the *Shower* is finally about the way a good man must live in a world that holds both good and ill. But, unlike any other poem discussed in this chapter, the *Shower* is that rare challenge to all readers and all critics: a truly great poem.

Because it is a great poem, the *Shower* has always attracted a lion's share of critical attention. Unfortunately, however, modern critics have generated two distinct but contrary views of the poem and these views have for some years now stood side by side unreconciled. The first, more traditional and more sanguine view results from what might be called a tonal interpretation of the poem. Irvin Ehrenpreis, in a recent reading of the *Shower*, provides a forceful example of such an interpretation: he de-emphasizes the *Shower*'s classical allusions; notes, but partly suppresses, the unpleasant items Swift lists in his depiction of London; and provides an emphatic and fully sensitive response to the vigorous and affirmative spirit of the depiction. Understandably, then, Ehrenpreis concludes his reading with the sanguine observation that though "Sewer stenches, aching teeth, drunken vomitings, meet us throughout the City Shower; yet they add up not to an indictment but to a cheerful acceptance of the urban scene."[23]

Undeniably, Ehrenpreis's reading of the poem does capture part of its truth, but his reading also oversimplifies the *Shower*'s paradox. Thus an entirely different view of the poem can be legitimately generated by merely reversing Ehrenpreis's critical priorities and emphasizing the poem's classical antecedents and general unpleasantness, while de-emphasizing its striking vigor. This procedure has been followed most successfully in

23. Ehrenpreis, 2:386.

two apparently independent but nevertheless related articles. The first of these, Brendan O Hehir's "Meaning in Swift's 'Description of a City Shower' "[24] was a pioneering work, for O Hehir was the first critic to point out that Swift's depiction of London awash in an autumn shower is continuously modeled upon far more disastrous depictions of storms and floods in classical literature, particularly in Virgil's first *Georgic* and in the ninth book of the *Aeneid*. The startling discovery that Swift's poem is thus lined with description of mighty disasters naturally led O Hehir to a rather grim (but somewhat confusing) summation of the poem's meaning: "The poem's import seems then to lie," he argued, "within its own terms, and to be primarily an oblique denunciation of cathartic doom upon the corruption of the city."[25]

More recently Roger Savage, apparently unaware of O Hehir's essay, presented an equally gloomy but somewhat different view of the poem's import in his highly sophisticated essay "Swift's Fallen City, 'A Description of the Morning.' "[26] To Savage, Swift's main concern in the *Shower* seems to be the painful difference between a refined and heightened belle nature, as presented by Virgil even in the most terrible of his storm scenes, and nature as Swift himself finds it, an affair of mud, stench, sprats, and cats. "[Swift's] basic grievance," Savage argues, "seems to be that Modern Town is not Ancient Country." But such a grievance, as Savage himself points out, "is as pointless as torturing oneself with the sad truth that the men one knows are not so virtuous as one's fantasy Houyhnhnms."[27] Therefore, Savage concludes, Swift's *Shower*, though not entirely without point, is basically a saddening and somewhat illogical record of Swift's own unhappiness, a record which may at best dent our own complacency a little.

Obviously it has proven difficult for recent critics to accept the fact that the two basic views of Swift's *Shower* they have produced—one reflecting "Swift's cheerful acceptance of the urban scene," the other emphasizing the dark and unpleasant elements of his description—are simultaneously true. Ehrenpreis, after all, wrote his essay on the *Shower* after O Hehir published

24. *ELH* 27 (September 1960):194–207.
25. Ibid., p. 206.
26. In *The World of Jonathan Swift*, ed. Brian Vickers (Oxford: Blackwell, 1968), pp. 171–94.
27. Ibid., p. 192.

his, and Savage formed his reading of the poem after both Ehrenpreis's and O Hehir's essays were in print. In the face of this divergence of opinion, my purpose is to argue that the two basic views represented in the three essays I have summarized are not only simultaneously true but true only when they are understood together. Of course the implication of my argument is that Swift's *Shower* does not provide us the sort of simply comprehensive and comprehensible vision of the world that its critics have sought to find in it. Rather I think the *Shower* began as a consequence of Swift's most mature awareness that the world cannot be reduced to such a vision.

Because of a piece of good luck, which we may improve with deduction, we can guess with considerable certainty what constituted the seminal idea of the *Shower*. The piece of good luck occurs in the *Journal to Stella*, in which, on October 12, 1710, Swift remarked that he had "finished [his] poem on the Shower, all but the beginning."[28] The deduction is as follows.

In its final form, the *Shower* consists of four brief sections, arranged chronologically; thus we begin with a description of the threatening shower (1–12) and then proceed to the shower's onset (13–30), its progress (31–52), and its aftermath (53–63). Since we know that Swift did not begin writing his poem with the first lines of its first section, it is reasonable though not necessary to assume he began with the first lines of its second section and thus wrote lines 13 through 63 in more or less the order in which they presently stand. Although theoretically Swift might have begun his poem at any point in it from line 3 on, nevertheless two separate arguments both strongly suggest that line 13 really marks Swift's point of inspiration.

The first argument was originally presented by O Hehir and derives its force from his convincing demonstration that Swift's *Shower* variously reflects the storm in harvest-time that Virgil portrayed in his first *Georgic*. Having demonstrated a number of correspondences between Swift's shower and Virgil's storm, O Hehir observes that if the *Shower* was written in the order we have suggested, then the order in which Swift composed it (first the storm's onset, then its progress, its aftermath, and finally, the signs that foretell it) corresponds with striking exactness to the order in which Virgil presented his own storm scene. Of course,

28. *Journal to Stella*, 1:53.

strictly speaking, this argument is circular. Still, its circularity is probably justified by the poem's less subtle georgic overtones and by the felicity with which it suggests a sweeping explanation for Swift's otherwise perplexing order of composition.

The second argument that supports line 13 as the seminal line of the *Shower* is both simpler and less sweeping—but it leads to a crucial problem in interpreting the poem. As has been often noted, Swift's thirteenth and fourteenth lines, "Mean while the South rising with dabbled Wings,/A Sable Cloud a-thwart the Welkin flings," unmistakably echo Milton's description, in Book XI of *Paradise Lost*, of the gathering of the clouds that presaged Noah's flood:

> Meanwhile the south-wind rose, and with black wings
> Wide hovering, all the clouds together drove
> From under heaven.   (XI.738–40)

Since, then, line 13 is the first line in the *Shower* to duplicate almost exactly the phrasing of a major author and since it is perhaps the most obvious example in the *Shower* of this technique, it represents a natural starting point for a poem which, as O Hehir has demonstrated, depends heavily upon allusion. At line 13, that is, we seem to stand at the beginning of an idea.

If, however, the Miltonic resonance of lines 13 and 14 tends to confirm them as the seminal lines of the poem, that resonance is not self-interpreting. Swift's *Shower* probably began because the first lines of Milton's epic flood rumbled in Swift's head in time to the thunder of some storm in London in the fall of 1710, but that having been said, the difficult problem still remains of determining what he made of the correspondence. Of course every reader of the poem knows that having set down a recognizable version of Milton's big lines, Swift abruptly turned to parody them so that his whole passage reads,

> Mean while the South rising with dabbled Wings,
> A Sable Cloud a-thwart the Welkin flings,
> That swill'd more Liquor than it could contain,
> And like a Drunkard gives it up again.   (13–16)

But the point of this parody is not at all clear; it may be directed at Milton, or London, or both, or neither.

In fact, the more one knows about this parody, the more vexing it becomes, for its erudite allusions complicate rather than illuminate the problem of identifying its target. In the *Metamorphoses*, at the beginning of his narration of Deucalion's flood, Ovid, like Milton and Swift after him, portrayed a personified south wind. Ovid's south wind, however, is a good deal more detailed than Milton's; complete with dripping wings, a black veil over its terrible countenance, a beard heavy with rain cloud, and locks that are actually a torrent, it comes near being a grotesque. Milton, aware of the power of Ovid's depiction, but also aware of its dangers, picked his way cleanly through it to form his own lines. But Swift, apparently conscious of what Milton had done, transformed Ovid's dripping wind into his own drunken, vomiting cloud and hurled it, comically, back at Milton again.

Swift's parody, then, finally has too many targets to have any real target at all. Playing Ovid off against Milton and both off against an actual city shower, Swift seems to be responding, in these seminal lines, not so much to Milton, or Ovid, or London in themselves as to a much more generalized sense that what we call "significance" is a good deal more whimsical than most of us will usually admit. Deflect Ovid's south wind slightly and Swift knows that it turns comic, blow it on Milton's lines and they become ridiculous, but pass Milton's lines through a normal city shower and it grows ominous. Swift's seminal lines, then, are themselves something like a flood; they obscure the familiar boundaries we have drawn to segregate tragic events from comic ones and great events from small; they render the world indistinct to us.

Obviously it is natural for us to resist the effect of these lines; that is why we seek to identify the object of their parody. We want them to be directed against Milton or Ovid or London or anything at all in order that we can determine their meaning. Instead Swift directs them and the entire section that follows them only against the very discriminations that we regard as the basis of meaning. Combining Ovid, Virgil, and Milton with the everyday events of London during a shower, Swift whirls up a storm which is at once funny and sad, ominous and cheery, delightful and frightening.

At every turn this storm defies our best attempts to define its significance. For instance, we want to laugh at Swift's ridiculous comparison of the first drops of his rain to "that Sprinkling which some careless Quean/Flirts on you from her Mop, but not so clean'' (19–20). But we cannot simply laugh at this comparison because, even if we fail to recognize that Swift's "careless Quean" is an absurd descendant of Ovid's implacable Iris, we can certainly see that she has inherited some part of that deity's watery mercilessness. Thus though "You fly, invoke the Gods; then turning, stop/To rail; *she singing, still whirls on her Mop*" (21–22, italics mine). Something, then, is not quite funny about Swift's comparison and its evocation of a rain that will not cease. It arrests us between laughter and real concern and it will not let us go.

Perhaps, however, the most striking instance of that frustrating irreducibility which characterizes Swift's entire description of the onset of his shower occurs in its final question:

> Ah! where must needy Poet seek for Aid,
> When Dust and Rain at once his Coat invade;
> His only Coat, where Dust confus'd with Rain,
> Roughen the Nap, and leave a mingled Stain.   (27–30)

Everything about this question calls out for somber interpretation. At some level, at least, the poet it describes is certainly Swift himself. His coat may be his very soul, an association made probable not only by its previous occurrence in *A Tale of a Tub* but by Swift's apparent pun in the variant of these lines that appears in Faulkner's 1735 edition of Swift's poems: "Sole Coat, where Dust cemented by the Rain/Erects the nap, and leaves a cloudy Stain." So understood, then, the coat's welfare and the stains that threaten it become serious matters indeed, and the lines containing them expand to portray the condition of every man who, caught in a world he cannot wholly control, understand, or escape, feels imperiled by it.

But, of course, all this is simply "made-up stuff "; it can be found in the lines only *in potentia*. In themselves, the lines are no more than an amusing caricature of (perhaps) Swift himself caught awkwardly between home and coffee-house in the one good coat he owned during the whole of his London years. Thus the lines create for us, as readers, much the same problem as that faced by the poet described in them. Like him, we are caught up in mingled elements, tousled, vaguely threatened, and mostly perplexed.

To put this another way, the lines crystallize for us, both in the person of their befuddled poet and in our own experience of them, that insight into our inability to bind the world to our own meaning which first precipitated the opening lines of Swift's *Shower*.

The confluence in Swift's mind of the motif of a flood with his special awareness that our usual categories of meaning are inadequate to define the power and sweep of the world we experience represents, of course, no novel piece of symbolization. From the earliest literature on, poets have depicted floods in order to illustrate man's frailty before a nature greater than himself. But, as I have been suggesting, Swift's use of this motif is somewhat different from most in that he compels us, as readers, to experience its force. Mulling Swift's lines, we grow weary with thinking and are lost in his shower.

Swift's poem, then, can be legitimately described as the recovery of a traditional motif through the powerful demonstration of its validity. Having said this much, however, we may properly ask what impelled Swift to attempt this recovery. Like all such speculative questions, this one can be answered only tentatively. But to attempt to answer it, however tentatively, is not idle. For the reason Swift wrote his poem in the terms he did rather than in others—the logic, that is, of his poetic choices—is enmeshed in the background against which he wrote. For all practical purposes, then, so is the meaning of his poem.

The background of the *Shower* is extensive. The way Swift saw the rain fall in London in 1710 probably has its roots in patristic times and in the way early Christian exegetes, beginning with Augustine, defended the literal truth of the Scriptural flood against the attacks of pagans and heretics who sought to undermine its veracity by questioning its mechanics.[29] The basis of this early defense was reason; that is, early exegetes undertook to answer pagan objections in pagan terms. Thus, rather than respond to the question "how did the inhabitants of the ark live during their watery voyage" by saying "God sustained them," Christian commentators sought to find room in the ark, as its

29. Throughout my discussion of the exegetical history of Noah's flood I am indebted to Don Cameron Allen's enduring study, *The Legend of Noah*, Illinois Studies in Language and Literature, vol. 33, nos. 3–4 (Urbana: University of Illinois Press, 1949).

dimensions are given by Scripture, for food to sustain its inhabitants.

This tactic, continued from age to age into the Renaissance, had three consequences. First, for Christians themselves, belief in Noah's flood came to mean only belief in its rational probability. Thus if it could not be proved that the flood at least might have happened, then most men would grant it did not happen. In other words, with respect to the flood, exegetical tradition made human reason the measure of divine possibility. Secondly, the notion that Noah's flood was a parable illustrating man's frailty and his dependence on God's grace almost wholly disappeared. Rather the flood came to matter only insofar as its demonstrable historical veracity seemed to relieve men of the necessity of frail belief. Thirdly, the legend of Noah was doomed to fall to the status of a child's fairy tale by the end of the seventeenth century, neither significant nor believed, for the details of its Scriptural narration seemed wholly incompatible with the findings of modern science.

By the time Swift wrote the *Shower*, then, the most significant flood narration in Western literature was no longer available as a poetic vehicle, its significance having been compromised, ironically, by something like the same spirit of willfulness that, according to the legend itself, brought the antediluvians to watery destruction. That Swift was aware of, or at least responsive to, this ironic circumstance is attested by the shards of broken flood legends, including Noah's, which float, deprived of their own narrative order and integrity, through his *Shower*. But from these shards, as we have already seen, Swift reconstructs for us that sense of human frailty and fallibility of which they told when they were whole and living legends. More remarkably still, Swift also recovers the sense of grace that was the center of the greatest of them.

Frankly, however, most of us require help to discover this aspect of Swift's achievement in the *Shower* since we ourselves are prone to see in the story of Noah an emblem of God's wrath and not his grace. To be sure, we recognize the force of Noah's salvation and the symbolism of the rainbow, but like Michelangelo as he painted his famous picture of the flood in the Sistine Chapel, we sympathize with the drowning antediluvians. Probably Milton was the last great English poet for whom this was not so and who could consequently see both the horror and the grace of the legend of Noah and grasp their connection. That is why even if the first lines of Milton's description of Noah's flood were not also implicit in the first lines that Swift composed of his *Shower*, Milton's narration would be a proper background to the study of Swift's poem.

As he composed his narrative, Milton stood in an enviable position with respect to the history of the legend of Noah. Writing after centuries of rational exegesis, but before the deluge of scientific tracts published in the 1690s, he possessed at once an instance of divine intervention, the historicity of which he could believe without contradicting a world of empirical evidence, and a story he could conceive as drama because it had already been prodded by a multitude of imaginative Christian commentators. To put this another way, in Noah's flood Milton possessed what he could receive as a perfect context in which to explore God's ways with man.

That exploration, however, has dismayed most of its modern readers. Milton, we recall, causes us to view Noah's flood through Adam's eyes and thus permits us to test our own emotions against Adam's. But almost inevitably our emotions fail to tally with his. To be sure, we are at one with Adam when, viewing the horrific destruction attendant on Noah's flood and "comfortless, as when a father mourns/His Children, all in view destroyed at once," he utters a lamentation which puts in doubt human knowledge, life itself, and God's ways with man: "O vision ill foreseen!" he keens,

> better had I
> Lived ignorant of future, so had borne
> My part of evil only, each day's lot
> Enough to bear. . . .
> . . . .
> . . . Let no man seek
> Henceforth to be foretold what shall befall
> Him or his children, evil he may be sure. (XI.763–66, 770–72)

But, having committed our hearts to Adam's complaint and shared its woe, we are appalled when he, apparently forgetful of the suffering he has witnessed, rejoices in the salvation of Noah's family and distressingly says,

                                 I revive
           At this last sight. . . .
           .   .   .   .

           Far less I now lament for one whole world
           Of wicked sons destroyed, than I rejoice
           For one man found so perfect and so just,
           That God vouchsafes to raise another world
           From him.   (XI.871–72, 874–78)

The transition is too quick for us. We find it heartless and we
blame Adam for it.

Such a reaction is natural and causes us to wonder at Milton's
apparent approval of Adam's response. But we stand at the verge
of a mystery here, and we must not judge it until we have tried to
understand its significance. What Milton drives us to see is that
no response we might wish Adam to make can be better than the
one he does make, for what we would add to his tears for the
wicked we must take from his joy for the just. Thus Milton forces
us to recognize that the flood simply extends beyond our capacity
to respond fully to it. Of course we may continue to mourn
stubbornly for the antediluvians, but if we do so we simply recreate their vain willfulness in our own breasts and suffer their
flood in our unceasing tears. That is why we must let them go,
and with them that stubborn desire to define and control the
world they emblemize. It is painful for us to do so, of course, but
necessary in order to see that truth which was always implicit in
the legend of Noah and which it is the whole point of Milton's
dramatization of that legend to make us see: that the way of our
own will is the way of death and must be relinquished, but that
having relinquished that way we can float like Noah and rejoice
like Adam supported by what before drowned us.

Swift knew this truth too. Unlike Milton, however, Swift had
no believed legend to confirm the truth's validity. To be sure, as a
young man writing the *Ode to the Athenian Society*, he did
attempt in a complex set of introductory lines to invoke Noah and
to insist on the authenticity of the flood. But though these lines
form a rather interesting opening to a poem in which, we remember, Swift praises the Athenians' almost Noachical trust in
Providence, the fact that he is very uncomfortable with the lines
is evidenced by the confusing and intrusive scientific "explana-

tion" of the flood which he parenthetically introduced to bolster them up. When, then, twenty years later, Swift returned to the motif of the flood, he had to seek its life-bearing message only in the fragments men had made of its legends and in the rain that fell on London.

Viewed through that rain, as we have already seen, the meaning of events grows less distinct than we usually suppose it to be: the monumental and the insignificant, the tragic and the comic blur together in a haze which obscures their significance even as it bestows upon the event itself a preternatural clarity. This is true not only of the confusedly referential description of the shower's onset with which Swift began his poem; it is true, too, of his subsequent descriptions of the shower's effects and of its aftermath. To be sure, in the Pisgah-like tableaux of London that Swift spreads before us in these descriptions we may certainly find isolated fragments of meaning, but these fragments can never be compacted into a single, substantial vision of Swift's flood without effecting just that sort of brutal interpretive force which in revealing itself overthrows itself. Thus, to take a somewhat extended example, we may properly remark that Swift's pleasantly mocking description of a "Templar spruce" who, caught by the storm, "Stays till 'tis fair, yet seems to call a Coach," and his thoroughly good-natured description of the "tuck'd-up Sempstress" who "walks with hasty Strides,/While Streams run down her oil'd Umbrella's Sides" (35–38), are both made ominous enough by the two lines which immediately follow them: "Here various Kinds by various Fortunes led,/Commence Acquaintance underneath a Shed" (39–40). For these last two lines, as the *Tatler* noted when the poem was first published, apparently echo Virgil's description in the *Aeneid* of that fatal meeting of Dido and Aeneas in a cave during a storm, and that meeting, as Brendan O Hehir has observed, carries "very strong overtones of a primal fall."[30]

> From this ill-omened hour, in time arose
> Debate and death, and all succeeding woes.[31]   (IV.245–46)

---

30. O Hehir, p. 200.
31. The translation is Dryden's. Quotation from *The Poems of John Dryden*, ed. James Kinsley, 4 vols. (Oxford: Clarendon Press, 1958), 3:1151.

Taken as a single unit, then, these six lines, which seemingly
conjoin templar and sempstress, Aeneas and Dido, form a vague,
covert, but sufficiently gloomy prospect on human dishonesty and
its subsequent catastrophes.

But to read these lines so, to insist on seeing in them the
imminent destruction of a hypocritical town, is not only to strain
the small hypocrisies they actually describe; it is also to neglect
the fact that these six lines need not be taken as a single unit at
all. Instead one may shear away the final two lines and fix them,
with both perfect good sense and respect for Swift's punctuation,
to the two succeeding lines. By this change in critical emphasis
the gloom of the passage is immediately taken off; the dark
Virgilian echo, because it is no longer relevant, disappears; and
one is left with nothing more dire than two amusing descriptions
of templar and sempstress caught in a shower, succeeded by the
description of the good, because chastening, consequence of the
shower.

> Here various Kinds by various Fortunes led,
> Commence Acquaintance underneath a Shed.
> Triumphant Tories, and desponding Whigs,
> Forget their Fewds, and join to save their wigs.   (39–42)

In these eight lines, then, we are presented with a scene that,
like the flood Adam viewed from atop Mount Pisgah, ultimately
defies either adequate response or definition. Of course, we may
view it, as we have done, by turns, and thus call it first funny,
then frightening, now sanguine, now sad. But what we cannot do
is to see it all at once, state its meaning, and march it, captured,
down the pathways of our minds; finally, its characters, their
actions, and the language Swift uses to describe them, all have a
life of their own.

To learn to respect that life, to value it as Swift himself values
it, is the "lesson" of the *Shower*, its floating ark. Until we learn
that lesson, the poem must appear simply a puzzle to us, frustrating in its insolubility. For example, so long as we seek for a
simple primary meaning in Swift's famous comparison of a London beau, trapped in his chair by the shower, with the "Bully
Greeks" imprisoned in their horse (43–52), so long the comparison must continue to yield us only a confusing farrago of mean-

ings. Thus, because by long literary tradition London is Troy-Nouvant, we may certainly find in the comparison of beau to Greek a dark warning of London's imminent peril, a repressed cry that the enemy is already within the gates. On the other hand, because this enemy is no invader but London's own wicked progeny, and because the storm seems to be directed with special force at him, we may see in Swift's description of his predicament an instance of providential purgation and a proof of divine justice. Furthermore, because this enemy is much diminished both by his circumstances and by the Greek warriors to whom he is compared, we may hear in the comparison primarily Swift's derisive laughter at a being malicious enough to destroy a civilization but impotent to commit more than base murder. But precisely because all these meanings and more exist suspended in Swift's comparison, none of them can be legitimately proposed as the primary import of that comparison. Rather, that import must be sought in Swift's own vibrant consciousness of the finally mysterious autonomy of life, a consciousness so sensitively aware of life's irreducibility that, even touching lightly on the old story of the Greeks in their wooden horse, it records its perception that as the Greeks entered Troy they were at once bullies and heroes, cowards and conquerors, bringers of death and the vital embodiment of civilization itself.

Of course, this consciousness is every way the reverse of that habit of mind which drove men to seek in the story of Noah the certifiable proof of the verity of their faith and thus of their own significance. For Swift's consciousness, as it is reflected in this poem, gives us no proofs at all but only paradoxes for us to wonder at. Yet as we wonder at them—caught between tears and laughter and bewildered by a city shower that is also, somehow, a terrible flood which nevertheless remains a city shower—we may discover as the poem's final paradox that we stand on the very grounds of faith for which the rational explicators of the legend of Noah sought in vain. Made newly, if grudgingly, aware of what such explicators forgot, that both life itself and such art as truly reflects life possess a power and an integrity independent of us, we recover in the admission of our awareness the terms of our own worth as living beings and the freedom to trust in what we know we cannot fully understand.

It is the exuberance of this freedom that we hear in the first

lines Swift wrote of the *Shower*. Delightedly aware that it was not
he who must make the world make sense, Swift could, like
Yeats's old man, simply clap texts and sing louder for every tatter
he found in his sole coat. Freed, too, of the intolerable burden of
judging the world, he could afford as he wrote the body of his
poem just to observe its mingled good and bad without longing
after resolution. Finally, having watched the last turnip top tumble down his flood in satisfying ridicule of the triplet form he
disliked, he could draw what he perhaps might have called the
application of his poem.

Clearly even as Swift drew this application, he intended it to
serve as an introduction to the complex vision that informs his
Shower. Yet admirably though it serves this function, it retains, too, something of its character as application. Consequently
it is probably true that until we ourselves live through the body of
Swift's poem, the full significance of the lines he wrote to introduce it must escape us. Only when we can measure Swift's
opening assertion that "Careful Observers may foretel the
Hour/(By sure Prognosticks) when to dread a Show'r" (1–2)
against our knowledge of Swift's awareness that man is not the
measure of all things can we hear at once both the laughter
implicit in Swift's sly parenthesis and the real trust, redolent of
Virgil's georgic faith, with which these lines explicitly affirm the
mutual reciprocity of man and a world he was meant to live in. Of
course the cheerful affirmation of these lines is immediately
qualified, even as it is in Virgil's *Georgics*, by Swift's awareness
that though man's proper role in the world is that of prudent
observation and response, neither careful observation nor prog-
nostication can eliminate the possibility of pain and sorrow. Indeed, as Swift describes it, the very act of observation itself
involves pain; for the signs by which a coming shower are an-
nounced range from those causing annoying offense—"Returning
Home at Night, you'll find the Sink/Strike your offended Sense
with double Stink" (5–6)—to those which produce pain as deep as
mortality: "A coming Show'r your shooting Corns presage,/Old
Aches throb, your hollow Tooth will rage" (9–10). But though
Swift knows, then, even as Adam did, that observation involves
pain and foresight may foresee ill, never does Swift say, with
Adam on Pisgah,

> Let no man seek
> Henceforth to be foretold what shall befall
> Him or his children.   (XI.770–72)

In fact, that response is assigned in the *Shower* only to Dul-
man, who, warned of the storm, merely "damns the Climate, and
complains of Spleen" (12). But Swift's posture in this poem does
accord with other words of Adam's, among his last in *Paradise
Lost*, uttered when he has attained what Michael calls "the sum
of wisdom." "Henceforth I learn," Adam says, choosing words
very different from Swift's, but possessing neither more measured
tension nor more of confidence,

> Henceforth I learn, that to obey is best,
> And love with fear the only God, to walk
> As in his presence, ever to observe
> His providence, and on him sole depend.   (XII.561–64)

3

"Left all below at Six and Sev'n"
Cadenus and Vanessa

BECAUSE HE SUPPRESSED nothing of the London he portrayed, Swift's *Description of a City Shower* is one of the greatest
brief celebrations in any language of the mingled human situation.
And because Swift usually could write completely and powerfully
about all that he saw, felt, and thought, his mature verse forms
one of the most vigorous and valuable collections of poetry in our
language. Occasionally, however, even in his mature work, individual poems suggest that Swift sometimes refused to acknowledge a part of his own experience. *Cadenus and Vanessa* is such
a poem, and it is consequently a failure. Nevertheless, in its very
failure the poem still exhibits Swift's proclivity to affirm richness
and possibility in life. For though he rejects what he should affirm
in *Cadenus and Vanessa*, Swift does struggle to delineate something of value in the poem, and he does so even at the cost of
producing outrageous self-contradiction.[1]

1. For interpretations of *Cadenus and Vanessa* that suggest in various ways that
the poem is successful, consistent, and informing, see Peter Ohlin's " 'Cadenus
and Vanessa': Reason and Passion," *SEL* 4 (1964):485–96; James L. Tyne's
"Vanessa and the Houyhnhnms: A Reading of 'Cadenus and Vanessa,' " *SEL* 11
(1971):517–34; Gareth Jones's "Swift's *Cadenus and Vanessa*: A Question of
'Positives,' " *EC* 20 (1970):424–40; and Peter J. Schakel's "Swift's 'dapper Clerk'
and the Matrix of Allusions in 'Cadenus and Vanessa,' " *Criticism* 17
(1975):246–61. Of these interpretations, Mr. Jones's and Mr. Schakel's seem to me
especially provocative and to require particular comment. Mr. Jones's reading can
be divided into two parts. First, he argues that the protracted and fruitless
dialogue between Cadenus and Vanessa is meant to demonstrate the inadequacy
of "naked reason" to tame "the chaotic world of sense and passion." This part of
Jones's argument is perfectly sound. Then, however (dropping the close reading
that characterizes most of his essay), Jones argues that the poem's closing section

If ever an occasion seemed contrived to provoke a fractured and contradictory poem, that occasion is the uneasy friendship Swift maintained with Esther Vanhomrigh from 1708 until her death in 1723. By 1713, the year in which Swift apparently composed *Cadenus and Vanessa*,[2] this friendship had become, if not actually a sexual liaison, at least a passionate relationship.[3] In this relationship, however, Swift and Esther were unequal participants. Esther entirely committed herself to Swift and to what she called her "inexpressible passion" for him.[4] She wished him to make a similar commitment to her. He would not do so. That he loved her is indisputable: "soyez asurée," he wrote her late in their relationship, "que jamais personne du monde a été aimée,

---

is constructed "to compel us, by tempting us ever and again to rest thankful in easy certainties of judgment, and then subverting those certainties, not merely to contemplate but to live the difficulties of our predicament." This is attractive argument. It would be true if applied to many of Swift's poems. But it can be made true of *Cadenus and Vanessa* only if we accept that the poem exhibits something hard to find in it—a hearty response to "the difficulties of our predicament"—and if we suppose that lines 818–27 present "an easy certainty of judgment" rather than a thorny conclusion. Both positions seem forced to me. So, too, does Mr. Schakel's high-handed response to lines 818–27. Schakel argues that Cadenus's rejection of Vanessa is clear *"in spite" of these lines*. Having made this claim, he is able to suggest that in *Cadenus and Vanessa* Swift at once says a firm "no" to Esther Vanhomrigh, places most of the blame for that "no" on himself, and indicates through allusions to Virgil and Ovid "the need for self-acceptance and self-sacrifice in love." Again, like Jones's, much of Schakel's argument is attractive. Swift often does supply the norms of his verse by allusion, and one could wish that in this poem he had demonstrated so sound a view of love as Schakel proposes. Unhappily, Swift does not. First, despite Schakel's asseverations, Swift's "no" to Esther remains debatable; lines 818–27 are at least ambiguous and they are the last lines in the poem on the subject. Secondly, despite a great deal of special argument, Schakel does not convince me that either Ovid's view of love or Virgil's treatment of Dido informs the poem very deeply. Venus finds these two sources hopelessly muddy on the very point she is trying to resolve and throws both texts back on the shelf before she appeals to experience. If any text, then, embodies an ideal for Swift in this poem, it is certainly neither of these. A possible candidate is the verse of Tibullus, whose works, we are told, are not to be found in Venus's wrangling court at all, and whose peaceful celebrations of placid love therefore may represent Swift's own permanent, unattainable, and debilitating dream.

2. Dates from 1713 to 1719 have been proposed for the completion of *Cadenus and Vanessa*. For a review of the problems involved see *The Collected Poems of Jonathan Swift*, ed. Joseph Horrell, 2 vols. (Cambridge: Harvard University Press, 1958), 1:388.

3. For a recent, and full discussion of this relationship see Ehrenpreis, 2:647.

4. *Vanessa and her Correspondence with Jonathan Swift*, ed. A. Martin Freeman (London: Selwyn and Blount, Ltd., 1921), p. 128.

honorée, estimée, adorée par votre ami que vous.''[5] But though
he loved her, he also knew beyond all forgetting the objections
reason could raise to his love. There were more than enough of
these: he was Esther's senior by nearly twenty years; he held a
position of spiritual authority in Dublin; he owed and felt loyalty
and devotion to Esther Johnson. Swift's case, then, was the sad
contrary of Esther's; in him prudence, reason, wisdom, whatever
one wants to call an objective view, necessarily opposed passionate choice. At his most harsh, Swift's experience of the contrariety of passion and prudence could make him snap such sentences
at Esther as "you used to brag you were very discreet. Where is
it gone?''[6] At his gentlest, that same contrariety begot *Cadenus
and Vanessa*.

The "lesson" Swift obviously meant to teach in *Cadenus and
Vanessa* is that reason and passion are absolutely antipathetic.
That is, the poem is Swift's attempt to explain and justify to
Esther the contradictions he felt by suggesting that those contradictions reflect the general human situation. This attempt fails
for a variety of reasons, each of which we will examine in its
turn. However, because the attempt structures both the opening
scene and much of the subsequent action in *Cadenus and
Vanessa*, it provides us our simplest entry into the poem.

Cadenus and Vanessa begins in Venus's Court where a group
of shepherds and nymphs are joined in formal debate before
Venus herself. The advocate for the nymphs complains that
shepherds have left off loving; the advocate for the shepherds
responds that the nymphs, having grown frivolous and degenerate, are no longer worthy of love. This debate is conducted with
full legal decorum, but it is patently, and comically, absurd. For
when both sides have finished presenting their cases and Venus
has consulted her law-texts and precedents, the debate stands
exactly where it began. The moral is obvious: matters of love
cannot be settled by legal debate, for love has nothing to do with
either law or reason.

Of course, the development of *Cadenus and Vanessa* depends
upon Venus's unwillingness or inability to grasp that moral.
Rather than do so, she decides to test the validity of the
shepherds' complaint by choosing a beautiful female infant and

5. Ibid., p. 133.
6. Ibid., p. 99.

endowing her with every imaginable virtue. Venus hopes that as the child, Vanessa, grows to maturity, she will inspire love among the shepherds and imitation among the nymphs and thus end the altercation between them. But, of course, the experiment is doomed. For the shepherds' complaint against the nymphs is based upon the assumption that there is (or, at least, ought to be) some real correspondence between love and rational appreciation of worth. In the context of *Cadenus and Vanessa* that assumption is false. Indeed, Swift so sets the terms of his poem that the very representatives of love and wisdom are unalterably antagonistic. Venus is able to procure the gifts of wisdom, knowledge, judgment, and prudence for Vanessa only by deceiving Pallas. And Pallas, once she is undeceived, prognosticates the failure of Venus's experiment with a single, wonderfully scornful question: "How can Heav'nly Wisdom prove/An Instrument to earthly Love?" (294–95).

In this poem the answer is, it cannot; in fact, wisdom proves to be a positive hindrance in matters of love. Vanessa grows up possessed of far too much prudence, wisdom, and grace for the mere men and women she must live among; they (with, perhaps, some reason) find her dull and she scorns them. Again, Swift's moral could hardly be clearer: among mankind love goes by liking; it is purely subjective and has nothing to do with objective worth. And this moral is driven all the way home in the final development of the poem. For when Vanessa finally does fall in love she is not motivated by reason; rather, she is compelled by one of Cupid's darts to love a man both too old for her and unwilling to reciprocate her passion—her tutor, the priest Cadenus.

Having fallen in love, Vanessa becomes Swift's principal example of love's fundamental unreasonableness. First, in radical opposition to her early acuity, she learns to gainsay the evidence of her eyes and ears:

> *Vanessa*, not in Years a Score,
> Dreams of a Gown of forty-four;
> Imaginary Charms can find,
> In Eyes with Reading almost blind;
> *Cadenus* now no more appears
> Declin'd in Health, advanc'd in Years.

> She fancies Musick in his Tongue,
> Nor further looks, but thinks him young.   (524–31)

Then, obviously unsettled in her own wits, Vanessa undertakes to prove to her reticent tutor that reason is her guide in love. As might be expected, her argument fails on two counts. First, her demonstration proves only that self-love, not reason, is the source of her passion:

> Self-Love, in Nature rooted fast,
> Attends us first, and leaves us last:
> Why she likes him, admire not at her,
> She loves herself, and that's the Matter.   (684–87)

Secondly, her argument leaves Cadenus as coldly out of love with her as he was before she started.

Of course, Vanessa's failure to provoke passion in Cadenus is not a direct consequence of the faults in her argument. Rather, both her faulty argument and her failure to move Cadenus's love result from this poem's iron law; because love and reason are antipathetic, love cannot be defended by reason and no one can be reasoned into loving. By the same token, no one can be reasoned out of loving either, and that is a point that Cadenus himself, reasonable as he pretends to be, misunderstands. Thus, just as Vanessa tries to defend her love by reason, he tries, by reason, to defend his failure to love. Consequently, his arguments are as illogical and as ineffectual as her own.

The real cause of Cadenus's failure to love is, of course, simply the cast of his own personality. Swift makes this perfectly plain:

> *Cadenus*, common Forms apart,
> In every Scene had kept his Heart;
> Had sigh'd and languish'd, vow'd, and writ,
> For Pastime, or to shew his Wit;
> But Time, and Books, and State Affairs
> Had spoil'd his fashionable Airs;
> He now cou'd praise, esteem, approve,
> But understood not what was Love.   (540–47)

Cadenus, however, is unwilling to accept the utter subjectivity of his feelings; instead, he attempts to rationalize them. Arguing that respect is better than passion and devotion superior to love, he ends by offering Vanessa "that Devotion we bestow,/When Goddesses appear below" (788–89). This offer, however, is the most outrageous of the entire poem; it is not only just what Vanessa does not want, it is also what no reasonable man ought even to consider offering to a mortal woman. In making this offer, then, Cadenus provides what is perhaps the poem's most ironic instance of Swift's thesis: when reason is applied to matters of love, it is not only inefficacious, it is in real danger of growing unreasonable itself.

Thus outlined quickly, *Cadenus and Vanessa* hardly appears to be an inconsistent poem; if anything, the dilemmas its characters continuously experience seem to form a too single-minded demonstration of the antipathy of love and reason. In fact, however, the poem does possess a vigorously buoyant counterthesis, which can be best understood if we begin not by tracing its appearance in the poem but rather by reminding ourselves of a few commonplace observations on the nature of love itself.

The first of these observations is that, despite Swift's poem, love and reason are not antipathetical. They are simply very different from each other. Of course, because they are so different it certainly can happen that they may be opposed in any given relationship. Thus sometimes reasonable people fall in love with most inappropriate partners. This fact, however, no more proves that love is unreasonable than the fact that sometimes reasonable people choose appropriate mates proves that love is reasonable. Rather, both facts demonstrate merely that love and reason are different from each other; and that, with the exception of one corollary, is all that can be said about their relationship.

The corollary is this: because love and reason are different, love cannot be judged by reason. Of course, an object of love can be so judged, but not love itself. Love itself can be judged only by our experience of it. And our experience tells us that love is good. Indeed, even when we find love painful, we know that it is good because no matter how painful it becomes—how offensive to our reason or injurious to our pride—we are unwilling to give it up. We savor even what is bitter in it.

Now, that love is a good in itself is a point Esther Vanhomrigh understood perfectly well. Thus in her correspondence with Swift she argued again and again that her passion had its own validity and truth, and that it possessed a substantive goodness which neither time nor circumstance could alter. For example, in probably her best letter to him, she pleaded with Swift, "Put my passion under the utmost restraint, send me as distant from you as the earth will allow, yet you cannot banish those charming ideas, which will ever stick by me whilst I have the use of memory. Nor is the love I bear you only seated in my soul, for there is not a single atom of my frame that is not blended with it. Therefore don't flatter yourself that separation will ever change my sentiments, for I find myself unquiet in the midst of silence, and my heart is at once pierced with sorrow and with love."[7] Certainly, this passage is beautifully plain. One would suppose that, even against his will, Swift could not have wholly failed to understand it.

And one would suppose, too, that at some level, though probably with great distress, Swift himself understood the power of passionate love to enrich and illuminate human experience. After all, he did remain more or less bound to Esther for a period of fifteen years. But he also felt—and evinced throughout his life—an overpowering distrust of passionate love. This distrust goes well past the usual Christian adjurations against uxoriousness. It is rather an inability to bless life itself in one of its aspects. The extent of this inability is made particularly plain in the following passage from *Thoughts on Religion*: "Although reason were intended by providence to govern our passions, yet it seems that, in two points of the greatest moment to the being and continuance of the world, God hath intended our passions to prevail over reason. The first is, the propagation of our species, since no wise man ever married from the dictates of reason. The other is, the love of life, which, from the dictates of reason, every man would despise, and wish it at an end, or that it never had a beginning."[8] Strictly speaking, of course, this passage is orthodox. In it Swift does affirm that physical passion is a good in that it assures procreation. But Swift offers this affirmation in so bitter a spirit that he almost transforms the blessing of life itself into a curse. Thus, even following the church on the topic of passionate love, Swift manages to be strikingly negative.

7. Ibid., p. 128.
8. *Swift's Prose*, 9:263.

In *Cadenus and Vanessa* Swift's inability to affirm the value of passionate love produces a variety of unfortunate results, and these, in their turn, lead to the poem's chief inconsistency. To begin with, because Swift would not dramatize that passion which—as their letters indicate—characterized part at least of the relationship between himself and Esther, the portrait he drew of each of them in *Cadenus and Vanessa* is a radically diminished and impoverished copy of its original. Thus Esther, whose letters prove her a woman of high intelligence as well as of a passionate nature, is reduced to a lovely, charming, but naïve schoolgirl. Similarly, Swift, who really did love Esther, is diminished to a rather silly pedant, incapable of passion. Neither character, then, is really very human, and the drama they play out between them is necessarily something less than and different from the human experience of love.

Of course, Swift was under no literary obligation to write fully about either his own or Esther's experience in love. Rhetorically, it was quite satisfactory for him to simplify and caricature himself, simplify and compliment Esther, and contrive their interaction so as to demonstrate again and again that division between reason and passionate love which always qualified his conduct towards her. Indeed, assuming that Swift's sole purpose in this poem was to tell Esther as gently as possible that he would not act on his love for her as she wished him to act, the poem's strategy is perhaps the best he could have devised. Only if Swift wished to affirm some part of the felt worth of his relationship with Esther would the poem's strategy become an embarrassment. In that case, however, Swift's diminution of himself and Esther must become an insurmountable bar to dramatizing the truth.

Yet for Swift to wish to affirm—even as he parted with Esther—something of the worth of his relationship with her is not only natural but also wise. For as his verse itself has taught us, one cannot hope to transcend a difficulty unless one first confronts it. Thus, to cite a traditional instance, one cannot escape one's mortality simply by refusing to hear of death. Instead, paradoxically, in order to live well and boldly, one must live regularly aware of mortality. By the same token, one cannot relinquish a love that circumstance makes impossible simply by saying it either does not exist or is not a good in itself. For to attempt to relinquish love this way is in fact to relinquish nothing at all. Rather, in order to put aside a love that cannot flourish, one must confront and affirm the good that one rejects. Only by doing this can one relinquish love or anything else. And only by doing this can one rescue something of value—charity, perhaps, or simple loyalty and honor—out of the pain inherent in relinquishment.

Thus, though Swift was under no obligation to tell the truth in *Cadenus and Vanessa* about his experience of love or about Esther's, he was obliged—in order to break cleanly with her—to affirm at some point the real value of their relationship. Of course, he might have effected this affirmation entirely in his own mind prior to composing the poem. However, the evidence in *Cadenus and Vanessa* suggests that he did not do so. Rather, he attempted to affirm the value of his relationship with Esther within the poem itself, and the consequence is necessarily unfortunate. For within *Cadenus and Vanessa* there is literally nothing that can be affirmed. Its characters are simply too narrow and too cold to permit Swift to dramatize through them any real richness of human experience. Consequently, given the impulse to affirm some part of his experience, all Swift could do in *Cadenus and Vanessa* was to suggest, not that love is a good in itself which may be celebrated even in renunciation, but rather that, perhaps when all is said and done, love may be rational after all.

Unhappily, in contradiction both to his poem's thesis and to its purpose, this is just what Swift does suggest in two separate but related ways in *Cadenus and Vanessa*. The first of these ways is essentially dramatic. By portraying Pallas as an insufferable scold—proud, unyielding and self-righteous—at the same time that he portrays Venus as a delightful though a deceived and deceiving woman, Swift guarantees that even if we accept his poem's basic thesis that reason and passion are antipathetic, we must simultaneously struggle uneasily against that thesis. For following the poem's emotional pull, we necessarily wish both for Vanessa's good success in love and for Venus's eventual triumph. Thus, will we, nil we, we are taught by the poem itself to long for the recovery of precisely that mythic, rational love which Swift so splendidly parodies in the shepherds' bathetic complaint. Further, led by Swift, we also learn to blame the world for Venus's inability to provoke such love among mortals. "Thus, to the

World's perpetual Shame," we say, "The *Queen of Beauty* lost her Aim" (432–33). In effect, then, against its very thesis, we are encouraged by the drama of this poem to dream after impossibilities.

Of course, because this is Swift's poem, it is tempting to suppose that the pressure its drama exerts on us to hope for a rational love is only a rhetorical ploy designed to teach us forcibly the futility of such hopes. The fact is, however, that the dramatic pressure of this poem instead represents Swift's own yearning for an impossible conflation of love and reason. This unhappy truth becomes transparently and distressingly clear in those lines near the close of the poem in which Swift sums up the debate between Cadenus and Vanessa. "But what success *Vanessa* met," the passage coyly begins,

> Is to the World a Secret yet:
> Whether the Nymph, to please her Swain,
> Talks in a high Romantick Strain;
> Or whether he at last descends
> To like with less Seraphick Ends;
> Or, to compound the Business, whether
> They temper Love and Books together;
> Must never to Mankind be told,
> Nor shall the conscious Muse unfold.   (818–27)

Everything about this passage is disturbing. To begin with, as a possible conclusion to the debate between Cadenus and Vanessa, it is simply illogical. For each of the three potential resolutions it suggests to that debate supposes some possible compromise between Cadenus's reason and Vanessa's passion—and it is exactly the impossibility of such a compromise which has been the whole lesson of Swift's poem. Further, as a revision of Swift's thesis that reason and passion are antipathetic, the passage is even less acceptable. For not only is its suggestion that love and reason may temper each other logically unprepared for in the poem, it is also experientially untrue. In fact, so different are love and reason from each other in human experience that it is much safer (though still false) to suppose that they are mutually hostile than it is to suppose that they are miscible. Finally, then, even if we consider the passage as but a piece of gallantry offered in consolation to a rejected woman, it is still deeply unfortunate. For its range of possibilities only could have encouraged Esther, impassioned as she was, to hope for some better outcome for her love than Swift ultimately had either means or will to offer her. Thus, cruelly, having written this poem to make clear to Esther that she must part from him, Swift draws it to its close by proffering her an empty and futile reprieve.

Sadly enough, Swift probably could not help committing this piece of unintended cruelty and futile dreaming. Such folly is the hallmark of any poem or any relationship that is not a celebration of the truth. Thus, in this particular case, because he either would not or could not dramatize the richness of passionate love itself, Swift had no choice but to attempt to define its felt worth in reasoned and reasonable terms. Such an attempt can have only two results, and both of them are lies. Either passionate love is discovered to be unreasonable—and hence worthless—or it is supposed to be reasonable—which is untrue. Caught between these two lies and unable to exhibit the truth, Swift floundered both in this poem and in his relationship with Esther to a conclusion that, as he says, left all things "at six and sev'n." One regrets the relationship, of course, with its long, futile pain for both Esther and Swift. But one is glad to have the poem. For though in *Cadenus and Vanessa* Swift does not tell much truth about love, he really does attempt to do so. Consequently, in his struggle to define the worth and the pain of passionate love, he both exposes his own errors and challenges us to test what we know of love against the confusions he engendered and endured.

4

"Believe me *Stella*"

The Poems to Esther Johnson

LIKE *Cadenus and Vanessa*, Sir Philip Sidney's *Astrophel and Stella* is an attempt to reconcile—in the face of a difficult relationship—those parallel and traditional polarities: reason and passion, body and spirit, divine and earthly love. Unlike *Cadenus and Vanessa*, however, *Astrophel and Stella* is a highly successful literary achievement. A large measure of its success is due to a single virtue: despite the fact that many of its individual sonnets are extremely derivative, almost all of those that speak directly to the tension between reason and passion do so with apparent fullness and honesty. Consequently, the values Sidney is able to wrest from the tensions his sonnets express seem always to be fairly won.[1]

Frequently, of course, Sidney is able to win nothing from the tensions he records. Thus he concludes poem after poem by reminding both himself and his obdurately chaste mistress that after all possible philosophizing "Desire still cries, 'Give me some food' " (Sonnet 71).[2] Occasionally, however, Sidney does discover a potential reconciliation in the impasse he portrays. This reconciliation is very different from the foolish hope Swift proffers Esther at the close of *Cadenus and Vanessa*, for it is

1. For a treatment of reason and passion in *Astrophel and Stella* which is different in emphasis from my own but very thorough, see Robert L. Montgomery, Jr., *Symmetry and Sense: The Poetry of Sir Philip Sidney* (Austin: The University of Texas Press, 1961), chap. 7.

2. Quotations from Sidney's *Astrophel and Stella* are from the Folio Society edition, notes by Kingsley Hart (London: Folio Society, 1959).

founded not on pedantic dreams of tempered love and reason but rather on passionately imaginative insight. Gazing into Stella's mortal eyes, Sidney catches there—without losing his sense of her flesh and his desire—a glimpse of passionate virtue and passionate chastity:

> O eyes which do the spheres of beauty move,
> Whose beams be joys, whose joys all virtue be
> Who, while they make Love conquer, conquer Love:
> The school where Venus hath learned chastity.   (Sonnet 42)

To be sure, such glimpses are as rare and ephemeral in *Astrophel and Stella* as they are moving. On the other hand, these glimpses are moving and believable precisely because they momentarily achieve a real, though intensely imaginative, harmony.

Whether Swift saw and appreciated this achieved harmony in *Astrophel and Stella* is a nice question. Eschewing passionate love, he certainly failed to produce in *Cadenus and Vanessa* anything like Sidney's compelling reconciliation of love and virtue. On the other hand, he does effect something very like Sidney's imaginative harmony in the poems he wrote to another woman: Esther Johnson, whom he, following Sidney, called Stella.

Of course, Swift's poems to Esther, unlike Sidney's to his Stella, are not much troubled by desire. They are, however, deeply concerned with the flesh. Annually occasioned, these poems were written to commemorate Stella's birthdays at an age when, Swift insisted, such commemorations could begin to mark only the stages of both his own and her physical decrepitude. Thus, just as Sidney refused to obscure the fact of desire in a mist of spirituality, so Swift refuses in these poems to turn away from the facts of age and mortality. Anxious to praise Stella's enduring virtues, he nevertheless makes it impossible, by the very occasions he chooses to celebrate her, for himself, or her, or us, to turn away from her physical frailties and growing disabilities. By that unwillingness, he sets the problem of his poems to her: what hope has man of being aught that will survive his illnesses?

To answer this problem, Swift moves towards a variety of statement as highly imaginative as Sidney's own, in which our enduring virtues are understood to be established on and nourished by our very ailments. Thus, in a passage reminiscent of that one in which Sidney momentarily glimpsed in his Stella's eyes an immortal reconciliation of virtue and desire, Swift, praising his own Stella's eyes, finds their growing dimness a stimulus for her virtue: "ev'ry Virtue now supplyes/The Fainting Rays of Stella's eyes" (*Stella's Birth-Day, 1720/21*, 21–22). Of course, the claim made in these lines is extravagant. That is the point, I think; for the Stella verse is truly fanciful poetry. Bacchus, Apollo, Hermes, Medea, Janus, Elijah, and Elisha are all alive in its lines and the solutions it proposes to the problems raised are all, in some sense, mythic. To be sure, such fancifulness is rare in Swift. Even as a young man, we recall, he was afraid that his airy muse might only be a lying slut. But for these poems, Stella herself was both inspiration and audience, and between Swift and her, I suspect, there obtained such closeness of thought and feeling that for her (and, perhaps, only for her) he could relax his grasp on demonstrable truth to portray the truths they both intuited.

No one, surely, could have been more Swift's own creature than Stella was. He first met her in 1689, when she was eight years old. He was a newcomer both to England and to the household of Sir William Temple at Moor Park. She was the daughter of Mrs. Bridget Johnson, a gentlewoman attached to that household. Quite possibly he was immediately assigned a large part of Stella's education: her handwriting, at maturity, rather resembled his, and habits of script are formed early. It is worth noting that Swift was inordinately pleased by this resemblance in their scripts: when once he was asked, on receiving a letter from her, if he was accustomed to addressing letters to himself, he reported the incident to Stella with some glee.[3] And just as he took care to form her script to resemble his, and then took pride in the accomplishment, so in matters of character and opinion, he also served her as both model and teacher.

By 1701, Stella reposed enough confidence in Swift to do a rather remarkable thing for a young woman of twenty at the beginning of the eighteenth century. Taking as her companion Mrs. Rebecca Dingley, a poor relation of the Temples, Stella left Moor Park, traveled to Ireland, and established residence in

3. *Journal to Stella*, 1:183.

Dublin under Swift's unofficial guardianship. Swift himself was
then thirty-four. Writing years after the event (and but a few days
after Stella's death) Swift records an eminently practical reason
for Stella's removal to Dublin. Noting that he was then, to his
own mortification, settled in Ireland, he reminds us of Sir
William's death in 1699 and explains that this death caused young
Stella some financial embarrassment. "Upon this consideration,"
he goes on, "and indeed very much for my own satisfaction, who
had few friends or acquaintances in Ireland, I prevailed with her
and her dear friend and companion, the other lady, to draw what
money they had into Ireland. . . . Money was then ten *per cent.*
in Ireland, besides the advantage of turning it, and all necessaries
of life at half the price. They complied with my advice, and soon
after came over."[4]

Swift's practical explanation of Stella's startling removal is
doubtless true. But biographers agree that Stella must have been a
young woman either much more or much less than human to have
marched the whole way to Swift and Dublin with no thoughts of
matrimony. And in this supposition Swift's biographers are supported by, among others, the Reverend Thomas Swift, Jonathan's
cousin, who inquired of a friend in 1706 "whether Jonathan be
married? Or whether he has been able to resist the charms of both
those gentlewomen that marched quite from *Moore-Park* to
Dublin . . . with full resolution to engage him?"[5] Nevertheless,
however ardently Stella may have desired it, she never became his
wife. She became instead, in Swift's memorable words, "the
truest, most virtuous, and valuable friend, that I, or perhaps any
other person ever was blessed with."[6] This friendship doubtless
offered Swift, as Irvin Ehrenpreis has convincingly argued, the
deepest emotional satisfaction of which he was capable.[7] Judging
from the poems Swift wrote her, it offered Stella a rather more
mixed blessing. On the one hand, she lived much of her life in the
companionship, and all of her life in the confidence, of the man she
most highly esteemed; because of him she moved constantly
amongst a pleasant, and occasionally amidst a brilliant company,
and through him her virtue and honor won both a contemporary

4. *Swift's Prose*, 5:228.
5. *Swift's Correspondence*, 1:56.
6. *Swift's Prose*, 5:227.
7. Ehrenpreis, 2:138.

and a lasting fame. On the other hand, Stella endured a passage from childhood to childless spinsterhood, and time has not quite effaced all traces of her discomfort.

Some of these traces are minor and normal: like most people, Stella regretted the loss of her youth and beauty, and when she mourned their passing publicly, Swift felt it necessary to remonstrate with her.[8] Some of the traces are more ominous: increasingly in the poems he addressed to her Swift felt it necessary to assure Stella that she had made of her life, childless spinster though she was, something of value. Her need for such assurance is made poignantly clear in a poem written shortly before her death: "*Say, Stella,*" Swift asks her, "feel you no Content,/Reflecting on a Life well spent?" (*Stella's Birth-Day, 1726/27,* 35–36). And, indeed, I suspect we owe the very existence of the poems we shall examine to Stella's increasing need for assurance that she had spent her life well. The poems celebrate her last birthdays because it was then, not earlier, she needed to be told that neither were her youth and beauty wasted nor were her age and ailments pointless, for all served to nourish a virtuous disposition which could in turn support her.

———

By arguing that in these poems Swift effected for Stella a particularly felicitous and imaginative reconciliation of the claims of flesh and spirit I may seem to be presenting a reading of the Stella poems that is in merely perverse contradiction to the reading of several of my predecessors. Certainly, a number of Swift's readers have held the view that in the Stella poems Swift effects no reconciliation at all, but simply contrasts the transient and finally unimportant flesh to the shining permanence of the spirit.[9]

This traditional view, while partly credible, has sometimes been supported by unfortunately infirm evidence. The fact, for example, that we cannot draw a profile of Stella's face after having read Swift's poems to her proves nothing. We do learn a good deal about her physically—she was fat, for example, in 1719, emaciated by 1723, grey by 1725, under heavy medication by 1727—and though

8. See, for example, *Swift's Correspondence*, 3:86.
9. Two particularly sensitive readings along these traditional lines were recently provided by Robert W. Uphaus, "Swift's Stella Poems and Fidelity to Experience," *Eire-Ireland* 5 (Autumn 1970):40–52, and James L. Tyne, "Swift and Stella: The Love Poems," *TSL* 19 (1974):35–48.

most of what we learn is neither beautiful nor pleasant, it is the truth, it is not being disregarded, and Swift presents it far too vigorously for us to say he is simply dismissing it.

More pertinent, however, is the argument that some of the advice Swift gives Stella in these poems seems to ask her to disregard not only her flesh and passions but her human individuality as well. As an example of such advice, we may cite that passage which, because he thought its admonitions neither desirable nor possible, both annoyed and amused Samuel Johnson.[10]

> In Points of Honour to be try'd,
> All Passions must be laid aside:
> Ask no Advice, but think alone,
> Suppose the Question not your own:
> How shall I act? is not the Case,
> But how would *Brutus* in my Place?
> In such a Cause would *Cato* bleed?
> And how would *Socrates* proceed?
>
> Drive all Objections from your Mind,
> Else you relapse to Human Kind:
> Ambition, Avarice, and Lust,
> And factious Rage, and Breach of Trust,
> And Flatt'ry tipt with nauseous Fleer,
> And guilty Shame and servile Fear,
> Envy, and Cruelty, and Pride,
> Will in your tainted Heart preside.
>
> (*To Stella, Visiting me in my Sickness*, 35–50)

There are, as we shall see, considerations that mitigate the uncompromising rigor of even this passage. But certainly this advice displays a distrust of the flesh, the passions, and of what men call the world, as profound as can be seen anywhere in Swift. If the attitude displayed in these lines usually informed Swift's Stella poetry, it would be impossible to maintain that those poems achieve a vision of human life in which the flesh and its passions are meaningfully included. But my contention is that these lines, so often taken as typical of Swift's Stella poetry, are, in fact, atypical. They display a black distrust of this world and of every-

10. Johnson's response to these lines was recorded by Hester Piozzi. See *Johnsonian Miscellanies*, ed. George Birkbeck Hill, 2 vols. (1897; rpt. New York: Barnes and Noble, 1966), 1:202.

thing that has to do with it which, I have already argued, Swift
could never wholly repress. But to attest that they do not represent the sum of what Swift taught Stella, I can bring the best of
possible witnesses: Stella herself. For in her one surviving birth-
day poem to Swift, *To Dr. Swift on his birth-day, November 30,
1721*, Stella states what she thought she learned from Swift, and
she provides an imitation, too, of the way in which Swift taught
it.

W. B. Yeats apparently knew Stella's poem to Swift well, and
his reaction to it provides, I think, a particularly fine introduction.
He quoted a few lines from the poem in his one-act play, *The
Words Upon the Window-Pane*, and put into the mouth of one of
his characters (a young Swift scholar) the observation that the
quoted lines are reminiscent of seventeenth-century poetry, of the
work of Donne, say, or Crashaw.[11] The lines Yeats cited are half
of that passage in which Stella enumerates the truths Swift taught
her; here is her whole catalogue:

> You taught how I might youth prolong
> By knowing what was right and wrong;
> How from my heart to bring supplies
> Of lustre to my fading eyes;
> How soon a beauteous mind repairs
> The loss of chang'd or falling hairs;
> How wit and virtue from within
> Send out a smoothness o'er the skin:
> Your lectures cou'd my fancy fix,
> And I can please at thirty-six.   (33–42)

Of course, these lines are not at all reminiscent of Donne's pros-
ody, or Crashaw's. But Yeats's observation seems proper because Stella displays in these lines an awareness, ubiquitous in
Donne and Crashaw, of that merger of flesh and spirit which
Donne, in *The Extasie*, called the "subtle knot which makes us
man." Stella is not saying, in these lines, that moral integrity may
serve to make a woman's company pleasant after she has lost her
beauty, though such a doctrine is good sense and might, perhaps,
be what each of us would say. Rather, Stella is arguing (and she

---

11. *The Variorum Edition of the Plays of W. B. Yeats*, ed. Russell K. Alspach
(New York: Macmillan, 1966), p. 941. Needless to say, I do not wholly agree with
Yeats's interpretation of Swift's character as it is dramatized in this play.

says she learned the argument from Swift) that moral sense literally prolongs youth, that an honest heart actually brightens eyes, and that wit and virtue can transform a complexion. Stella, that is, is arguing that the flesh and spirit are tied together with so subtle a knot that the deficiencies of the former can be supplied by the abundance of the latter.

We may say, of course, that this doctrine is merely "pure poetry," not good sense at all, certainly not what we have come to think of as "Swiftian." And, indeed, if we say so, we will be pretty close to the truth. For Stella's whole poem is so constructed as to move us almost insensibly past a number of sensible barriers.

The poem opens with an invocation to St. Patrick's Dean; it mentions both Ireland's and Stella's own indebtedness to him, and then passes on to a traditional request:

> Let me among the rest attend,
> Your pupil and your humble friend,
> To celebrate in female strains
> The day that paid your mother's pains;
> *Descend* to take that tribute due
> In gratitude alone to you.   (3–8, italics mine)

All this seems ordinary enough. The only thing that might possibly startle us in these lines is the verb "descend." Such a verb, one might think, would be more properly addressed to a god or to a saint than to a man: at least, it makes us wonder where Swift is. But it will not be until we reach the conclusion of the poem that the uneasiness this verb causes us can bear any fruit. For it is certain enough that here, in the first part of her poem, Stella is addressing a mortal, a man born in pain.

In fact, almost the entire first third of Stella's poem is taken up with the painful fact of human mortality. For, once Stella has addressed Swift and acknowledged him to be her early and her only guide, she goes on to depict the fate of those beauties who have not had his tutelage and who live, therefore, the ephemeral lives of beings with "no endowments but a face." Stella's portrait of beauty's decay is not so powerful as those Swift could draw (Stella's invokes a more obvious pathos than his do), but her point is the same as his, that flesh rots quickly.

Behold that beauty just decay'd,
Invoking art to nature's aid;
Forsook by her admiring train
She spreads her tatter'd nets in vain.   (15–18)

Stella's sketch, then, and the grim point she makes with it, might
have led her very logically to renounce all concern for the useless,
transient flesh, and to opt through the rest of her poem, for the
virtues of pure virtue. But she does not do so. Instead, the second
third of her poem contains those lines quoted above, in which the
flesh is understood to be a part of the subtle human knot, deriving
at least a measure of permanence from its association with the
timelessness of wit, truth, and virtue. To move, then, from the first
to the second third of Stella's poem is to move from a realm in
which time's grasp on flesh seems absolute, to a realm in which
that grasp has been somewhat relaxed. It is to move from what we
like to call realism towards those kinds of unprovable hopes which
find their fullest expression in myths.

It is natural, therefore, that as Stella closes the second section of
her poem she presents her hope that flesh may be supported by
virtue in an eminently recognizable mythic shape. "Oh! turn your
precepts into laws," she begs of Swift,

Redeem the women's ruin'd cause,
Retrieve lost empire to our sex,
That men may bow their rebel necks.   (49–52)

Stella's touch is both delicate and comic in these lines; we distort
them if we do not recognize that. But we misread them, I think, if
we do not see that Stella has built her whimsical vision of a female
paradise from elements of a larger hope for an empire, once lost, to
be redeemed, in which men will be no longer rebellious and flesh
will die no more.

This hope for the abolition of time through virtue receives its
most transparent form in the final section of Stella's poem. In it
Stella wishes Swift a long life, but she knows that he is mortal, that
Eden is not yet come again, and that he must die. Yet the way in
which Stella chooses to depict his death both accepts that death
and transcends it.

Late dying may you cast a shred
Of your rich mantle o'er my head;
To bear with dignity my sorrow,
One day *alone, then die to-morrow*.   (55–58)

It is the fate of Elijah that Stella describes here, to whom it was
given to transcend the boundary which divides mortal from immortal. Elijah steps alive into heaven's chariot and, obliterating for an
instant the line between flesh and spirit, heaven and earth, drops
his mantle to Elisha below. By closing with these lines, which unite
Swift and herself in a death which transcends death, Stella turns
her poem back to its beginning, to her request of Swift that he
"*Descend* to take that tribute due/In gratitude alone to you," and
to the hope which that request foretold.

———————

Swift was apparently so delighted with Stella's poem that he felt it
necessary to assure those to whom he showed it that it was all
purely Stella's and had not had a jot of his correction.[12] There is no
reason to doubt the truth of Swift's protestation, but we should
note that he was pleasantly aware of much in the poem that might
have been his own. Stella herself gladly confesses that the poem's
doctrine is what she learned from Swift. What Swift probably recognized is that to present his doctrine, Stella chose his own
methods: moving from a world of truths that could be validated
towards a realm of mythic statement, Stella's poem moves along a
path Swift had already opened in the first lines of his earliest poem
to her, *On Stella's Birth-day, 1718/19*.

Stella this Day is thirty four,
(We won't dispute a Year or more)
However Stella, be not troubled,
Although thy Size and Years are doubled,
Since first I saw Thee at Sixteen
The brightest Virgin on the Green.   (1–6)

I should note that I have broken off this passage before its
proper conclusion. In the lines immediately following these Swift

12. See Deane Swift, *An Essay on the Life, Writings and Character of Dr.
Jonathan Swift* (London: Charles Bathurst, 1755), p. 81.

tells Stella why she ought not to be troubled. But the efficacy of that explanation depends, I think, upon our understanding the lines I have already cited. And the first thing worth knowing about these lines is that, on the day that they were presented to Stella, she was not thirty-four but thirty-eight.

This sort of slip is not unusual for Swift: getting Stella's age wrong, in fact, getting most dates wrong most of the time is what he did constantly in casual reference. He himself was aware of this penchant, and he complained all his life of a bad memory. But, in fact, Swift's was a selectively bad memory. He could, when he cared to, remember a date with great exactitude: he was said to have memorized the whole of Butler's *Hudibras*, and a glance at his account books easily convinces one of the precision of which he was capable. The truth, apparently, is that there were some things that Swift preferred not to remember too clearly, and among these, as Sir Harold Williams suggested years ago, was the age of the woman he loved.[13]

This curiously intentional forgetfulness produces extraordinary poetry. On the one hand, Swift bluntly tells Stella that she has grown to middle age, a fact that he wants both of them to face. On the other hand, by a combination of mistake and gallantry, he apparently undercuts the very meaning of time's passage. Refusing to "dispute a year or more," Swift sets one wondering how many years, exactly, he was capable of discounting, and whether, finally, the passage of years means anything at all in his poem.

This ambivalent attitude towards what most of us consider the ineffable truth of time's passage colors each of the six lines I have cited. In them Swift is truly telling Stella that she has grown old and fat, but he is telling her this in a fashion so contemptuous of mere facts and simple numbers as to make one doubt the reality of age itself. All his arithmetic is flamboyantly wrong. He tells Stella that her age has doubled since he first met her, but (leaving aside the fact that Stella is not thirty-four) the sum of sixteen and sixteen is only thirty-two. Furthermore, Swift did not meet Stella when she was sixteen; he met her, as she knew very well, when she was eight. Under the guise, then, of supplying facts, what Swift has really done is to create just the sort of muddle in which fact tends to dissolve. And to speed the dissolution, he added a dash of vague

13. *Swift's Poems*, 2:721.

pastoralism (on what green did Swift see Stella?) and an estimate of her increase in girth which is purely outrageous.

Yet, for all their levity, these lines do show Swift's awareness that youth fades, that the process "troubled" Stella, and that, though his levity and false quantities might jostle her morbid awareness of age and its effects, he could not dispel age itself. He could only remind Stella, as his levity ought to remind us, that we are not so much time's creatures as to be unable to jest with time. But that reminder is enough, for it prepares us to reject our morbid picture of man as a spirit trapped in an alien and relentlessly aging flesh for the more hopeful view Swift proceeds to offer Stella. "Be not troubled," he advises her,

> Although thy Size and Years are doubled,
> · · · · · · · · · · · · · · ·
> So little is thy Form declin'd
> Made up so largly in thy Mind.   (4, 7–8)

This advice, like the lines we have just examined, tells us that Stella has grown fat with age; Swift insists yet again that her form, being so large, is but little declined. But the words "large," and "little declin'd" function in these lines as near-puns; they refer to Stella's increased girth but also to her breadth of mind, and thus they view her broadened form, not as an encumbrance but as a testimony to her virtue. What Swift demonstrates in these lines, then, and recommends to Stella, is a vision that transforms even the infirmities of flesh into human good, and turns a solid antagonist into a malleable part of that "subtle knot" which makes us man.

Swift ends his poem by putting in an ageless form his own hope that time and its effects on flesh may be translatable into human good.

> Oh, would it please the Gods to split
> Thy Beauty, Size, and Years, and Wit,
> No Age could furnish out a Pair
> Of Nymphs so gracefull, Wise and fair
> With half the Lustre of Your Eyes,
> With half thy Wit, thy Years and Size:
> And then before it grew too late,
> How should I beg of gentle Fate,

(That either Nymph might have her Swain,)
To split my Worship too in twain.   (9–18)

Unfortunately, there is no way of knowing whether Swift knew the symbolic ceremony that Frazer, under the title of "Sawing the Old Woman," described as once widespread through Europe and still practiced in the seventeen-thirties in France.[14] To this ceremony, traditionally acted at mid-Lent, was brought a wooden effigy. When the effigy had been clothed in the costume of an old woman, it was placed on the public scaffold, and, to borrow a phrase from Aristophanes, split up the middle. I know of no one who has speculated whether this ceremony predates Lent. Certainly, it scarcely needs its lenten context to make obvious its commemoration of the death of the old to make way for the new. And thus, though it is as crude as Christ's triumph over time and death is profound, this little ceremony nevertheless shares a common hope with that far greater mystery.

It would be pleasant to know if Swift had either heard of, or been witness to, a variant of the ceremony Frazer describes, but such knowledge is not, I think, crucial. Probably, if Swift knew of such dramas, he disapproved of them. Quite possibly, he would himself deny any connection between the crudely acted drama at the scaffold, and his witty, sophisticated prayer for some mythic god to make, from his and Stella's age, pairs of youthful nymphs and swains. Yet for all that, and with appropriate respect for its skillful raillery, we should see that Swift's prayer is still a type of the human dream that time and age may someday yield flesh up to eternity. That is why his prayer is a proper conclusion to a poem intended to teach Stella a use for her own "superfluous" flesh.

In both Stella's poem to Swift and Swift's first poem to her I have traced a pattern which structures, though with variations, most, though not all, of Swift's Stella poetry. These poems, beginning with a morbid, though wittily put, sense of age and the corruptibility of flesh, first find a use even for infirmity and then, on the basis of that success, move to a more general statement of man's promised immortality. But though these poems have a

14. Sir James George Frazer, *The Golden Bough*, 3d ed., 13 vols. (1911–36; rpt. New York: St. Martin's, 1966), 4:240–45.

common pattern of development, they vary considerably in poetic merit. Two of them, *Stella's Birth-Day. A great Bottle of Wine, long buried, being that Day dug up*, and *Stella's Birth-Day, 1724/25*, seem to me particularly fine, and they illustrate the flexibility Swift could achieve within a single pattern.

Swift's celebration of his restored and restoring bottle of wine is easily the most intellectually teasing of the group. The poem begins, as each of the poems does, with a complaint against age, but in this poem, the complaint is Swift's own: his power of verse, he says, has grown enfeebled.

> Resolv'd my annual Verse to Pay
> By Duty bound, on *Stella's* Day;
> Furnish'd with Paper, Pens, and Ink,
> I gravely sat me down to think:
> I bit my Nails, and scratch'd my Head,
> But found my Wit and Fancy fled.   (1–6)

Becoming increasingly desperate, Swift calls upon Apollo, as god of poetry, to help him out of his predicament, but for some time the god simply lets Swift sit and stew. When Apollo finally deigns to answer, he advises Swift first to gather together his household and his friends. Then, utilizing the particular talents of each, Swift must seek out the tomb of a long-buried bottle of wine. Once exhumed and drunk off, the wine, Apollo claims, will give Swift the power to invoke his muse and "to crown the year" with Stella's praise.

The poem divides neatly into two parts—Swift's statement of his problem and Apollo's solution—and the latter is precisely the mythic counterpart of the former. Through the whole first half of his poem, we remember, Swift complains of his poetic enfeeblement. For all we know, that complaint may reflect some real compositional problems. But as Swift makes his plea to Apollo, those problems become both subject and inspiration for his poem. Like the phoenix, Swift's wit rises from its own ashes in the first half of this poem and thus illustrates that proper use of adversity which Swift, through all these poems, attempts to teach Stella.

Apollo's answer merely puts into broader, mythic terms the solution to the problems of age and enfeeblement that the poem's very existence portrays. For Apollo's bottle of wine, the proposed inspirer of Swift's song, is a very type of death and rebirth. First, like Swift's poem itself, the bottle's tomb can be found only through the proper use of adversity. Swift's housekeeper, Mrs. Brent, is assigned this ritual and, indeed, since the bottle could be found only by a seeker capable of "nine ways looking," she was the only person proper for the search. "She had," as Swift dryly noted in his copy of the poem, "a cast in her eye." Secondly, the bottle presents, as Swift describes it being exhumed, a perfectly contrived picture of life sprung from death. "See!" Swift commands us, "as you raise it from its Tomb,/It drags behind a spacious Womb" (67–68). Lastly, that spacious womb contains, as Swift carefully tells us, the work of Bacchus, and Bacchus is not only a god who is annually regenerated but (as Patrick Delany reminds us in the Latin verse he wrote to accompany Swift's poem) the only god to be twice born. Rent from Semele's womb as she lay on her funeral pyre, Bacchus, as the myth runs, was sutured in Zeus's thigh to be reborn an immortal.

Whimsical though it is, then, this poem is tightly made. With a bottle of wine for its subject, it presents a Bacchic rite of regeneration in which Swift himself, rising from his infirmities "to crown the year," plays Bacchus. And further, Swift is at some pains to make us understand that in his regenerative Bacchic character he is playing a role in what he understands to be the way of the world. For in the creation of the poem's emblematic bottle of wine are involved, we learn, all the elements of the world—earth, air, fire and water—and to this bottle Swift is led by Apollo himself. This last touch is very nice indeed, for it recaptures the wisdom that led the Greeks to center at one place, Delphi, the worship of both Apollo, the god of clear reason and the high arts, and Bacchus, the god of exuberant, fleshy, and constantly renewing life.

Stella's Birth-Day. A great Bottle of Wine, long buried, being that Day dug up, is doubtless Swift's most spectacular showcase both for the great truth of all his Stella poems—that of our adversities we must make our advantages—and for the reconciliations of flesh and spirit, this world and the next, which that truth makes possible and requires. *Stella's Birth-Day, 1724/25* is, on the other hand, a much quieter achievement, but it is the more movingly human poem.

The first half of the poem is devoted to the now familiar

complaint of age. Giving their ages, this time, almost correctly, Swift wistfully asks Stella,

> At Fifty six . . .
> Am I a Poet fit for you?
> Or at the Age of Forty three,
> Are you a Subject fit for me?　　　　　　　(23–26)

The answer to both questions, Swift concludes, is no.

> Adieu bright Wit, and radiant Eyes;
> You must be grave, and I be wise. .
> Our Fate in vain we would oppose,
> But I'll be still your Friend in Prose.　　　　　(27–30)

But this is the same trick, yet more boldly executed, that we have seen before. Swift here makes his very adieu to poetry serve him as subject for half a poem.

Yet, for all the similarity between the opening of this poem and the opening of *Stella's Birth-Day. A great Bottle of Wine, long buried, being that Day dug up*, the two passages strike the ear with different tones. We know that in the interim between the two poems, Stella suffered a dangerous bout of illness. Perhaps as a consequence, Swift's opening in this later poem, though able to transform adversity to advantage, conveys a deeper sense of his awareness of age and flesh's frailty.

Perhaps too, one's reading of the first half of this poem is colored by a second half that presents, not an exuberantly Bacchic rebirth, but a much more sober estimate of the human condition. Stella has aged, Swift admits, but then his eyes have "somewhat dimmish grown." And in a passage which I must not shorten Swift willfully believes the evidence of his own half-ruined eyes, trusting the fate which has dimmed his vision:

> But, *Stella* say, what evil Tongue
> Reports you are no longer young?
> That *Time* sits with his scythe to mow
> Where erst sate *Cupid* with his Bow;
> That half your Locks are turn'd to Grey;
> I'll ne'er believe a word they say.
> 'Tis true, but let it not be known,

My Eyes are somewhat dimmish grown;
For Nature, always in the Right,
To your Decays adapts my Sight,
And Wrinkles undistinguish'd pass,
For I'm asham'd to use a Glass;
And till I see them with these Eyes,
Whoever says you have them, lyes.   (35–48)

Of course, this denial of what everyone else can see may seem
merely fanciful; so, too, may Swift's concluding lines.

No Length of Time can make you quit
Honour and Virtue, Sense and Wit,
Thus you may still be young to me,
While I can better *hear* than *see*.   (49–52)

But if this is only fancy, it is haunting fancy. For though, unlike
Swift, we may choose to use glasses—and though we may improve on our senses in ways Swift never dreamed of—yet we can
never, any more than Swift, guarantee that what we sense is all
there is. Indeed if, like Joseph Glanvill (an author Swift knew),
we contrast our senses with that Edenic perfection of sense by
which prelapsarian Adam was supposed to see at a glance the
whole of "Coelestial magnificense" and to hear its music, then
not only are we all, like Swift, half-blind, but he, like us, is
near-deaf.[15] And only, I think, by feeling the force of Glanvill's
contrast, and by remembering how deeply ingrained it was in the
seventeenth century, can we grasp the point of Swift's poem and
what it affirms.

Swift chooses, in a way that may appear eccentric at first, to
school his worse eyes by his better ears and to believe the results.
But that, after all, is what all men must do, for though all men (by
Adam's standard, at least) suffer under some degree of sensory
imperfection, none can afford to abandon his senses. This only
difference, then, obtains between Swift and most of us—Swift is
at once aware that his flesh and its senses are imperfect and yet,
trusting that the very disabilities of his senses have been
"adapted" to his needs, he is willing to labor through those

15. *The Vanity of Dogmatizing*, ed. Moody Prior, reproduced from the 1661
edition for the Facsimile Text Society (New York: Columbia University Press,
1931), pp. 4–5.

senses towards what he can know of timeless honor and virtue, sense and wit. This is the height of Swift's wisdom, I think, and, movingly, his careful yet trusting adjustment of ear and eye does not go unrewarded in this poem. Rather, it brings a glimpse of eternal youth to his darkened sight.

To seek in ruined flesh with ruined flesh for immortal truth requires superb trust in nature's, or fortune's, or God's way with man. Swift's trust was powerful, but it was so, as I have argued in other contexts, because it was much exercised by his doubts. Of those doubts, not surprisingly, we see a good deal in these intensely personal poems. We are, in fact, constantly reminded of what Swift knew very well: that the special vision that sees traces of immortality in this world is both tenuous and dependent. "Oh, ne'er may Fortune," Swift prays at the end of the poem we have just examined, "shew her Spight,/To make me *deaf*, and mend my *Sight*" (53–54).

Two poems particularly, *To Stella, Visiting me in my Sickness*, and *Stella's Birth-Day, 1726/27*, seem to display the sort of doubt that puts in question the very truths and reconciliations that characterize the Stella poems. *Stella's Birth-Day, 1726/27*, is a tightly and compassionately made answer to the doubts that afflicted Stella on her deathbed. It is the best poem of the group and a proper close to this study. *To Stella, Visiting me in my Sickness*, on the other hand, is a loosely made, almost rambling poem, which fascinates because it shows the strength of Swift's own distrust of the world and the flesh he yet knew he had to trust.

Unlike most of the poems in the Stella group, more like *Cadenus and Vanessa*, *To Stella, Visiting me in my Sickness* begins with an impromptu myth.

> *Pallas* observing *Stella's* Wit
> Was more than for her Sex was fit;
> And that her Beauty, soon or late,
> Might breed Confusion in the State,
> In high Concern for human Kind,
> Fix *Honour* in her Infant Mind.   (1–6)

But this is a far more propitious beginning than the one Swift wrote for *Cadenus and Vanessa*. For in this poem, though Pallas displays an acute awareness that flesh, particularly beautiful flesh, can breed confusion, she also demonstrates what she entirely lacked in *Cadenus and Vanessa*—a "high Concern for human Kind"—and a vigorous willingness to work amidst it.

Curiously, however, with this myth but well begun, Swift abruptly breaks it off to define, in abstract terms, "the idea of Honour."

> But, (not in Wranglings to engage
> With such a stupid vicious Age,)
> If Honour I would here define,
> It answers Faith in Things divine.   (7–10)

This is really a sudden shift, both in tone and style, and it is strange to see Swift here more set against his age than Pallas herself. It is as though, with his poem already begun, Swift is still casting about for a perspective. And, as he plunges on, he finds a very dangerous one.

The definition of honor Swift finally supplies—"It answers Faith in Things divine"—resembles nothing so much as the definition of piety which Euthyphro gave Socrates: "Piety [is] that part of justice which attends to the gods, as there is the other part of justice which attends to men."[16] And it is worth listening to Socrates' criticism of this definition, for it applies to Swift's as well. "That is good, Euthyphro," Socrates begins; "yet still there is a little point about which I should like to have further information, What is the meaning of 'attention'? For attention can hardly be used in the same sense when applied to the gods as when applied to other things." What Socrates is accusing Euthyphro of forgetting is that divinity is qualitatively unique. And the same criticism can be leveled at Swift's equivalence of honor and faith, which, by making man's relationship with God but another type of man's general relationships, overlooks all the frailties that distinguish man from God. It is but a short step from the definition to the passage which follows it, a passage filled with Swift's

16. *The Works of Plato*, trans. Benjamin Jowett, 3d ed., selected and edited by Irvin Edman (New York: Random House, 1956), p. 50.

terrible impatience with human frailties and ended by his famous, silly advice: if you would act with honor, act as if you had no private interests and no selfish passions, as if, that is, you were a god.

This advice (already quoted above), though it has often been cited as typical of Swift's thought, has never been examined in context, as the conclusion to a whole passage. But, in fact, the whole of the passage in which this advice is incorporated may well have reminded Stella of one possible source for the advice itself: Plutarch's *On Moral Virtue*. We do know that Swift admired Plutarch's moral essays and they may quite possibly have been a resource he shared with Stella.[17] In the description, then, of an all-comprehensive honor with which Swift begins this passage Stella may have heard an echo of an all-comprehensive virtue with which Plutarch began his essay. Here is Swift:

> Those num'rous Virtues which the Tribe
> Of tedious Moralists describe,
> And of such various Titles call,
> True Honour comprehends them all.   (15–18)

And here is Plutarch:

> Virtue [is] one in substance. . . . For Virtue, when
> it considers what it ought to do and what it ought
> not to do, it is called prudence; and when it curbs
> passion, and sets a fit and proper limit to pleasure,
> it is called self-control; and when it is associated
> with our dealings and covenants with one another,
> it is called justice; just as a knife is one article,
> though at different times it cuts different things in
> half.[18]

Similarly, Swift's very advice to Stella that "In Points of Honour to be try'd,/All Passions must be laid aside" (35–36) may be grounded in Plutarch's observation that "reasoning without passion has a direct tendency to justice. . . . But the deliberations

17. A possible (though whimsical) demonstration of this can be found in the *Journal to Stella*, 2:601.

18. *Plutarch's Morals*, trans. Arthur Richard Shilleto (London: G. Bell and Sons, 1888), p. 98. Plutarch is here summarizing the arguments of Menedemos, Aristo, and Zeno as a preface to his own discussion.

and judgments and arbitrations of most people as to matter of fact being mixed up with passion, give reason no easy or pleasant access, as she is held fast and incommoded by the unreasonable, which assails her through pleasure, or fear, or pain, or desire."[19] Indeed, Plutarch's last few words here—"through pleasure, or fear, or pain, or desire"—may well have been in Swift's mind as he wrote his own vigorously expanded command:

> Drive all Objections from your Mind,
> Else you relapse to Human Kind:
> Ambition, Avarice, and Lust,
> And factious Rage, and Breach of Trust,
> And Flatt'ry tipt with nauseous Fleer,
> And guilty Shame, and servile Fear,
> Envy, and Cruelty, and Pride,
> Will in your tainted Heart preside.   (43–50)

Yet, for all their similarity, Swift's advice differs radically from Plutarch's essay, and *On Moral Virtue* is, finally, a better antidote to than an illumination of Swift's lines. Plutarch's thesis in *On Moral Virtue* is that virtue can be attained only by yoking the soul's passions to the soul's reasons. "If the passions," Plutarch states, "were entirely removed . . . reason would become in many duller and blunter, like the pilot in the absence of a storm."[20] Unfortunately, Swift's advice on trying "points of honour," so reminiscent of parts of Plutarch's essay, does not resemble *On Moral Virtue* in this crucial observation. Instead, Swift advises us that as we try "points of honour," we ought first "lay aside" passion and then allow reason to solve our problem. Since, however, as Swift describes them, "points of honour" arise only when passion and reason have come to cuffs, his advice is not only humanly impossible, it is logically absurd. Simply put, if passion is laid aside in solving points of honor there is no problem and, hence, nothing for reason to work upon. That is to make reason a "dull pilot" indeed. Swift's advice, then, means no more than this: if you get rid of your problem, you will have no problem.

Obvious tautologies, such as this one, are rare enough in Swift's poetry, but then so is the sort of plain didactic statement

19. Ibid., p. 110.
20. Ibid., p. 117.

that can plunge to tautology. Swift's poetry simply is not, either in general, or at its best, a poetry of statement. Usually, when Swift writes downright didacticism it is, as here, an attempt to lighten the burden of human paradox by supplying a simple formula for conduct. And while the results of that attempt are not always as silly as are these lines, in which Swift's possible source actually exposes the weakness of Swift's lines, the results are generally unfortunate. At least as unfortunate, I think, has been a tendency of Swift's critics to take those results as typical of Swift's thought and thus to come away with the chaff and leave the grain.

Such critics to the contrary, Swift's *To Stella, Visiting me in my Sickness* does not conclude with the fifty lines we have examined; in fact, it can hardly be said to have come to its subject. That subject is Stella as she visits Swift in his sickness, and when, close to its conclusion, Swift turns his poem towards her, he recaptures at once the richness of his opening lines. Those lines, we recall, portray Pallas as she, "in high Concern for human Kind," stooped to instill honor in Stella's infant mind. The warmth of that portrait remains suspended through the barren, abstract center of this poem—that is what is wrong with it. But when Swift finally describes Stella's ministrations to him at his bedside, he reflects again the truth implicit in her honor's geniture: that honor is a response to flesh and the passions, not an avoidance of them.

As Swift describes them, the duties Stella chose to assume were onerous and, practically speaking, futile. Swift was—he himself admits it—a querulous patient at best, and he had reached an age when recovery from illness is both slow and painfully temporary. Yet, for all that, Stella's efforts on his behalf were valuable, and though the worth of those efforts is not didactically demonstrable, it is perfectly portrayed in the little round of Stella's ministrations with which Swift closes his poem.

The passage opens with Swift's description of himself, impatient and in pain, before one of Stella's visits:

> . . . on my sickly Couch I lay,
> Impatient both of Night and Day,
> Lamenting in unmanly strains,
> Call'd ev'ry pow'r to ease my pains.   (97–100)

Swift's impatience here is hauntingly familiar. It derives, I think, from a scriptural passage to which he was always drawn: Job's shrill lamentation, in the agony of his flesh, against the day of his birth and the night of his conception.[21] "Let that day perish wherein I was born, and the night in which it was said, there is a man child conceived. Let that day be darkness. . . . As for that night, let darkness seize upon it" (3:3, 4, 6). I do not argue that Swift here has "intentionally" assumed Job's posture; in fact, I suspect that the passage we are examining is entirely beyond the reach of Swift's conscious art. It has been preceded by a poem in which Swift has given vent to his impatience with the terms of human life. Impatient, he has willed away the passions, the flesh, and cursed all their attendant frailties. Impatient, he has commanded Stella to live above the reach of "mere Human Kind." But after he has done all that, he knows (if it can be called knowledge) that he has uttered Job's complaint against the very terms of existence, and that he must abide Job's answer.

Job is answered by God's voice speaking to him out of a whirlwind. He is told, we recall, that all the conditions of his life are from God's hands and that, therefore, it is only incumbent upon him to accept, undisputed, His dispensation. "When thy right hand can save thee," God tells him, "then will I confess thee unto me."

Swift is answered in a manner more ambivalently divine; having "call'd on ev'ry pow'r to ease [his] pain," he sees Stella run to his relief. But though Stella's presence contrasts whimsically with God's awful whirlwind, Stella embodies, no less truly for all that, God's answer to Job. As Stella ministers to Swift she works, he sees, with "chearful Face," but "inward Grief." Pained by his pain she accepts her pain and turns it to good:

> And, though by Heaven's severe Decree
> She suffers hourly more than me,
> No cruel Master could require
> From Slaves employ'd for daily Hire
> What *Stella* by her Friendship warm'd,
> With Vigour and Delight perform'd.   (103–8)

21. Swift's well-documented attachment to the Book of Job admits of several different interpretations. For one directly opposed to my own see John M. Bullitt, *Jonathan Swift and the Anatomy of Satire* (Cambridge: Harvard University Press, 1953), p. 9.

This patient, uncomplaining acceptance of "Heaven's severe Decree" is what Stella teaches Swift. It is a bitter draught, as nauseous as his medicine, but like that medicine, it is healing. In four beautifully compact lines, Swift shows us Stella administering both:

> I see her taste each nauseous Draught,
> And so obligingly am caught:
> I bless the Hand from whence they came,
> Nor dare distort my Face for shame.   (113–16)

This is a simple act, simply described, but it catches entire that "True Honour" which comprehends all virtues and which, amidst man's allotted pain and frailties, both gives and receives blessings.

The poem has come full circle. The honor that Pallas, "in high Concern for human Kind," placed in Stella's infant mind, emerges in Stella's actions as, again, "high Concern for human Kind." Early in the poem, we recall, Swift defined honor like this: "Honour . . . answers Faith in Things divine." It is a dangerous definition because, blurring the line between man and God, it tempts man to try to live as if he were God. Yet it is true that, at the end of this poem, Stella's ministering to Swift does recall Pallas's ministering to her. There is no contradiction here; it is just that, as generations of Christians have affirmed, though the way up is only the way down, the way down is the way up.

This paradox is hard to seize, but it is harder still to hold. And before this poem closes we see it start to slip Swift's grasp again. "Best pattern of true Friends, beware," he warns Stella;

> You pay too dearly for your Care;
> If, while your Tenderness secures
> My Life, it must endanger yours.
> For such a Fool was never found,
> Who pull'd a Palace to the Ground,
> Only to have the Ruins made
> Materials for a House decay'd.   (117–24)

It is almost as if Swift has forgotten that in ministering to him, Stella has been blessed. But then, because this is a hard truth for doubting man to remember, it is a measure of Swift's faith that a few years later, when he had to, he could in his turn teach it to Stella.

Stella's Birth-Day, 1726/27 is the last poem of the Stella group, and it is the most moving of them. In it Swift develops the motifs typical of the group—recognition of age, the uses of frailty, the mythic statement—but he uses these motifs with an earnestness proper to the poem's occasion. The poem was written as Stella lay on what both she and Swift knew was probably her deathbed, and though it begins with the touch of bravado we have come to expect, that bravado now only poignantly emphasizes the inevitability of age and death:

> This Day, whate'er the Fates decree,
> Shall still be kept with Joy by me:
> This Day then, let us not be told,
> That you are sick, and I grown old,
> Nor think on our approaching Ills,
> And talk of Spectacles and Pills;
> Tomorrow will be Time enough
> To hear such mortifying Stuff.   (1–8)

Swift can still jest in these lines, of course, but his jests are within that tradition of grim humor indigenous to the *memento mori*.[22] Stella, dying, would see the point of his starkly comic name for pills and spectacles—"mortifying Stuff." And attuned to the decorum of sacramental service by an intimate thirty-year friendship with Dean Swift, Stella must have also recognized, in the request her friend and yearly poet makes to appear to her this year in his clerical robes, a preamble to what could only be a poetic "Communion of the Sick." "From not the gravest of Divines," Swift asks, "Accept for once some serious Lines" (13–14).

That Stella, apparently near death, was truly in need of Swift's priestly ministrations is made painfully clear very early in the poem. For Swift, seeking a common ground from which to prepare Stella to face death with that faith emblemized by his office,

---

22. For a discussion of this tradition see Louis Martz, *The Poetry of Meditation*, 2d ed. (New Haven: Yale University Press, 1962), pp. 135–44. Also see pages 155–59 below.

must begin very far indeed from faith. He must begin by granting the possibility that "future Happiness and Pain" may be a "mere Contrivance of the Brain"; that is, he must begin by casting into doubt a tenet crucial to Stella's very salvation. And were this not enough, he must also put in doubt all earthly efficacy of human virtue by granting at least the possibility that virtue, though it is often "stil'd its own Reward,/And by all Sages understood/To be the chief of human Good" (26–28), may, in its very action, die.

Further, Swift ministers to Stella in this poem, not with his customary moral force, but as if she were an at least potentially hostile communicant. The special pleading which is observable in his initial request of Stella to "accept, for once, some serious Lines," recurs at the beginning of almost every major unit of thought in the poem. "Say, *Stella*," Swift asks but a few lines later in the poem, "feel you no Content,/Reflecting on a Life well spent?" (35–36). Again, not many lines later, we hear

> Believe me *Stella*, when you show
> That true Contempt for Things below,
> · · · · · · · · · · · · · · ·
> Your former Actions claim their Part,
> And join to fortify your Heart.   (67–68, 71–72)

Finally, all these instances of what one might call a submerged ethical appeal surface, at the close of the poem, in a cry so open as to expose both the depth of Stella's rancor and Swift's pain in the face of it. "Take Pity," he exhorts her,

> on your pitying Friends;
> Nor let your Ills affect your Mind,
> To fancy they can be unkind.
> Me, surely me, you ought to spare.   (80–83)

This special pleading reflects, at least in part, I suspect, the disastrous conclusion of Swift's romantic attachment with Esther Vanhomrigh. Swift, we know, took pains to conceal that relationship from Stella, but by April 1726 several copies of *Cadenus and Vanessa* were in circulation and we can guess that the poem seriously compromised Swift and jeopardized his friendship with Stella. We have, of course, stories in plenty of Stella's nightly weeping herself to sleep, and of stormy confrontations and secret marriages. But perhaps the best evidence we have of Stella's distress is the ethical and theological despair that Swift, having so probably contributed to as a man, exhibits here as a poet, in order to heal as a priest.

Because, then, Swift was probably one cause of the despair he is trying to cure, a real problem for him in this poem must have been just to get Stella to listen to him. And, therefore, the basic strategy of the poem, which is not to praise virtue in the abstract, but is, rather, to give an extensive list of Stella's virtues, ought to be understood first as a prudent example of hortatory tact. But it is also something more than tact; for if Swift in this poem spread before Stella a pleasing tapestry of her own virtues—her cure of the sick and care of the convalescent, her bold fidelity in friendship, her courage and generosity and purity—only in order to entice her eye, still the very fact that such a list may gratify her provides at least one appeal from her thoroughgoing despair. If Stella is pleased by this poem, she demonstrates in herself that virtue can be at least its own reward. And thus Swift earns the right to ask her, towards the close of his poem, "who with reason can pretend,/That all Effects of Virtue end?" (65–66).

In still another way too, Swift makes his whole poem, or, more exactly perhaps, the very existence of his poem, an argument proving that virtue is its own reward. First of the virtues Swift attributes to Stella is her cure of the sick, her

> skilful Hand employ'd to save
> Despairing Wretches from the Grave;
> And then supporting with [her] Store,
> Those whom [she] dragg'd from Death before.   (37–40)

We know, of course, that Swift himself was the most constant of Stella's patients. Indeed, Swift completed this last poem to her with that acknowledgement—and an offer to

> give my Scrap of Life to you,
> And think it far beneath your Due;
> You, to whose Care so oft I owe,
> That I'm alive to tell you so.   (85–88)

But while these closing lines do not tell us, then, nor surely did they tell Stella, anything we did not know, they are argument nevertheless. For even as these lines acknowledge the impossibility of Swift's actually giving his "Scrap of Life" to Stella, they remind us that she has empowered him to do something even better; if Stella has derived any comfort from the poem that precedes these lines, that comfort is what she herself gave before. In her previous care of Swift, and in her "skilful Hand" which averted Swift's "despair," was the source of her present consolation.

Pleasing as this consolation might have been to Stella, it does not, however, include all the elements of this poem, much of which is devoted to refuting the opinion, apparently harbored by Stella on her deathbed, that a future state, entailing judgment, is merely chimerical. Thus, Swift moves in this poem from the brave declaration with which he first addresses Stella: "This Day, whate'er *the Fates decree*,/Shall still be kept with Joy by me" (1–2, italics mine), to the similarly worded, and yet very different, pious exhortation with which he concludes his argument: "O then, whatever *Heav'n intends*,/Take Pity on your pitying Friends" (79–80, italics mine).

Curiously, however, just in this crucial argument, Swift's poem, so delicate in its delineation of the state of Stella's soul, and so gentle in its consolations, seems, initially at least, to be simply assertive. Thus, for example, even as Swift grants the possibility that "future happiness and pain" may be a "mere Contrivance of the Brain," he hastens to add that such a position would be argued only by atheists to entice

> And fit their Proselytes for Vice;
> (The only Comfort they propose,
> To have Companions in their Woes.)   (22–24)

This coda seems, one must say, fair neither to Stella nor to the argument. But it is typical of Swift's procedure in this poem. To his description of Stella's cure of and subsequent care for her patients, Swift gratuitously adds these lines: "(So Providence on Mortals waits,/Preserving what it first creates)" (41–42). And thus he apparently begs the question by making Stella a type of the very providential care which is in doubt. Because, then, Swift's arguments for a future state appear so uncharacteristically weak, his final consolation to Stella, that Virtue "at [her] sickly Couch will wait,/And guide [her] to a better State" (77–78), while perhaps deeply moving, may also seem unearned and unconvincing.

Yet the apparent weakness of Swift's argument for faith is finally, I think, only apparent; the assertive method of his poem does not reflect a weakness in his argument, but rather identifies for us the type of argument he has employed to convince Stella of the existence of providence, judgment, hell, and heaven. It is an argument both venerably ancient and yet so readily accessible to Swift as to have been practically part of the air he breathed. Indeed, if we listen sympathetically to Swift's claim that only a vicious man would argue against a future state, we can hear, in reversed form, and stated as an irrefutable fact, the view of faith that both determines and explains the strategy of this poem: faith is apparent to the virtuous man, and therefore the assent to faith is to be made, not through subtle argument but through the practice of virtue.

The idea that virtue opens the eye to faith was already part of Swift's intellectual character when, as a young man tutoring Stella and writing his *Ode to Dr. William Sancroft*, he affirmed with Plotinus that "never did eye see the sun unless it had first become sunlike, and never can the soul have vision of the First Beauty unless itself be beautiful."[23] And apparently this Neo-Platonic faith never entirely separated, in Swift's mind, from the Platonic imagery in which he probably first saw it expressed; for such imagery permeates this poem. Shall your virtues, Swift asks Stella, "like empty Shadows pass,/Or Forms reflected from a Glass?" (51–52). No, he assures her, they shall "leave behind"

> Some lasting Pleasure in the Mind,
> . . . .
> And strongly shoot a radiant Dart,
> To shine through Life's declining Part.   (29–30, 33–34)

But not all the imagery of this poem is typically Platonic. The idea that virtue is at once a good in itself, its own reward, and that yet it illuminates a higher good and leads man towards it is also the substance of the two most characteristically Swiftian

23. Plotinus *Enneads* (trans. Stephen MacKenna, 4th ed., rev. B. S. Page, London: Faber and Faber, 1969) 1.6.9.

similes in this poem. "Does not the Body thrive and grow," Swift asks,

> By Food of twenty Years ago?
> . . . .
> And, is not Virtue in Mankind
> The Nutriment that feeds the Mind? (55–56, 61–62)

The point of this homely comparison is at least partly obvious: it is another attempt to convince Stella that virtue does sustain us in this life. But we miss part of the force of the comparison, I think, if we forget that it is after all a comparison of virtue to food, and that a man does not live to eat, but rather eats to live. Implicit, that is, in Swift's choice of things to be compared is the suggestion that virtue, like food itself, may serve both as a temporary end and as a higher means.

This same suggestion appears, perhaps more clearly, in the second simile that Swift constructed to describe virtue in this poem. "Virtue in her daily Race," he says,

> Like *Janus*, bears a double Face;
> Looks back with Joy where she has gone,
> And therefore goes with Courage on. (73–76)

Again, the point of the simile is so apparently obvious, and Janus is so physically appropriate to represent virtue's habitual and self-sustaining action, that the simile almost discourages further investigation. But it is well to remember, I think, what Swift, whose library contained two editions of Ovid, would almost certainly have known: that the two-headed deity Janus is the god of all beginnings and the very porter of Heaven. Thus, at the opening of the *Fasti*, Ovid asks, "Why, Janus, while I propitiate other divinities, do I bring incense and wine first of all to thee?" And Janus responds, "It is through me, who guard the thresholds, you may have access to whatever Gods you please."[24] Thus, by comparing virtue with Janus, Swift covertly suggests again what he will overtly claim just a few lines later: that virtue will wait at Stella's "sickly Couch" and guide her to a better state. Indeed,

24. Ovid *Fasti* (trans. Sir James George Frazer, 5 vols., London: Macmillan, 1929) 1.13.

seen from the perspective of the two similes which have preceded it, Swift's overt claim does not seem nearly so arbitrary: it is, rather, the poetically valid conclusion of twenty lines of poetic argument.

Finally, the way in which overt and covert meaning flow through these two similes towards an assertion of belief provides us, I think, a sketch in miniature of both the mode and purpose of Swift's Stella poetry. For just as these similes suggest that virtue is its own reward and also a means to a yet higher good, so each aspect of this poem—its consolations, its "ethical appeals," its argument for the earthly efficacy of human virtue, and its insistence on the justice of Providence—is subordinated to the single great purpose of Stella's salvation. Encouraging her to be at peace with herself and with her friends, the poem constantly recommends those very acts of virtue through which Stella's eye can see, plain before it, the evidence of her immortality and future reward. Indeed, by closing his poem still exhorting Stella to pity and to spare him, Swift transformed even his own frailties and weaknesses, those faults which were both a probable cause of Stella's despair and an almost insurmountable bar to Swift's effectively ministering to her, into a means for her salvation. For by offering himself to Stella as an object for her pity, he provided her both an occasion for and a model of that practical virtue which he believed would "guide [her] to a better State."

5

" 'In Princes never put thy Trust' "

Verses on the Death of Dr. Swift

EVEN THE BRIEFEST outline of the *Verses on the Death of Dr. Swift* must highlight the great single problem that the poem has always presented to those who have read it with care. That problem is to discover the relationship between the panegyric with which Swift's poem ends and that maxim of La Rochefoucauld which, Swift tells us in his headnote, occasioned the entire poem: "In the Adversity of our best Friends, we find something that doth not displease us."[1]

The first section of the *Verses* (1–72)—the section that Swift himself calls a "proem"—is Swift's demonstration of the universal scope and applicability of the maxim; his proof that, even with the best of us, "The strongest Friendship yields to Pride,/Unless the Odds be on our Side" (37–38). The second section of the poem (73–299) is an application of the maxim to a specific and extreme case: Swift imagines the niggling comforts and ignoble sentiments his death will stimulate in most of his friends. But the final, panegyrical section of the poem—which Swift imagines spoken after his death and by "one quite indiff'rent in the Cause"—seems to exist in flat contradiction both to the maxim and to the first two sections of the poem. For in the final section

---

1. Swift's translation; in French the maxim reads thus: "Dans l'adversité de nos meilleurs amis nous trouvons quelque chose, qui ne nous deplaist pas." As Sir Harold Williams notes (*Swift's Poems*, 2:553n7), "This maxim was xcix in the first edition of *Réflexions ou sentences et maximes morales*, 1665, and, together with a number of others, was suppressed by the author in later editions. It will be found in modern editions among the 'Réflexions Supprimées.' "

152

Swift offers himself as that man to whose actions La Rochefoucauld's maxim is not applicable, as that man who, far from
finding his private ends in his friends' misfortunes, "Without regarding private Ends,/Spent all his Credit for his Friends"
(331–32).

Of course, from Swift's day to ours there have been numerous
attempts to "explain" the apparently egotistical and contradictory
conclusion of this poem.[2] To my mind, however, the most chal-

2. As noted in the preface, an earlier version of this chapter was published in
RES 21 (November 1970):422–41. At that time perhaps the clearest statement of
the poem's central contradiction had been rendered by Ronald Paulson in *The
Fictions of Satire* (Baltimore: Johns Hopkins Press, 1967), pp. 189–94. At that
time, too, the range of interpretive responses to the poem could be defined (as
Arthur J. Scouten and Robert D. Hume later did) by noting three contrasting
essays. In the earliest of these, John Middleton Murry suggested that the poem
was badly flawed by the incongruous self-laudation of its panegyric (*Jonathan
Swift: A Critical Biography* [London: J. Cape, 1954], pp. 454–60). A few years
later Barry Slepian argued that the panegyric's objectionable overplus of praise
was ironic and meant to demonstrate Swift's own pride ("The Ironic Intention of
Swift's Verses on His Own Death," *RES* 14 [August 1963]:249–56). Finally, in
1965, Marshall Waingrow, responding to Slepian's essay, found the panegyric to
be a model of moral perception offered in "the decorous third person" ("*Verses
on the Death of Dr. Swift*," *SEL* 5 [1965]:513–18). Though Waingrow's essay is
open to objection, I thought his response the soundest place to begin further
investigation of the poem. I still do. Since 1970, however, several new essays on
the *Verses* have appeared. A number of these essays (like Ronald Paulson's
earlier one) seem to me to share—with helpful variations—the view Waingrow
articulated. Among these are Hugo Reichard's "The Self-Praise Abounding in
Swift's *Verses*," *TSL* 18 (1973):105–12; Robert W. Uphaus's "Swift's 'whole
character': The Delany Poems and 'Verses on the Death of Dr. Swift,' " *MLQ* 34
(December 1973):406–16; and Donald C. Mell's "Elegiac Design and Satiric Intention in *Verses on the Death of Dr. Swift*," *CP* 6 (December 1973):15–24.
Additionally, and very recently, Peter J. Schakel in "The Politics of Opposition in
'Verses on the Death of Dr. Swift,' " *MLQ* 35 (September 1974):246–56, has
suggested a genuinely new interpretation of the panegyric which I describe later in
the body of this chapter. Finally, Arthur H. Scouten and Robert D. Hume
published an essay, "Pope and Swift: Text and Interpretation of Swift's Verses on
His Death," *PQ* 52 (April 1973), which is sharply critical of the earlier version of
this present chapter. As its title suggests, Scouten and Hume's essay is an attempt
to generate a reading of the *Verses* based in part on its textual history. The
reading so generated amounts to this: in the *Verses* Swift mingled exaggerated
self-praise, half-genuine apologia, and satiric attack in order simultaneously to
exemplify the rightness of La Rochefoucauld's maxim and to remark his own
moral righteousness. From my perspective, this reading is tenable but incomplete.
For to suppose that in the *Verses* Swift merely persuades us to accept an attractive picture of himself amidst an attack on others' selfishness is to reduce the
poem to only a rhetorical trick. Scouten and Hume are perfectly willing to accept
such reduction. Thus, summing up the poem's achievement they remark that
"what makes the poem so delightful, and the irony so delicious, is our constant
awareness of the game Swift is playing." I, however, think that if the poem
contains much game, it contains much earnest, too. Therefore, though I have

lenging argument so far to appear was offered by Professor Marshall Waingrow in an article entitled, *"Verses on the Death of Dr. Swift."* Waingrow argues that Swift's *Verses* is purposely contradictory, executed so as to compare that world full of men corrupted by self-interest, and properly described by La Rochefoucauld, with Swift, whose very life stands as a refutation of La Rochefoucauld's cynicism.

Waingrow's approach to the poem is not, as we shall presently see, without its own difficulties, but it does allow him to see, and to state with great clarity, a crucial point about Swift's final panegyric on himself. That panegyric, Waingrow argues, is a model of altruistic behavior: in it Swift generously takes the occasion of his own death not only to demonstrate the selfish responses of most men to their fellows' suffering, adversity, and death, but also to provide men an example (apparently desperately needed) of a life well lived. Thus, Waingrow insists, Swift's panegyric rises as far above the charge of petty egotism as Swift himself, viewing his very death as an occasion for others' instruction, rises above his own mortality.

Waingrow's insight into the purpose and effect of Swift's panegyric forms, it seems to me, the natural starting point for further thought on Swift's poem. But Waingrow's article, as a whole, is somewhat misleading, because, in his desire to show us that Swift's panegyric is a moral exemplum, he has presented both a more perfect Swift and a more corrupt world than does Swift's poem itself. Swift, in fact, records sharply enough his own selfishness in the very opening lines of the poem; and if, later, he can savage the selfishness even of his friends, he can commend their selflessness, too. When, for example, he comments that at his death "Poor *Pope* will grieve a Month; and *Gay*/A Week; and *Arbuthnott* a Day . . ." (207–8), his clear-eyed recognition that "no passion burns forever in so frail a lamp as man" only adds lustre to his friends' real capacity to mourn at all.[3] By blurring

---

responded to their criticisms both by illustrating more of the poem's gamesomeness than I had previously done and by attempting to clarify several sections in my argument which they appear to have misunderstood, I have not significantly changed my conclusions. The case between us finally must stand like this: they think Swift quoted Scripture in the *Verses* because "he was, after all, a clergyman" and presumably could not help talking Bible; I think Swift quoted Scripture in order to teach us how to transform what is base in us into virtuous conduct.

3. For this view of these lines I am indebted to Maynard Mack's discussion of

this sort of complexity in Swift's poem, Waingrow partly defeats his own argument, for he makes Swift seem finally a model of what is apparently inimitable virtue. Portraying Swift as a man of only public ends—and identifying no way by which he became so—Waingrow places Swift beyond the grasp of us poor mortals whom, he argues, Swift is trying to teach.

But that is Waingrow's error, not Swift's. Swift's panegyric on himself is qualified, not only by the ironic undertones that run through it, but, as we shall see, by the entire progress of the poem which has led up to it. That is why I think that before the *Verses on the Death of Dr. Swift* is instructive satire and a model for us, it is a personal, deeply searching and, at the same time, very traditional consideration by Swift of the implications of his own death. And if we can learn from Swift's meditative exercise, that is because, I think, he has followed the command—*memento mori*—and has drawn from his meditation that truth which is the traditional end of such meditation: "Happy is he that hath the God of Jacob for his help, whose hope is in the Lord his God" (Psalm 146:5).

That Swift thought often on his own death we know both by inference and by direct statement. "When I was of your age," Swift wrote to Pope, when Pope was forty-five, "I thought every day of Death, but now [at sixty-six], every minute."[4] Even the briefest examination of Swift's correspondence makes clear that this apparently hyperbolic statement lacks little of being absolute truth. From a surprisingly early period of his life, and to all manner of correspondents, Swift observed that he was one who "must expect to decline every month, like one who lives upon his principal sum which must lessen every day."[5]

Further, themes of mortality and of the generally transitory character of this world not only color Swift's correspondence but are early and often repeated themes in his poetry. Exiled—from his point of view—from England, Swift arrived in Dublin in 1714 both sick and lonely, to assume his deanship. His sickness was

them in *Major British Writers*, ed. G. B. Harrison et al., 2 vols. (New York: Harcourt, Brace and Company, 1954), 1:665.

4. *Swift's Correspondence*, 4:152. For similar remarks written to Lord Boling-broke see 3:354, 382.

5. Ibid., 4:477.

not, his correspondence indicates, really dangerous, but, characteristically, he projected his sickness and loneliness into the deathbed poem, *In Sickness*, which, though it was composed thirty years before his death, ends with this final request:

> Ye formal Weepers for the Sick,
> In your last Offices be quick:
> And spare my absent Friends the Grief
> To hear, and give me no Relief;
> Expir'd To-day, entomb'd To-morrow,
> When known, will save a double Sorrow.   (23–28)

Swift's tendency to make his own illnesses, the illnesses and deaths of his friends, indeed, even the wearing out of his old cassocks, occasions for reflections on his own end is partly attributable, perhaps, to his own particular affliction, Ménière's syndrome. To be subject any moment to severe, protracted, and inexplicable attacks of deafness, extreme dizziness, and nausea might well influence a man to think often on the frailty of his own flesh. Surprisingly, however, Swift's reflections on death have little of either the fear or the horror one would naturally expect in thoughts stemming from painful physical disabilities. Neither did Swift's imagination dwell upon vivid deathbed scenes or upon the circumstances of final corruption, although, as we shall see, he knew very well the tradition in which such description was commonplace. Rather, his serious reflections on death seem to focus finally, and easily, on its providentially benevolent nature. "It is impossible," he concludes in *Thoughts on Religion*, "that anything so natural, so necessary, and so universal as death, should ever have been designed by providence as an evil to mankind."[6] And this conclusion is natural for Swift because, I think, his tendency to reflect often on death owes at least as much to the seventeenth-century traditional meditation on death as it does to his own afflictions.

It is difficult to delineate the precise form of traditional meditations on death, for seventeenth-century meditators produced a bewildering variety of texts. As Louis Martz points out in *The Poetry of Meditation*, of all the forms of meditation spawned by the Counter Reformation in England, the meditation on death was

6. *Swift's Prose*, 9:263.

certainly "the most widely and intensely cultivated."[7] And because the form itself was so popular, the meditation on death came to serve many purposes. Some of these meditations were obviously undertaken as truly mystical exercises, attempts to pierce through death, so as to see, now, as "face to face." Many meditations, however, were less exalted; they were exercises, as Robert G. Collmer puts it, in "hard, close thinking" about death;[8] they were intended to extract wisdom from the grave "where," Fray Luis de Granada assured readers throughout the seventeenth century, "almighty God is wont to teach those that be his."[9] Of these latter, less exalted meditations, there is also a wide variety of types: those intended first to cure the natural fear of death, those that most encourage a true repentance for sin, and those that emphasize a true contempt of the world and a desire for godliness.

But though there is no "typical" meditation on death, there are certain themes that most such meditations share. First, although each meditation has a particular emphasis, most at least touch on three related moral topics: they encourage the repentance for sin, they insist that the concerns of this world are transitory, and they teach men to put their trust in God. Secondly, many of these meditations share, particularly in their description of the corruption to which man's flesh is heir, a kind of wry irony. This irony or "grim humor," which is fully documented with examples in Professor Martz's study, can be illustrated from what is perhaps the best-known group of seventeenth-century meditations on death, Donne's *Devotions upon Emergent Occasions and Several Steps in my Sickness*. Donne, describing the dissolution of the body, often turns to jest a topic that might equally well inspire horror: "*Now* all the parts built up, and knit by a lovely *soule*, *now* but a *statue* of *clay*, and *now*, these limbs melted off, as if that *clay* were but *snow*; and *now* the whole *house* is but a *handfull* of *sand*, so much *dust*, and but a *pecke* of *rubbidge*, so much *bone*. If *he*, who, as this *Bell* tells mee, is gone now, were some *excellent Artificer*, who comes to him for a *clocke*, or for a *garment* now? or for *counsaile*, if hee were a *Lawyer*? If a

7. 2d ed. (New Haven: Yale University Press, 1962), p. 135.
8. "The Meditation on Death and its Appearance in Metaphysical Poetry," *Neophilologus* 45 (October 1961):325.
9. *Of Prayer, and Meditation*. Cited from Martz, p. 135.

Magistrate for *Justice?*"[10] Finally, these meditations shared an enormous popularity. Well into the eighteenth century, discourses on death that strongly reflect the meditative tradition were being composed and sixteenth- and seventeenth-century meditations were being translated and, in many cases, retranslated. As an indication of the continuing vitality of the tradition in the eighteenth century one may note that not only did Swift's friend the playwright Nicholas Rowe aid in the translation of an edition of meditations published in 1709, but, in 1703, he used a book of formal meditations as an important property in the death scene of *The Fair Penitent*.[11] Presumably Rowe could count on an eighteenth-century audience's familiarity with the formal meditation on death.

It would be strange, therefore, if Swift, who as a relatively young man "thought every day of death" and, as an older man, "every minute," were unaware that in so reflecting on his own death he was participating in that great meditative tradition according to which precisely those persons are blessed "that ever have the houre of death before their eyes, and that everie daye dispose themselves to die."[12] Further, there are lines within the *Verses on the Death of Dr. Swift* which indicate that he was fully conversant with the common motifs of the meditative tradition. Swift's wry assumption, for example, that after his death his writings would be turned to mean ends by disreputable printers is, I think, an intentional, comic, yet finally quite serious evocation of one of the most constant themes of Christian meditation: the inevitable decay and ignoble end of the body. By simply using the word "remains" ambivalently in the following passage, Swift makes his lines both a satiric lash and a moral lesson on the final disposition of *all* human remains:

> Now *Curl* his Shop from Rubbish drains;
> Three genuine Tomes of *Swift's* Remains.
> And then to make them pass the glibber,
> Revis'd by *Tibbalds, Moore, and Cibber*.   (197–200)

Such instances of Swift's comic adaptation of meditative materials

10. *Devotions Upon Emergent Occasions*, ed. J. Sparrow and G. Keynes (Cambridge: Cambridge University Press, 1923), p. 105.
11. L. H. Wyman, "The Tradition of the Formal Meditation in Rowe's *The Fair Penitent*," *PQ* 42 (July 1963):412–16.
12. *The Imitation of Christ*. Cited from Martz, p. 136.

are numerous in the *Verses*, and they are important. Still more important, however, there is a connection between Swift's *Verses* and formal meditation which goes beyond these wry echoes; finally, I think, Swift's poem was written for the same purpose as were formal meditations, and, therefore, in something like the same form.

"In omnibus operibus tuis memorare novissima tua et in aeternum non peccabis" (Ecclus. 7:40). This text from Ecclesiasticus was the touchstone for the whole tradition of meditation on death: in the very fact that man must die to the world was, for the Christian meditator, the secret of how to live well in it. And the same paradoxical vision informs Swift's poem. Swift's *Verses*, which begins with La Rochefoucauld's observation that in the adversity of our friends there is that which does not displease us, ends by asserting what is both the most extreme form of that maxim and the central tenet of all meditations on death—in the sickness and death of our friends (and of ourselves) is our strongest moral instruction.

Further, the progress of the *Verses* to this truth—the poem's three-part structure—is controlled, though unobtrusively and with great delicacy, by the three traditional topics of the meditation on death: recognition of and repentance for sin, a true contempt for that which is purely worldly, and, finally, the reliance on God that makes possible charity towards man. Beginning with a painfully clear vision of that sinful and worldly nature he shares with every man, Swift ends with a demonstration of what can be made of it. Swift demonstrates, that is, through the contemplation of his own death, those lessons that he, earlier in his life, had prayed Esther Johnson might learn in her last illness: "Almighty and most gracious Lord God, extend, we beseech thee, thy pity and compassion towards this thy languishing servant: Teach her to place her hope and confidence entirely in thee; give her a true sense of the emptiness and vanity of all Worldly things; make her truly sensible of all the infirmities of her life past, and grant to her such a true sincere repentance, as is not to be repented of."[13]

In the fall of 1725 there passed between Swift and Pope one of those bagatelles which great men seem occasionally to contrive only to tease out of thought men yet unborn. The exchange was

13. *Swift's Prose*, 9:256.

begun by Pope who, knowing apparently very well the Dean's admiration for the maxims of La Rochefoucauld, sent the Dean a proposal to write "a set of Maximes in opposition to all Rochefoucault's principles." The Dean, in turn, vigorously replied: "I tell you after all that I do not hate Mankind. . . . I am no more angry with [Walpole] Then I was with the Kite that last week flew away with one of my Chickins and yet I was pleas'd when one of my Servants Shot him two days after, This I say, because you are so hardy as to tell me of your Intentions to write Maxims in Opposition to Rochefoucault who is my Favourite because I found my whole character in him, however I will read him again because it is possible I may have since undergone some alterations."[14] In this reply, Swift is, of course, obviously and deliberately repaying Pope's raillery in kind: he is first too cold-blooded, then too enthusiastic, and finally too demurring to be believed. But if the railing tone of this passage makes Swift's exact sentiments hard to guess, that tone does not obscure his obvious regard for La Rochefoucauld. Therefore, despite Waingrow's conclusion that the *Verses* is "a direct rebuttal of La Rochefoucauld's maxim,"[15] I think we must believe that Swift is being perfectly truthful when, in the first paragraph of his poem, he tells us that

> As *Rochefoucault* his Maxims drew
> From Nature, I believe 'em true:
> They argue no corrupted Mind
> In him; the Fault is in Mankind.   (1–4)

This assumption that mankind is essentially selfish and profoundly flawed is not, we should begin by remarking, incompatible with the traditional Christian view of fallen human nature. La Rochefoucauld himself, responding to the early criticism that his unflattering view of our nature had stimulated, remarked that this view was really "nothing else than an abridgement of such morals as are entirely conformable to the thought of several fathers of the church."[16] And, because this early defence did not suffice to

---

14. *Swift's Correspondence*, 3:118.
15. Waingrow, p. 517.
16. *Oeuvres Complètes de La Rochefoucauld*, ed. L. Martin-Chauffier (Paris: Gallimard, 1964), p. 397.

silence those who found his low estimate of human nature "un-Christian," La Rochefoucauld took occasion, in later editions of the *Maxims*, to remind his critics that Christianity has always distinguished between humanity as described in his maxims, in "that deplorable state of nature corrupted by sin," and humanity as it may be illuminated by "une grâce particulière."[17] Not surprisingly, the whole of La Rochefoucauld's *Maxims* can be read (as I think Swift read them) as a long, witty but traditionally grounded argument written to drive man from a love of his own fallen nature to a trust in divine grace.

But traditionally Christian as is this view of man as selfish and flawed, both it and the Christian terms in which it was normally couched were under severe attack even as Swift asserted it as his own. Through the last quarter of the seventeenth century and into the eighteenth century, the doctrine of original sin—with its insistence on man's profoundly flawed condition—met tremendous philosophical resistance.[18] Shaftesbury, to cite a primary example, forcibly argues that if the Fall, with its consequent disasters for man and nature, had really occurred, it would be impossible to exonerate God. Further, neither Shaftesbury, nor men like him, found much reason to postulate a fall. Heartened by, among other things, Newton's harmonious discoveries, they looked at nature and saw, not the ruined effects of sin, but an exquisitely articulated creation. In this creation it seemed to them impossible that only man should be askew. If in fact, they argued, man seemed faulty, that was because he had persistently blinded himself to his own worth. Preeminently social from birth, man thought of himself as the selfish, sinful result of a fall and thereby missed, it seemed to many in Swift's age, that very sociability which was his primary characteristic, and which united him with nature's harmony. That this benevolist vision achieved a rapid popularity is understandable: men could not but be pleased at being told, as Richard Cumberland (in an exact contradiction of the maxim of La Rochefoucauld that begins Swift's *Verses*) told them, that

17. Ibid., p. 399.
18. I am here particularly indebted to Ernest Tuveson's "Shaftesbury on the Not so Simple Plan of Human Nature," *SEL* 5 (Summer 1965):403–34, and to Stanley Green's *Shaftesbury's Philosophy of Religion and Ethics: A Study in Enthusiasm* (Athens: Ohio University Press, 1967).

"there are in mankind, considered as Animal-beings only, Propensities of Benevolence towards each other. . . ."[19]

Thus, in choosing to begin the *Verses* with a defence of La Rochefoucauld's vision Swift has involved himself and his poem in a lively argument. Further, he does nothing to make his view more palatable to a benevolist when he insists not only on the truth of La Rochefoucauld's maxim but on the truth of its corollary as well. Not only, Swift argues, are men not displeased at the misery of friends, but so self-interested are they that they are themselves made miserable by their friends' successes:

> What Poet would not grieve to see,
> His Brethren write as well as he?
> But rather than they should excel,
> He'd wish his Rivals all in Hell.   (31–34)

And while Swift argues very gently, in the first paragraphs of the *Verses*, for the validity of that view of man he is defending—he begins whimsically by asking "Who wou'd not at a crowded Show,/Stand high himself, keep others low?" (15–16)—ultimately his initial gentleness serves only to make his final conclusion all the more crushing. Self-love, he asserts, conditions all human relationships, even the strongest friendships, by both making them possible and limiting their strength.

If this conclusion seems as unacceptable to us as it was to many of Swift's contemporaries, that is partly because we are, in some vaguely uncomfortable way, the intellectual heirs of the benevolists. But we must nevertheless remember that within the traditionally Christian ethic from which Swift was working, it is possible, without contradiction, to grant the existence of real friendship and yet understand the strongest of friendships to be limited. This is true because the Christian conception of even the strongest friendship is linked indivisibly to self-love: "thou shalt love thy neighbour as thyself" is both the beginning and end of the Christian counsel of friendship. And Swift drew bluntly enough the consequences of this commandment at the beginning of his sermon *Doing Good*: "Nature directs every one of us, and God permits us, to consult our own private Good before the

19. *A Philosophical Enquiry into the Laws of Nature*, trans. John Towers (Dublin: Samuel Powell, 1750), p. 211.

private Good of any other person whatsoever. We are, indeed, commanded to love our Neighbour as ourselves, but not as well as ourselves. The love we have for ourselves is to be the pattern of that love we ought to have towards our neighbour: but, as the copy doth not equal the original, so my neighbour cannot think it hard, if I prefer myself, who am the original, before him, who is only the copy."[20] Given Swift's traditionalist view that the love we have for our friend is founded in our own self-love, it follows that "the strongest Friendship [must] yield to Pride,/Unless the Odds be on our Side."

But as Swift moves towards this conclusion he is moving in the realm of paradox: self-love ultimately limits the strength of the strongest friendship, yet self-love also provides the pattern and the reason that makes "strong friendship" a possibility. Further, for Swift, even the meanest effects of self-love—envy, say, or avarice—bear a perverted testimony to our felt communion with other human beings. Thus, although in the first forty lines of the *Verses* Swift insists on showing us that we glory in the misery and are miserable in the glory of other men, he simultaneously shows us that, as Waingrow observes, "ironically, what appear to be the most self-regarding of emotions are . . . in fact . . . utterly dependent upon the condition of others."[21] This paradoxically social quality of selfishness is amply demonstrated in Swift's mock protest, "Give others Riches, Power, and Station,/'Tis all on me an Usurpation" (43–44). A man who makes this stingy observation (and, Swift insists, we all occasionally do) is not, of course, being very sociable, but he is being social: he does recognize, though in a clearly perverse way, that his lot is somehow related to that of his fellows.

Envy and magnanimity then, while different in their effects, come to seem in the proem not so different in their origins; they are both self-interested responses to the condition of other human beings. Indeed, Swift demonstrates how close they are by actually translating, before our eyes, his own envy into magnanimity. "In *Pope*," he says,

I cannot read a Line,
But with a Sigh, I wish it mine:

20. *Swift's Prose*, 9:232.
21. Waingrow, p. 514.

When he can in one Couplet fix
More Sense than I can do in Six.   (47–50)

Obviously, these lines on Pope (as well as the similar lines on Gay, Arbuthnot, and Pultney) are a confession of Swift's envy. Just as obviously these lines are handsome praise and an act of true magnanimity.[22] With this capacity to transform his meanest selfishness into praise, Swift did not need Cumberland's assumption that men possessed a "benevolent impulse" in order to propose a standard of moral conduct for men. In fact, for Swift, the assumption that man naturally possessed a benevolent disposition only obscured man's real moral task; to draw from his potentially dark and selfish nature a truly generous conduct.

But to recognize that Swift's willingness to confess his envy transforms that envy into a generous praise is to raise another question—how can one account for Swift's willingness to work this transformation? The beginnings of an answer to this question can be found, I think, in the two ironic lines that conclude Swift's oblique praise of his friends: "If with such Talents Heav'n hath blest 'em/Have I not Reason to detest 'em?" (65–66). These lines are ironic, of course, since the answer to the question they pose is necessarily "no." But the reason why it must be "no" informs Swift's magnanimity. Swift himself discusses this reason in numerous places, most notably in his sermon *On Mutual Subjection* where he states clearly the doctrine, only ironically implied by the lines above, that not only the division of talents, power, and riches among mankind, but the entire condition of each man—his health, wits, and all—is granted not by chance but by Divine dispensation.[23] From this doctrine Swift, in this sermon, draws several conclusions with respect to envy. First, to envy a man possessed of apparently greater gifts than oneself is a blasphemous act because it is ultimately to challenge the wisdom of Heaven. Secondly, to envy another man is to contradict one's

---

22. I cannot resist the temptation to remark once more the character of Professors Scouten and Hume's particular criticism. Attacking my treatment of the lines on Pope they state that "The lines on Pope, Gay, and Arbuthnot [Fischer] reads as a 'confession of Swift's envy.' " Then, having neglected the sentence to which this footnote is appended, they continue: "But look at the passage. . . . the whole passage is a graceful compliment to Swift's friends and an ironically self-deprecating joke." Thus, they deprive me of my own argument, strip it of its moral implications, and then make it themselves.

23. *Swift's Prose*, 9:145–46.

own best self-interest, for if the man envied uses his gifts as he ought (as Pope, Gay, Arbuthnot, and Pultney clearly have done), then these gifts will manifest themselves as social good. Finally, to envy a man who abuses his talents and uses them viciously is madness, for it is only to envy him his own viciousness. Therefore what Swift's ironic question—"Have I not Reason to detest 'em?"—evokes by implication is an understandable reason for his willingness to transform his own envy into magnanimous praise. In the light of his ironic question Swift's envy appears as a blindly self-interested and hence unprofitable response, while his magnanimity appears as a response not necessarily less self-interested but much more finely attuned to conditions fixed by Divine dispensation.

The import of the proem, then, can be summarized as follows: first, it is an argument to demonstrate that the motivation for all our actions and relationships is always self-interested; second, it shows us that, though we are by nature selfish, we are by our very selfishness involved in the condition of others; last, it obliquely reminds us that our condition as well as the condition of everyone else is granted by Divine dispensation—a fact which, if we are to follow our true self-interest, must affect our response to those conditions. Thus, while the proem is not directly prescriptive, the sum of its arguments does lead to the moral position that it is not only permissible (indeed, inevitable) to seek one's own interest in one's dealings in this world, but it is important to succeed. Success, however, depends upon remembering, first, one's communion with other men, and second, that all things in this world are of God.

The irony of the second section of Swift's *Verses* is not, then, that his friends are so willing to seek their self-interest in Swift's illness and death; the irony is that they are *unable to find their self-interest*. For, if in the prosperity of our friends our own self-interest leads us to assert our community with them, then the same lesson should be, if anything, more clear in our friends' adversities. Donne, in his *Devotions*, makes this point in a way that illuminates the misguided responses of Swift's friends: "We scarce heare of any man *preferred*, but wee thinke of our selves, that wee might very well have beene that *Man*; Why might not I have been that *Man*, that is carried to his *grave* now? Could I fit my selfe, to *stand*, or *sit* in any mans *place*, and not to lie in any mans *grave*? I may lacke much of the *good parts* of the meanest, but I lacke nothing of the *mortality* of the weakest: They may have acquired better *abilities* than I, but I was borne to as many *infirmities* as they."[24] It is precisely this extremely self-interested wisdom that Swift's friends (trying, for the most part, to escape the fact of their own mortality) ironically fail to discover in Swift's death. The irony of the situation is established from the first lines of the second section:

> The Time is not remote, when I
> Must by the Course of Nature dye:
> When I foresee my special Friends,
> Will try to find their private Ends. (73–76)

It is, of course, precisely their own ends that Swift's friends ought to be able, but seem unwilling, to foresee in Swift's own. Rather, most of them view Swift's decline and "hug themselves, and reason thus;/'It is not yet so bad with us' " (115–16).

In this failure Swift's friends seem remarkably obtuse, for Swift has imagined his own death in such a way as to make its universally fatal implications extremely clear. When the Dean's knell is tolled it immediately involves whole communities. The news runs through Dublin, begets a race of elegies, spreads to London, invades the Court, inspires activity at Curll's, reaches out to Twickenham, and finally filters through a female card party. The spreading of the news itself becomes emblematic: no human scene, it is clear, is completely exempt from a passing-bell. Further, the universality of death is what Swift emphasizes in the way he imagines his own, for the Dean dies of no unique disease; his death is, rather, in accord with "the Course of Nature" to which all men must submit; a neighbor can be readily imagined who might "feel a Pain, / Just in the Parts, where I complain" (135–36).

But, as clearly as Swift points the moral of his death (that any man may lie down in the grave prepared for Swift himself), nevertheless he imagines this moral to be almost universally disregarded. Even that very neighbor whose pains presage his ap-

24. *Devotions*, pp. 92–93.

proaching end is pictured inquiring, not after the "way to die," but frantically after ways to live—"what Regimen I kept;/What gave me Ease, and how I slept" (139–40); while the rest "give a Shrug and cry,/I'm sorry; but we all must dye" (211–12), and pass over with that shrug both the seriousness and the moral of the truth they have uttered.

Repelled, then, as Swift's companions are by the thought of their own deaths, it is hardly surprising that they prove almost aggressively indifferent to the news of their friend's, mingling that news with cards and politics and talk of heirs. But it is not really for their indifference to his own death that Swift is satirizing them: that indifference is only symptomatic of their greater failing. Swift's satire of them is based upon their failure to grasp the significance of the admonition that follows immediately upon the imagined advent of Swift's death—"O, may we all for Death prepare!" (153). That warning is, within the Christian scheme, the great moral of Swift's and every man's death. It is the moral stressed in that "departing prayer" which, as it was traditionally read at each Anglican's death, Swift imagined read at his: "teach us, who survive," says that prayer, "in this and other like daily spectacles of mortality, to see how frail and uncertain our own condition is, and so to number our days, that we may seriously apply our hearts to that holy and heavenly wisdom, whilst we live here, which may in the end bring us to life everlasting."[25] In their failure to avail themselves of Swift's death as a reminder of their own, and thus as a warning to be mindful of ultimate values, most of Swift's friends desert, not Swift, but their own self-interest. They therefore become part of that group which has always been the object of satire—the group of men who, not knowing themselves, do not know their own good.

Of course, Swift does distinguish between his friends' varied responses to his death. Between those who amuse themselves by predicting the day of Swift's death and, say, Pope, who will mourn Swift for a month, there is a world of difference. The former fail in both compassion and comprehension. They fall to counting the days remaining to Swift's life when, in fact, the event of his death should teach them to number their own days. That is why they are subject to Swift's satire. There is, on the

25. "Visitation of the Sick," *The Book of Common Prayer* (London: John Baskett, 1727).

other hand, as we have already seen, a high compliment for Pope in Swift's recognition that "Poor *Pope* will grieve a Month." But, as different as are these two imagined responses to Swift's death, they have one thing in common: they both remind Swift (and us) of what most of his friends have forgotten, "how transient are all things below."[26] Thus even Pope, Swift's warmest friend, will mourn his death but for a month, while Arbuth . . . , physician and realist, will grieve (in Swift's outrageous pun) for ". . . nott a day."[27] The punning jokiness itself of this last line only more strongly reinforces the moral that has been evident through all the imagined responses to Swift's death: "Where's now this Fav'rite of *Apollo*?/Departed; *and his works must follow*" (249–50).

Indeed, the transience of men and things is the whole burden of lines 243–98, the concluding lines of the second section. Of course, these lines do possess a painful sort of gaiety, and the scene they describe is one Swift certainly knew to be exaggerated. Nevertheless both the dark gaiety of these lines and their exaggerations point to a moral truth: the world of men is inclined towards negation, that is, towards evil; what is good in it is often lost and what is evil seems to flourish. Thus, just as earlier in the poem Swift imagined that his literary remains would pass through the soiling grasp of Tibbalds, Moore, and Cibber, so in the last fifty lines of its second section he supposes that but a short year after his own death, his archfoe Walpole will find a vindication, and Henley an audience, and Woolston, who showed "That *Jesus* was a Grand Impostor," a pension. In effect, then, no seventeenth-century meditator, caught up in the theme of *contemptus mundi* and demonstrating through the comic but wormy circumstances of death the absolute corruptibility of all worldly things, could put the point more clearly than Swift has put it here. For in his imagined description of the hypocritical mourning of some of his friends, the limited mourning of the best of his friends, and the apparently unlimited triumph of his wicked enemies, Swift's laughter verges on despair for this world and everything in it. How anything of lasting value can be done or gained in such a world is almost impossible to conceive. And yet, it is precisely at this point that Swift, donning the disguise of an

26. The line is from Swift's poem *The Journal, Swift's Poems*, 1:283.
27. I am indebted to my colleague Jack Gilbert, who made me laugh to see this pun.

"impartial" narrator, chooses to pen a panegyric on himself the basis of which is the good that he has accomplished in this world.

A relatively simple problem in this panegyric has caused what I think to be an astonishing amount of difficulty in its interpretation. The problem is that, throughout its length, the panegyric is exaggerated in its praise of Swift, and in several particulars it is untrue. Since this problem has obscured for many readers what is central in the panegyric, it must be dealt with first.

In a recent article, Peter J. Schakel provides us a useful place to begin.[28] Having reminded us that the speaker of the panegyric is not Swift, Schakel suggests that its speaker is instead a Tory zealot who, true to La Rochefoucauld's maxim, overpraises Swift to serve his own ends. This is a fine suggestion and a wholly convincing one as long as we remember that the speaker of the panegyric, like all of Swift's personae, is not a substantial character but a bias which Swift can manipulate in dozens of ways in order to insinuate, through falsehoods, what is true. Thus some of the speaker's falsehoods—like Falstaff's lies—are gross and palpable. But much of what the speaker says merely casts Swift's life in a flattering light.

Of the gross fictions in the panegyric two observations should be made. The first is that each such fiction works so as to force us to distinguish between what is permanently valuable and what is not. For example, when the panegyrist begins his praise of Swift by claiming that "The Dean, if we believe Report,/Was never ill receiv'd at Court" (307–8), we laugh at the claim not simply because it is blatantly untrue but because, seen against the integrity of Swift's real career, it is also vulgar and trivial. Similarly, when the panegyrist boasts, in stolen lines, that Swift's poetry is wholly original (317–18), we are amusingly taught to value less the proud individualism which makes such boasts (though, oddly enough, Swift's special use of these lines does make them original). Finally, when the panegyrist states—contrary to the evidence of this very poem—that Swift "lash'd the Vice but spar'd the Name" (460), we are compelled to reconsider this traditional satiric nicety and urged to recognize that, by Swift's standards at least, its general practice exhibits too much

28. "The Politics of Opposition in 'Verses on the Death of Dr. Swift.' "

care for personal pride and too little for public virtue. Thus, each outright lie in the panegyric functions, when it is compared to the truth of Swift's life, in such a way as to make us discredit not only its biographical content but the sort of worldliness that stimulates the lie as well.

Once we see that the outright lies in the panegyric function in this way, then it should be easy to see also that these lies do not undermine but rather support that large bulk of the panegyric which, if flattering to Swift, is biographically sound. For it is precisely for those virtues which we automatically attribute to Swift as we correct the narrator's lies that Swift is praised through most of the panegyric. Thus, the occasional and obvious lies in the panegyric validate the truth of most of it. That is why, once the outright lies are set apart, along with the equally obvious instances of exaggeration which protect the panegyric from a charge of *simple* boastfulness, it is no longer necessary for us sharply to distinguish between Swift's voice and that of his some-times fatuous narrator. Rather, having achieved this much insight into the way the panegyric works, our sole business is to seek in Swift's description of the good he has done for the means by which he has done it.

This search is not really a difficult one; for throughout the panegyric Swift "explains" his good works by referring to his faith, consistently describing the former in the scriptural language of the latter. Thus when he tells us, for example (echoing Christ's words in Luke 18:2), that his defense of Ireland brought him into conflict with a judge " 'Who long all Justice had discarded,/*Nor fear'd he GOD, nor Man regarded*'' (421–22), he obviously does more than indicate that this judge is a very wicked fellow. Rather, he indicates something about the basis of his own conduct. Unlike his antagonist, he presumably does fear God and care for man. And that, his lines suggest, is why he acts well.

In effect, then, the panegyric teaches precisely that lesson for which we have been prepared earlier in the poem. For just as Swift's graceful transformation of envy to magnanimity (which we examined in the proem) was rendered explicable by those lines in which Swift obliquely reminded us that the gifts of his friends had been assigned them by heaven, so in the panegyric the good Swift records of himself is made instructive and meaningful by those allusions to Scripture through which that good is told and which commend with particular force a trust in God. To careful readers, then, the chief lesson of the panegyric should come as no surprise. For, after all, this lesson—that men act well for themselves and others when they observe the will of heaven—is the lesson of the whole of Swift's *Verses*.

Indeed, perhaps the most perfect instance of this lesson occurs not in the panegyric at all, but rather in that passage in the second section of the *Verses* in which, unvexed by lies and exaggerations, we watch Swift open the matter of his intended will. Later on in the poem, of course, we shall learn that Swift intends to endow a "House of Fools and Mad." At this point, however, Swift keeps the object of his charity general, identifying its recipients only as "Strangers." This apparent vagueness serves him well, for through it he simultaneously effects two ends. First, he allows himself to draw as sharply as possible the difference between his general generosity and the meanly self-interested response he supposes that generosity will evoke:

> "To Publick Use! A perfect Whim!
> "What had the Publick done for him!
> · · · · · · · · · · · ·
> "And had the Dean, in all the Nation,
> "No worthy Friend, no poor Relation?
> "So ready to do Strangers good,
> "Forgetting his own Flesh and Blood?"   (157–58, 161–64)

Secondly, by telling us only that he will leave his money to "Strangers," Swift enables us—with a small feat of memory—to identify the motive for his generosity. It is a most practical motive. For as the Psalter assures us in a variety of ways and places, both the rich and the poor will die and leave their money to strangers.[29] In effect, then, since the logic of the Psalter's point is indisputable given a generation or two, Swift's charity amounts to no more than this: he willingly does that which he knows ultimately he must do. Of course, the benevolent Richard Cumberland might not have approved of such charity. But John Donne would have understood it perfectly. For Swift's charity exhibits precisely that truth which is repeated again and again in all traditional meditations on death—that because men do die,

29. E.g., Psalm 49:10.

virtue and enlightened self-interest command the same conduct. It is this lesson that Swift, reviewing his life as if he were dead, also teaches us repeatedly through the truths and falsehoods of his panegyric.

The panegyric begins with a brief defence of Swift's satire, to which topic we will return at the close of this study. Immediately after this defence Swift plunges us into those lines of the panegyric which are so often cited as exemplary of an overweening pride. He begins by claiming that

> "He never thought an Honour done him,
> "Because a Duke was proud to own him:
> "Would rather slip aside, and chuse
> "To talk with Wits in dirty Shoes:
> . . . .
> "He never courted Men in Station,
> "*Nor Persons had in Admiration*;
> "Of no Man's Greatness was afraid,
> "Because he sought for no Man's Aid.   (319–22, 325–28)

Of course, there *is* a sort of pride in this claim. Furthermore, it is not strictly true: Swift was human and sometimes did court men in station to serve his own ends. If we wish, then, we can choose quotations from Swift's correspondence which seem to explode this claim, and then assign it with special prejudice to Swift himself or to a foolish narrator. But if we do this, though we exactly serve biographical truth, we abuse the point of the claim abominably.

For the fact of the matter is this: Swift really did toady less to titled or stationed greatness than any other man one might readily name. Certainly, then, the independence he claims for himself always was his ideal. That he has here embodied that ideal in himself so absolutely may reflect his own pride, of course, but if so, he has already admitted to that pride. Far more important, the way Swift has portrayed himself serves a significant moral purpose. For first, Swift's portrait reminds us that, considered in itself, independence is an absolute virtue and enviable in its possessor precisely because it frees him from all small considerations. Further, Swift's portrait is designed to suggest to us how we may achieve this enviable good. For in telling us that he did not court men in station "*Nor Persons had in Admiration*," Swift does not simply boast of his own integrity. Rather, by his wording he directs us to that passage at the close of the Book of Jude in which Jude, having charged an unidentified group of heretics with inverting all religious values, ends his charge with the assertion that these heretics disregarded God "having men's persons in admiration." In effect, then, Swift reminds us that though, finally, neither he nor any man may be utterly independent, all men may choose whether they will depend on other men and be afraid, or upon God and achieve such freedom as Swift so powerfully portrays for us in his own life.

It is this choice that Swift presents to us again and again in the panegyric. For an example, we may examine Swift's famous claim that

> "Fair LIBERTY was all his Cry;
> "For her he stood prepared to die;
> "For her he boldly stood alone;
> "For her he oft expos'd his own.   (347–50)

A number of readers have taken this claim to be either a piece of intentional self-satire, or evidence of Swift's egomania. To understand his claim, however, we must appreciate how his use of the word "liberty" is qualified by the lines that introduce his claim. In those lines Swift tells us he

> "With Princes kept a due Decorum,
> "But never stood in Awe before 'em;
> "He follow'd *David's* Lesson just,
> "*In Princes never put thy Trust.*   (339–42)

The "lesson" is found in Psalm 146: "Put not your trust in princes, nor in the son of man, in whom there is no help. His breath goeth forth, he returneth to his earth; in that very day his thoughts perish. Happy is he that hath the God of Jacob for his help, whose hope is in the Lord his God" (Psalm 146:3, 4, 5). And with this "lesson" as his moral guide it is small wonder that Swift was provoked at the sight of a "slave in power." Trust in God, not subjugation to princes "in whom there is no help," is Swift's ideal of a "liberty worth dying for." Possessed of this "liberty" Swift could claim of himself, from the center of his own moral values if with biographical exaggeration, that

". . . Power was never in his Thought;
"And, Wealth he valu'd not a Groat.   (357–58)

For understanding the transience of power and fame and worldly
station Swift knew that ultimately he, and we, could afford to lose
them.

Neither the panegyric, then, nor the whole of the *Verses* should
be understood as an ironic praise of Swift's fortitude in impossible
circumstances, but rather as a demonstration of his ability, which
we may emulate, to translate common, human adversity into
good. Take, for example, the adversity on which Swift dwells so
often in this poem, the limitations and vagaries of human friendship. The coldness of most of Swift's friends at his death plays a
prominent part in the second section of the *Verses*, and Swift
returns to the ultimately undependable nature of human friendship
in the panegyric, remarking that he knew a time

"When, *ev'n his own familiar Friends*
"Intent upon their private Ends;
"Like Renegadoes now he feels,
"*Against him lifting up their Heels*.   (403–6)

No doubt this betrayal pained Swift deeply, but the terms in
which he expressed it indicate that he knew how to find his own
true self-interest even in this most painful form of adversity. For
the italicized sections of this quotation are drawn from Psalm 41:
"Yea, mine own familiar friend, in whom I trusted, which did eat
of my bread, hath lifted up his heel against me"; and the whole
argument of this psalm is relevant to Swift's poem.

The psalm begins with a statement of faith: the Lord will show
mercy to the charitable man. Then it becomes a highly personal
narration which, something like Swift's *Verses*, begins with a
confession: "I said, Lord, be merciful unto me: heal my soul; for
I have sinned against thee." Quickly we learn that the narrator is
sick both in soul and body and that his friends have chosen this
moment of his adversity "to speak evil of " him and to plot
against him: "All that hate me whisper together against me:
against me do they devise my hurt. An evil disease say they,
cleaveth fast unto him: and now that he lieth he shall rise up no
more." The similarity between these friends of the narrator (who

actually "devise his hurt") and Swift's friends who, if they do not actually devise his hurt, anticipate his death with unseemly indifference is, I think, obvious. Swift himself acknowledges the similarity by forming his own complaint out of the words of the psalm. But the relevance, for us, of the intersection of Swift's *Verses* with Psalm 41 lies in the conclusion of that psalm, a conclusion which both is, and is not, like the conclusion of Swift's poem: "But thou, O Lord, be merciful unto me, and raise me up, that I may requite them [my unfaithful friends]. By this I know that thou favourest me, because mine enemy doth not triumph over me." The narrator of this psalm knows that in his adversities his only refuge is the Lord. But the narrator—who is an Old Testament narrator—conceives of God's graciousness manifesting itself towards him by permitting him to take vengeance on his enemies. Swift, on the other hand, recognizes that it is also a mark of grace to die in charity with those who have sinned against one. It is this good that, now, he chooses to draw from those who have betrayed him:

> "Ingratitude he often found,
> "And pity'd those who meant the Wound:
> "But, kept the Tenor of his Mind,
> "To merit well of human Kind.   (359–62)

Over and over this transforming choice is repeated as Swift, in the panegyric, draws from all the adversities of his life—the political jars of his friends, his exile to Ireland, Wood's halfpence—the list goes on and on—his own true good. And that good is a good, not only for him, but, because it is founded on his trust in God's way with men, a good for all the members of God's community. Even out of the flaws of his own character Swift can draw good. He had long intended, he wrote to many friends, to effect with his will one last, grand, public charity. And he made clear to at least one man his reason for making his last endowment absolute: "I will tell you," he wrote to Samuel Garrard, "the whole scheme of an hospital for lunatics and idiots, a charity I find it the hardest point to settle well. I will never leave anything to any other use; I will leave the whole to God's providence how it will be disposed of, who will forgive me if my good intentions miscarry."[30] Now

30. *Swift's Correspondence*, 4:296–97.

Swift did have, as he admits in his *Verses*, "too much Satyr in his Vein" (456) and, others might add, too much vanity as well. But even that overabundance of satire he made serve what he conceived to be the uses of Providence: he built that

". . . House for Fools and Mad:
"And shew'd by one satyric Touch,
"No Nation wanted it so much.   (480–82)

And from a combination of satire and vanity he drew no less a piece of charity than the *Verses on the Death of Dr. Swift* itself, which, as much as any seventeenth-century meditation on death, can instruct one how to find in the greatest earthly adversity, death itself, that true good "which may in the end bring us to life everlasting."[31]

31. "Visitation of the Sick." Too late to note in my text, it occurred to me that the word *debtor* in the penultimate line of the *Verses*, " 'That Kingdom he hath left his Debtor, / 'I wish it soon may have a better," may have resonated in Swift's mind against the debts and debtors mentioned in the Lord's Prayer. If so, then these compressed, agrammatical lines remind us, first, that Ireland really did owe Swift a debt, second, that Swift needed to forgive that debt, because, last, like Ireland and all the nations of mankind, Swift was indebted to One better than himself.

6

"Caetera desiderantur"

On Poetry: A Rapsody

ACCORDING TO SWIFT HIMSELF, who is seconded by Dr. William King, Queen Caroline was the first notable reader of *On Poetry: A Rapsody* to identify the poem's critical problem—that of defining its point of view. However, the Queen identified the problem only by stumbling over it: she assumed that the panegyric to royalty with which the poem concludes is seriously meant and she continued under that delusion until (as King puts it) Lord Hervey took "some pains to teach her the use and power of irony."[1]

It is, of course, proper to laugh at the Queen's proud naïveté.

1. For King's account of this incident see his *Political and Literary Anecdotes* (London: J. Murray, 1818), p. 15. Swift's account is preserved in a piece of Anglo-Latin writing (Huntington Library, Forster no. 530, pp. 22–23) which was recently printed and commented on by George Mayhew in *Rage or Raillery: The Swift Manuscripts at the Huntington Library* (San Marino, Calif.: The Huntington Library, 1967), p. 113. Mayhew's decoding is as follows.

(Sheridan) The captack [?] knows you
to be an enemy
I'll say no more.
(Swift) I value not a' vile tongues, I'm
a loyal Dean to his
Majesty as well as the
Queen. (Sheridan) you think so
On account of your panegyric
in your *Rapsody*, I
suppose. (Swift) Not at all; Queen
Carolina   For Queen Carolina
Was pleased.

177

But it is also perhaps unfortunate that Lord Hervey's explication did not survive. For though no reader since Caroline has publicly suggested that the poem's final panegyric is meant as praise, neither has any subsequent reader suggested precisely what the poem is about.[2]

Yet, complex as it is in its particulars, the *Rapsody* is thematically a simple poem. Its thesis is that what is not of God cannot stand. And its form, seen whole, is a demonstration of its thesis. Thus, when the "old experienc'd sinner," who is the nominal narrator of nearly the whole of the poem, arrives at that final denial of God's providence towards which his advice has tended from the outset, his voice, along with the world he has described, disappears into the frightening hiatus with which the *Rapsody* concludes.

Both morally and formally, then, the *Rapsody* draws the contrapositive of Swift's most usual poetic pattern. Normally Swift's poetry demonstrates his own power to draw good out of ill in imitation of and submission to divine providence. But in the *Rapsody*, Swift demonstrates that this is God's world by illustrating the catastrophic consequences involved in choosing one's own will in preference to God's. This unusual strategy was more or less forced on Swift; it is the consequence of his wish to depict in the *Rapsody* the serious flaws he found in Edward Young's group of seven "characteristical satires," *Love of Fame: The Universal Passion*.

Swift first read Young's satire in the mid-twenties and his initial reaction to it was curiously mixed. On the one hand, he deftly satirized Young's work as being "not merry enough nor angry enough."[3] On the other hand, he spoke of Young as being one

2. I know of no extended reading of the *Rapsody* that responds to it as a whole. However, there are several recent treatments of the poem which, though either too partial or too brief, are especially interesting and informative. C. J. Rawson provides a suggestive discussion of the poem's imagery of circles and spirals in *Gulliver and the Gentle Reader: Studies in Swift and Our Time* (London and Boston: Routledge and Kegan Paul, 1973), pp. 60–83. James L. Tyne explores some of the background figuring in the poem's panegyrics to Walpole and George II in "Swift's Mock Panegyrics in 'On Poetry: A Rapsody,' " *PLL* 10 (Summer 1974):279–86. Finally, David Ward comments illuminatingly on the poem's concern with "the fitting, the harmonious, the relevant, the 'Natural' " in *Jonathan Swift: An Introductory Essay* (London: Methuen, 1973), pp. 197–200. Mr. Ward's remarks are very brief; had they not been so, this chapter might have been unnecessary.

3. This quotation provides the "bite" for a very funny passage in which Swift

(though the gravest) of that exclusive group of satirists in which he included himself, Pope, Gay, and Arbuthnot.[4] Swift's judgment of men and books is not usually so mingled. In this case, however, the very contrariety of his response comes near to characterizing the mixed essence of Young's major satire. Not until he wrote the *Rapsody*, however, did Swift wholly succeed in defining both the damning limitations of Young's work and the implications of those limitations.

The controlling thesis of the *Love of Fame*—that most human misery is of human begetting, pride being the progenitor of our follies—is of course a perfectly valid satiric insight. It is either a corollary to or exactly the same as the thesis of Swift's *Rapsody*, and within the first four lines of the *Rapsody*, Swift acknowledges that his satiric target is the same as Young's. But even as Swift makes this acknowledgment he ambiguously suggests that Young's recent attack was not wholly satisfactory. "*Young's* universal Passion, *Pride*," Swift observes, "Was never known to spread so wide." Implicit in these teasing lines is both the suggestion that Young did not adequately define the range of human willfulness, and the suggestion that the pride Young attacked is *his* "universal Passion" not merely because he attacked it but also because he is possessed by it.

Both of these suggestions (accusations, actually) are grounded in real shortcomings in Young's satire, satire which, despite the soundness of its initial premises, is weak both in the particulars of its execution and in its general strategy. To begin with, Young directed the satirical parts of his poem, not against real persons, but only against what Swift called "the harmless alphabet." And the consequence of Young's meek gentility is that instead of

---

chides Pope (to whom he is writing) as well as Young. "All things in verse good or bad that London produces, are printed here, among the rest, the Essay on Man, which is understood to come from Doc^tr Young. No body names you for it here (we are better judges, and I do not railly). It is too Philosophical for me, It is not equall, but that author our friend, never wants some lines of Excelent good sense. *What is, is best.* is the thought of Socrates in Plato, because it is permitted or done by God. I have retained it after reading Plato many years ago. The Doctor is not merry enough nor angry enough for the present age to relish as he deserves." *Swift's Correspondence*, 4:153. Swift also satirized Young in two short poems written (probably) in 1726: *On Reading Dr. Young's Satires, called the Universal Passion*, and *A Copy of Verses: Upon two Celebrated Modern Poets*.
4. *Swift's Correspondence*, 4:53.

employing the poet's power of praise and blame to distinguish the good from the bad, "to teach love to virtue and hatred to vice"[5] as Dryden succinctly put it, Young merely further confounded distinctions in a society that was already quickly losing the capacity to distinguish at all. Swift sums up the effect of the kind of imprecise blame that Young deals in like this:

> On A's and B's your Malice vent,
> While Readers wonder whom you meant.
> A public, or a private *Robber*;
> A *Statesman*, or a South-Sea *Jobber*.
> A *Prelate* who no God believes;
> A [Parliament], or Den of Thieves.
> A Pick-purse at the Bar, or Bench;
> A Duchess, or a Suburb-Wench. (159–66)

Unhappily, the whole effect of the *Love of Fame* is very much like the effect of Young's alphabetical blaming; it all tends to confuse the crucial question of what really constitutes moral behavior. Further, and worse, not all the defects in Young's satire can be excused on the grounds of Young's simple, supine amiability. Rather, most of the poem's moral shortcomings are apparently the consequence of Young's laziness in combination with his ambition. Swift captures a remarkable instance of Young's slothful ambition and delineates its confounding consequences in those lines (219–32) in which he ironically instructs potential poets that should they write an encomium for a king who happens to die, that same encomium can, unaltered, be properly offered to his successor. In this ironic instruction Swift precisely recapitulates the fantastic history of that panegyric to George II with which Young concludes the seventh and final satire in the *Love of Fame*. Young had, in fact, previously published that same panegyric in praise of George I and Swift makes it abundantly clear that such slovenly assignment of praise blurs all real distinction both between good and bad and between man and man. By Young's panegyric habits, Swift laconically suggests, it is apparent that

5. *Of Dramatic Poesy and Other Critical Writings*, ed. George Watson, 2 vols. (London and New York: J. M. Dent and Sons, E. P. Dutton and Co., 1962), 1:213.

A Prince the Moment he is crown'd
Inherits ev'ry Virtue round,

· · · · · · · · · ·

Is gen'rous, valiant, just and wise,
And so continues 'till he dies.   (191–92, 195–96)

Finally, then, because Young was committed to the sort of moral shuffling implied by his willingness to substitute George II's name in a panegyric designed for George I, the *Love of Fame* is, despite its nominal morality, a poem that praises not the eternal good, not what should be, but merely what temporarily is. Thus, Young concluded his Sixth Satire with a praise of Queen Caroline and his Seventh Satire with a praise of George II and Robert Walpole. And these praises are so palpably gross that Swift was able, with only slight exaggeration, to readapt them to his own ironic purposes in the panegyric to royalty that concludes the *Rapsody*. For example, where Young likens the royal house of Brunswick to a flood of blessings—"In Brunswick such a source the muse adores,/Which public blessing thro' half of Europe pours" (VII, 207–8)[6]—Swift simply literalizes Young's implicit metaphor: "The Remnant of the royal Blood,/Comes pouring on me like a Flood" (437–38). Again, where Young observes that George "burns with such a godlike aim/Angels and George are rivals for the fame" (VII, 209–10), Swift first extends the hypocritical blasphemy of Young's observation by comparing George with Christ and then pushes the resultant comparison to the following question and response.

Yet, why should we be lac'd so straight;
I'll give my [monarch] Butter-weight.
And Reason good; for many a Year
[Christ] never intermeddl'd here.   (487–90)

By such parody, then, Swift exposes the pompous immorality and blasphemy of Young's praise. Ultimately, however, the *Love of Fame* raises some problems that parody cannot deal with by itself. Young's poem offers us the lamentable spectacle of a satirist who, though pretending to satirize a poisoned age, is instead poisoned by it and becomes in his turn a contributor to its

6. Quotations of Young's poetry are from *The Poetical Works of Edward Young*, ed. the Rev. J. Mitford (London: William Pickering, 1852).

corruption. Watching Young wield the satirist's sacred weapon of praise and blame in the mere service of the court, "Where," Swift observes, "Y[oung] must torture his Invention,/To flatter *Knaves*, or lose his *Pension*" (309–10), one cannot help wondering whether there is any limit at all to the power of corruption. And the gravity of this question is only increased when one remembers that Queen Caroline took seriously even Swift's openly ironic praise of herself and her family, praise that if intended seriously would have been profoundly blasphemous.

It is to the question of whether the power of corruption is absolute or not that the *Rapsody*, seen whole, finally addresses itself. Swift tries that question by stating essentially the same values that are nominally defended by Young in the *Love of Fame* and then consciously and blatantly offering them up to corruption. Swift, that is, does absolutely what Young does insidiously, and the result of Swift's trial is a demonstration that because this is a just and providential world, corruption ultimately destroys itself.

Of course, Swift's demonstration is only a piece of art, a highly controlled fiction reflecting not necessarily what is, but rather what Swift thought should be. And seen one way, life, through the blunt realities of this imperfect world, always defeats art either by corrupting the artist (as in Young's case) or by providing a Queen Caroline whose naïve but not innocent reading of the *Rapsody* seems to threaten the very validity of its demonstration. Seen another way, however, and it is finally the right way, art survives life. Young and Queen Caroline are dead, but Swift's poem remains to warn a world that can threaten but not disprove the poem's thesis.

For Swift the basic facts of God's providence as it relates to men were simple, vocational, and irrevocable. He stated those facts with particular clarity in his sermon *On the Duty of Mutual Subjection*: "God hath contrived all the works of Nature to be useful, and in some manner a Support to each other, by which the whole frame of the world under his Providence is preserved and kept up; so among Mankind, our particular Stations are appointed to each of us by God Almighty, wherein we are obliged to act, as far as our Power reacheth, towards the Good of the whole community."[7] From this basic and quite rigid notion of human vocation Swift built up the series of corollaries that fill out his sermon. Thus, he argues that insofar as a man uses his particular advantages of wealth, power, wisdom, or strength for the good of his neighbor, so far they prove a "blessing to him." But, he continues, should a man "not perform that part assigned to him towards advancing the Benefit of the Whole" he becomes at once a burden to himself, and "a very mischievous member of the Public." Such folly, he memorably concludes, is "the true principal cause of most Miseries and Misfortunes in life."

The first seventy lines of the *Rapsody* are really no more than a poetic restatement and extension of this view of vocation. Swift begins the poem by flatly contradicting the variety of theriophily that suggests that man, unlike lesser creatures, cannot plainly perceive what is proper conduct for him (1–24). Rather, Swift argues, man differs from brutes (who *do* "find out where their Talents lie") not because he is worse informed than they are, but merely because he is the "only Creature,/Who, led by *Folly*, fights with *Nature*." On this topic, then, Swift is perfectly plain: human error and its consequent disasters are for him, in this poem at least, the mere result of willed perversity.

In its full sweep, the *Rapsody* depicts the corrupt effects of human perversity at every level of English society. But, from its title on, Swift's critique of willfulness is contained and controlled by its special examination of the mad desire of all men to abandon their proper callings and become poets. Thus, the *Rapsody* begins with the observation that "All Human Race wou'd fain be *Wits*,/And Millions miss, for one that hits," and its title suggests that Swift's chief concern is with the power of this crazed aspiration to debauch the very art of poetry into mere wanton rhapsody.[8]

7. *Swift's Prose*, 9:142.
8. Though the pun on "rap" is obvious, the significance of the word "rapsody" may be somewhat obscured for the modern reader since both the connotation and denotation of that word have changed considerably since Swift used it. For us, the word "rhapsody" commonly denotes a type of music which exhibits agreeable lyrical freedom. In the eighteenth century, however, the word was often used to refer to any work distinguished by an unhappy disorder. Thus, Pope, writing to Swift in 1729, defined by the word "rhapsody" the opposite of true wit's creative and orderly process. "This letter . . . will be a rhapsody; it is many years ago

The enormous consequence of such debauchery is what Swift seeks to impress on us early in the poem. In a passage entirely unlined by irony, he states clearly and with striking allusive power his vision of poetry's requirements and function:

> Not *Empire* to the Rising-Sun,
> By Valour, Conduct, Fortune won;
> Nor highest *Wisdom* in Debates
> For framing Laws to govern States;
> Nor Skill in Sciences profound,
> So large to grasp the Circle round;
> Such heavenly Influence require,
> As how to strike the *Muses Lyre*.   (25–32)

At a bare minimum, these lines are an impressive statement of Swift's belief that poetry is a vocation, requires heavenly influence, and is, indeed, the rarest and most graced of callings. But, in fact, the lines suggest far more than they state, for their comparisons, vocabulary, and syntax all participate in a special language, that language in which poets since Horace have insisted upon the power of poetry to preserve civility and teach virtue as no other art or science can do. Thus, the language of Swift's lines evokes a whole shower of remembered passages which themselves all echo Horace's claim in his *Eighth Ode, Book Four* (*The Power of Verse*), that

> Not Marble, though chiselled by sculptor of worth,
> Whose fame reaches out to the ends of the earth,
> . . . .
> Not Hannibal, threatening, back driven in flight,
> Nor impious Carthage, with torch fires alight,
> Imparted a lustre so bright to his name
> Who Africa conquered, victorious came
> To our shores, as the Muses of Poetry.[9]

Among these remembered passages we may include, I think, not

---

since I wrote as a Wit" (*Swift's Correspondence*, 3:362). As Swift, then, would have understood the words of his title, *On Poetry: A Rapsody*, that title delineates the process his poem describes; a debasing and disordering of the very art that traditionally taught the proper end of things and men.

9. Alfred B. Lund, trans., *The Complete Works of Horace*, ed. Casper J. Kraemer (New York: Random House, 1936), p. 286.

only those that directly imitate Horace, such as Shakespeare's delicately allusive lines in Sonnet 55,

Not Marble, nor the gilded monuments
Of Princes shall out live this powerful rhyme,
. . . .
Nor Mars his sword, nor war's quick fire shall burn:
The living record of your memory,[10]

but also those that clearly participate in the spirit of Horace's claim, such as Ben Jonson's staunch declaration that he "could never *thinke* the study of *Wisdome* confined only to the *Philosopher*, or of *Piety* to the *Divine*, or of *State* to the *Politicke*: But that he which can faine a *Common-Wealth* (which is the *Poet*), can gowne it with *Counsels*, strengthen it with *Lawes*, correct it with *Judgements*, inform it with Religion and Morals, [and hence] is all these."[11]

These passages, when their claims are once evoked by Swift's lines, illuminate in their turn the lines that evoked them. The poet, they insist, is and must be graced beyond the practitioners of the world's other great vocations, the makers of empires, framers of laws, seekers of scientific truth, because all other arts presuppose the poet's art. Singer of "ancient rights" whose powerful rhymes make value and beauty visible, the poet teaches what Horace calls "the native and proper use of things" on which all civilization rests and which would be truth were there no civilization at all. Thus, the madly crowding men whose foolish pursuit of poetic laurels the *Rapsody* begins by satirizing and ends by illustrating are at war not only with their own particular vocations but with that art the subject of which Swift knew to be the ineluctable nature of things, the art that always teaches the very lesson false poets, deserting their proper stations, have forgotten:

. . . much happier he who knows
How to enjoy the good that Heaven bestows,
Accepts its gifts and wisely uses all.[12]

10. *The Sonnets*, ed. John Dover Wilson for the syndics of The Cambridge University Press (Cambridge: Cambridge University Press, 1966), p. 30.

11. *Critical Essays of the Seventeenth Century*, ed. J. E. Spingarn, 3 vols. (Bloomington: Indiana University Press, 1957), 1:28.

12. These lines are from the ninth ode of the fourth book of Horace, trans. John Sargeant, in *The Complete Works of Horace*, ed. Kraemer, p. 289.

Swift suggests something of the nature and the effect of the corruption wrought by uncalled poets in the difficult passage immediately succeeding his claim that poetry is a specially graced vocation. In this passage Swift continues the rhetoric of negative comparison that structures his claim for poetry's power, but he gives that rhetoric a new and radical twist. Not the poet's high calling, but rather his blighted lot is the point of Swift's insistence that

> Not Beggar's Brat, on Bulk begot;
> Nor Bastard of a Pedlar *Scot*;
> Nor Boy brought up to cleaning Shoes,
> The Spawn of *Bridewell*, or the Stews;
> Nor Infants dropt, the spurious Pledges
> Of *Gipsies* littering under Hedges,
> Are so disqualified by Fate
> To rise in *Church*, or *Law*, or *State*,
> As he, whom *Phebus* in his Ire
> Hath *blasted* with poetick Fire.   (33–42)

Several readers of the *Rapsody* have expressed dismay with this passage and have argued that when we compare it, as Swift clearly intended we should, with the exalted lines that immediately precede it, the result is a muddle from which it is impossible to guess what Swift's view of poetry really was as he wrote the *Rapsody*. The situation is not, in fact, so desperate as that, but it is true that Swift was trying to do too many things at once within this short passage. On the one hand, he was savagely mocking the ironically misguided selfishness of such men as leave their proper callings in order to pursue so unremunerative a vocation as poetry. On the other hand, he was angrily lashing an age grown so corrupt that it starves its true as well as its false poets. Individually, of course, neither Swift's mockery of false poets nor his anger with his age conflicts with his preceding claims for the profound significance of poetry. But it must be admitted that Swift's further attempt to draw a clear connection between the activity of false poets and the corruption of a world that starves its true poets does produce such a conflict. Momentarily adopting as his own the techniques of false poets, Swift takes the special rhetoric with which true poets have traditionally defended their calling and jams that rhetoric with ugliness, corrupting it in order to define a corrupt world. Regarded in one way, this technique is brilliantly successful; it simultaneously shows us a poisonous rhetoric and lashes the age that rhetoric poisons. But, by shifting his ground so rapidly, Swift is asking a great deal of his reader. Thus when, not many lines later, he compares the plight of poems to that of chickens, quickly devoured and as quickly forgotten (61–70), it is hard to remember that he is satirizing, not poetry itself, but rather the similes that bad poets make and that his age unthinkingly swallows down.

By line seventy, that is, both Swift's strategy in the *Rapsody* and the particular difficulties inherent in that strategy have emerged. Loosing in his own lines, against the moral stance of his own poem, the sort of incongruous comparison and corruption of poetic vocabulary he found destructive in Young's satire, Swift illustrates brilliantly the capacity of poetic abuse to transform sense into nonsense, moral wisdom into folly. But the brilliance of Swift's illustration inevitably comes near to ruining its effectiveness. For such is the destructive and self-destructive power of poetic nonsense that within Swift's first seventy lines it threatens to overwhelm that view of human vocation and poetic function with which the poem began, and thus to make of the *Rapsody* not a controlled illustration of the power of corruption but simply a muddle.

By line seventy, however, Swift himself was aware of the threat that his technique posed to the sense of his poem. And his response to this threat was, though abrupt, effective enough. He merely shifted the narration of the poem from his own voice to that of a new narrator, who is introduced as an "old experienc'd Sinner." This shift in narration does not, in fact, noticeably affect the primary narrative technique of the *Rapsody* as it has been established by the first seventy lines of the poem. Through the sinner's voice, Swift continues to illustrate the effects of poetic abuse by demonstrating that abuse in action. But, because Swift's new narrator is specifically and unmistakably labeled an "old experienc'd Sinner," his corrupt lines illustrate poetic abuse without threatening the moral basis of Swift's poem. Further, because the sinner is introduced as an instructor, his entrance into the poem gives it a sense of direction and organization which its first seventy lines noticeably lack. The poem assumes the easily recognizable shape of that genre of instructional poetry of which

Horace's *Ars Poetica* is both the progenitor and the chief glory. Like Horace, who undertook the *Ars Poetica* in order to teach one or more of the Pisos to know his own poetic strength, the experienced sinner of Swift's *Rapsody* is introduced to us as one who is to teach fledgling poets

> Of diff'rent Spirits to discern,
> And how distinguish, which is which,
> The Poet's Vein, or scribling Itch.   (72–74)

Thus, from the sinner's introduction follows the general ordonnance of the remainder of the poem as it passes from instruction in the arts of poetry, propaganda, and criticism to a survey of the present state of letters and a concluding exemplary panegyric.

Of course, the sinner's rhapsody is like Horace's *Ars Poetica* in general ordonnance only. For the sinner's voice is designed to be exactly what Swift's voice was before—an active demonstration of the power of poetic abuse to translate sound doctrine into chaos and blasphemy. Thus, even the sinner's opening instructions to his protégés significantly damage the Horatian advice from which they are drawn:

> Consult yourself, and if you find
> A powerful Impulse urge your Mind,
> Impartial judge within your Breast
> What Subject you can manage best;
> Whether your Genius most inclines
> To Satire, Praise, or hum'rous Lines;
> To Elegies in mournful Tone,
> Or Prologue sent from Hand unknown.
> Then rising with *Aurora's* Light,
> The Muse invok'd, sit down to write;
> Blot out, correct, insert, refine,
> Enlarge, diminish, interline;
> Be mindful, when Invention fails,
> To scratch your Head, and bite your Nails.   (77–90)

To a reader conversant with Horace's *Ars Poetica* much of this advice must seem familiar. The first eight lines, for example, closely parallel in import the following Horatian advice:

Let poets match their Subject to their Strength,
And often try what Weight they can support,
And what their Shoulders are too weak to bear,
[For] After a serious and judicious Choice,
Method and Eloquence will never fail.[13]

And again the sinner's exhortation to his pupils to "Blot out,
correct, insert, refine" is, in its very wording, reminiscent of
Horace's admonition in the *Ars Poetica*, not to praise any poem
which has not been through many days and many blots, *multa
dies et multa litura*.

But, in fact, it is our very familiarity with and reverence for
Horace's advice that make the final, jingling, meaningless couplet of the sinner's counsel so disturbing. For while the sinner's
sudden collapse into trivia does not really detract from the validity of the Horatian advice he has mouthed, it does muddy that
advice. Horace's counsel, after all, is founded on his belief that to
be excellent, both poets and poems must reflect the nature of
things as things really are: thus, the poet must follow his proper
calling, the poem must truly illustrate its subject. But the sinner's
counsel covertly suggests that there really is no "nature of
things" at all. For by mindlessly appropriating Horace's advice
and then mixing in his own nonsense to make the whole serve
him as an impressive opening, the sinner insidiously undermines
the moral view of poetry's nature and function that Horace's
advice both inculcates and assumes. The sinner's method, that is,
is itself a sly argument based on the premise that since anything
can go anywhere, the end of poetry is not truth but show.

This perverse premise becomes increasingly apparent as the
sinner develops his advice. For him, it becomes clear, poetry has
no end but to enhance the reputations and fill the purses of its
practitioners. "Fame" or "profitable Game" are his sole terms
for poetry's proper goals. By a poem's success or failure to
achieve these goals he judges its worth; indeed, he bends the very
terms of traditional poetics so that they can achieve these goals
only, allowing the commitment to ordered reality which once
informed those terms to simply leak away. Thus, for example, to

13. Translation by Wentworth Dillon, fourth Earl of Roscommon. *Poems by the
Earl of Roscommon* (London: J. Tonson, 1717), p. 187.

the sinner as well as to Horace, the ability of poets to praise
and blame is an essential element of their poetic craft. For
Horace, however, the poetic function of praise and blame is
subservient to the teaching of moral universals, to teaching "love
to virtue and hatred to vice." But for the sinner there are no
moral universals. Rather, for him good and evil, true and false,
virtue and vice are only so many names—terms of vague approbation or disapprobation to be assigned in accordance with the
selfish interests of a particular poet. Thus, he claims (and Edward
Young's practice seems to support his claim) that a prince is not
to be called virtuous only when he actively participates in real
virtue. Rather, "A Prince," he instructs his pupils, "the Moment
he is crown'd" is said to inherit "ev'ry Virtue round" because to
say so is one of the ways to thrive.

The sinner's advice, then, though couched in Horace's terms
and in the format of the *Ars Poetica*, is finally an absolute perver-
sion of Horatian counsel. Horace encouraged men to see that that
which is absolutely good is also necessarily their own good. The
sinner encourages his pupils to determine their own good on the
basis of immediate cash value. But to say that the sinner perverts
Horace's counsel is not necessarily to prove that the sinner is
wrong. For just as Horace's poetry inculcates and assumes a
view of the world that is decorous, ordered, and vocational, so the
sinner's advice presupposes its own world view. Like Hobbes,
the sinner proposes that nature is fundamentally lawless and consequently savage. "*Hobbes* clearly proves," the sinner states,

> that ev'ry Creature
> Lives in a State of War by Nature.
> The Greater for the Smallest watch,
> But meddle seldom with their Match.   (319–22)

And the frightening thing is that the sinner's view has much to
recommend it. The *Rapsody* itself, after all, was written because
men do praise bad kings, defend bad ministers, plagiarize, lie,
cheat, steal, and murder. Men live, that is, as if Hobbes were
right and there were no common rule of good and evil to be taken
from the nature of things themselves. It is not, then, that the
sinner is wrong in his observations of the actions of men. There,
it is to be feared, he is right enough. But he is wrong about
nature.

In the *Rapsody*, Swift offers us three different modes through which we can perceive the quality and significance of the sinner's wrongness. Of course, the three modes tend to overlap: the *Rapsody*, after all, is all one poem. Nevertheless, it is useful to distinguish these modes, to observe that the first is didactic (Swift refutes what the sinner says), that the second is figurative (Swift illustrates what is wrong with what the sinner says by the images he makes him use to say it), and that the third is dramatic (Swift demonstrates the effect of the sinner's advice by showing us what becomes of the sinner).

Of these three modes, the didactic appears at first to be the least well integrated into the structure of the poem. Nominally, at least, the last 400 lines of the *Rapsody* are all spoken by the old experienced sinner. Yet, because the sinner is merely a creature of Swift's necessity, Swift felt no real commitment to maintain the integrity of his voice. Rather, quite often in the course of the poem, Swift interrupts the sinner in order to state what are clearly his own sentiments. For example, in the lines immediately preceding the poem's final panegyric Swift exclaims (in radical opposition to the sinner's earlier advice about princes),

> O, what Indignity and Shame
> To prostitute the Muse's Name,
> By flatt'ring [kings] whom Heaven design'd
> The Plagues and Scourges of Mankind.
> Bred up in Ignorance and Sloth
> And ev'ry Vice that nurses both.   (405–10)

Considered in itself, this outburst is nearly awkward in its obvious didacticism. Its sole purpose, so considered, is to provide us a standard by which to understand the blasphemous perversity of the sinner's panegyric to royalty which immediately succeeds it. But this passage should not be considered only in itself. It is, after all, one of a group of similar passages. For example, when the sinner maintains that "*Law* and *Gospel* both determine/All Virtues lodge in royal Ermine" (227–28), Swift immediately adds his own damning qualification to that opinion: "(I mean the Oracles of Both,/Who shall depose it upon oath)" (229–30). Or again, when the sinner advises young poets to

Display the blessings of the Nation,
And praise the whole Administration,
Extoll ye Bench of Bishops round,
Who at them rail bid God Confound,

Swift immediately undermines his advice by extending it:

To Bishop-Haters answer thus
(The only Logick us'd by Us)
What tho' they don't believe in Christ
Deny them Protestants—thou ly'st.[14]

Because, then, such interruptions are continuous through the sinner's counsel, they tend to become absorbed into the sinner's voice itself. So, in the following advice to unsuccessful poets, we do not readily distinguish between the first five lines, which are in character for the sinner, and the last line, which is clearly Swift's:

. . . tho' you miss your third Essay,
You need not throw your Pen away.
Lay now aside all Thoughts of Fame,
To spring more profitable Game.
From Party-Merit seek Support;
The *vilest* Verse thrives best at Court.   (181–86, italics mine)

Rather, we hear one voice in these lines, a voice that speaks at despairing cross-purposes with itself. Vacillating between practical advice and moral disgust, that voice achieves the bitterly cynical tone that marks it throughout the poem. And significantly, that tone is a perpetual antidote to the sinner's poisonous advice; for it suggests the miserable dilemma into which his own counsel has led him.

In fact, then, within the full sweep of the *Rapsody*, Swift's simple, didactic refutations of the sinner blend almost completely with the figurative and dramatic modes by which Swift illustrates the sinner's wrongness. Ultimately, that is, the end of all three modes is to make us see that to suppose, as the sinner does, that nature is savage, aimless, and improvident does not make her so

14. These lines are among those Swift omitted in the version of the poem printed during his life. The reason for their omission is obviously political. But see Sir Harold Williams's headnote, *Swift's Poems*, 2:639.

but does render our lives miserable. Thus, to pass to Swift's second mode, the images with which the sinner seasons his perverse advice to young poets are not only corruptions of traditional images used in classic advice; they tend to be disastrously self-fulfilling prophecies as well.

For example, the most striking, insistent, and frightening of the patterned metaphors that inform the sinner's advice is that one by which he brings all the acts and arts of life down to the single level of fornication. This process of metaphorical flattening begins early in the poem, when the sinner, debauching the traditionally commendatory image of the poem as child, identifies poetry instead as "The Product of your Toil and Sweating;/A Bastard of your own begetting" (115–16). By this piece of metaphorical adulteration the sinner deprives a traditional image of its real import; that is, he obliterates the distinction between legitimate and illegitimate art which the image originally suggested.[15] And what we must see about this debauchery is that while it is crude it is not arbitrary. Rather, it is the logical consequence of the sinner's basic assumptions; for to assume as the sinner does that nothing is, in itself, naturally good or ill is to effectively obliterate all distinction. Thus, by the end of the poem we learn that for the sinner, gypsies littering under hedges, poets writing panegyrics, and princes promiscuously generating heirs "*Britain* to secure/As long as Sun and Moon endure" are all engaged in essentially the same activity. Applying his metaphorical leveler to a multitude of human activities, the sinner reduces them all to basic animal sexuality. Thus, the sinner's imagery illustrates *first* the terrible poverty of his own vision; in his vision of the world all distinctions disappear—duchesses, suburb wenches, kings, poets, cuckolds, graceless children, and spawn are all huddled together beneath his terrible contempt.

Of course, a large part of the terror implicit in the sinner's metaphorical flattening of all human activity to one bastardized level is that it reflects more than the merely logical consequences of his own assumptions. To be sure, given those assumptions, the sinner can see the world no other way than he does; that is why his metaphors illustrate, before anything else, the dreadful wrong-

15. For the history and significance of this simile see Ernst Robert Curtius, *European Literature and the Latin Middle Ages*, trans. Willard Trask, Bollingen Series, no. 36 (New York: Pantheon, 1953), pp. 132–34.

ness of his own vision. But, the sinner is not only a corrupt man; he is a corrupt man in a corrupt society. Therefore, the wildly reductive images by which he depicts his society not only illustrate the poverty of his own assumptions; rather, his imagery also rightly portrays an England that at one end of its social spectrum experienced a remarkable increase in gypsy population,[16] while at the other end of that spectrum it was ruled by a king of whose father men at Oxford once cried "the King a cuckold: the prince a bastard."[17] Thus, frighteningly, the sinner's depiction of England is at once illustrative of his own depravity and strictly true. In the sinner, that is, Swift created England's perfect satirist; for through the sinner's depiction of England, Swift shows us both *how* the sinner's Hobbes-like assumptions about nature flatten human experience, and *what* the consequences of such assumptions must be in human folly and suffering when they are adopted by a whole society.

Finally, however, as we watch the depraved sinner depict a depraved England, we are led back to that question which, I have suggested, Edward Young's *Love of Fame* raised in Swift's own mind. For though the sinner's portrait of England overrun by a tattered mob of bastards, poets, godless prelates, princes, and peers damningly illustrates both his own corruption and its effects, it simultaneously raises the question whether there is any end to such corruption, any limit below which the sinner and the mad society he depicts cannot sink.

Of course, for the sinner the answer to this question is "no." Thus, though he views with contempt the vicious world he depicts, the sinner nevertheless both cultivates and recommends that others cultivate precisely that savage and improvident view of nature and human nature that, when acted upon, produces that world. The sinner, that is, because he is corrupt, is locked by his own perverse will into the set of assumptions that Swift thought was responsible for "most of the miseries and misfortunes in life."

But Swift himself was not similarly bound, And, therefore, he was able to make of the *Rapsody* something infinitely more posi-

16. See Michael Walzer, *The Revolution of the Saints* (Cambridge: Harvard University Press, 1965), particularly pp. 216–18.
17. For a narration of this incident see John David Griffith Davies, *A King in Toils* (London: L. Drummond, 1938), p. 41.

tive than a mere demonstration of the misery attendant upon the sinner's assumptions. In itself, such a demonstration could, at best, only induce us to believe that the sinner's assumptions are wrong. But, seen whole, the *Rapsody* is a positive, dramatic demonstration of Swift's belief that this is God's world.

Of course, it is precisely against Swift's belief in a provident and vocational world that all the sinner's assumptions about nature and human nature finally militate. Indeed, in the very lines with which Swift first introduces the sinner, he covertly suggests that for him there is no God but man, no law but human will. In those lines, we recall, Swift introduces us to an instructor who offers to teach new attempters

> Of diff'rent Spirits to discern,
> And how distinguish, which is which,
> The Poet's Vein, or scribling Itch. (72–74)

That the offer sounds very like Horace's offer to teach his pupil to know the scope and function of his poetic gifts is what we have already remarked. In fact, however, this offer is both the complete reverse of what Horace offers to teach and a piece of absolute blasphemy.

What makes this offer blasphemous is the sinner's willingness to try to teach precisely the *gift* "of diff'rent Spirits to discern"; for that is not a gift to be taught. Indeed, that gift is alluded to in what is perhaps the most famous Christian statement on the nature of vocation. Writing to the Corinthians, Paul urges each man among them to be satisfied with his own particular spiritual gifts since, he argues, "while there are diversity of gifts . . . it is the same God which worketh all in all." Illustrating this thesis Paul asserts that although "to one is given by the Spirit the working of miracles; to another prophecy, *to another the discerning of spirits* . . . [nevertheless] in all these worketh that one and the self-same Spirit, dividing to each man severally, *as He will*" (1 Cor. 12, italics mine). Thus, in Paul's context, since the gift "of diff'rent Spirits to discern" rests in God's hands to be given or withheld, it would be presumptuous for any man to offer to teach it. Therefore, by introducing the sinner as one who will attempt to teach this gift, Swift delineates from the outset the atheistical bent of the sinner's advice.

What we must remember, then, as we read the sinner's tortuous advice, and the equally tortuous depiction of his society which accompanies that advice, is that neither the miserable cynicism of his tone nor the miserable state of affairs he depicts is an inevitable consequence of the human situation. Rather, both his tone and the effects of his advice are the consequences of preferring one's own will before the harmonizing spirit of God as St. Paul depicts it. So to prefer one's will is, quite literally, to create one's own hell; for traditionally hell is merely where God is not. And that multitudes of Swift's contemporaries had indeed made their own hells is evident from the sinner's depiction of them. In their perpetual coil of aimless, swarming, darkling war their state differs from that of hell itself only in that they have not yet died. Vocationless, they stumble through a nightmare landscape deprived of all guidance save that provided them by a king who "As soon as you can hear his Knell,/ . . . turns *Devil* in Hell," and by a court which at the king's death will be similarly "transform'd to Imps" and translated to a hell "Where, in this Scene of endless Woe,/They [will] ply their former Arts below" (205–6, 208–10). To choose to please such a court, to try to live by its fashion, is equivalent to choosing utter damnation; indeed, according to the example of Edward Young (who "must torture his Invention,/To flatter Knaves, or lose his *Pension*"), it is to live the hellish life of Tantalus.

Of course, it is towards precisely this hellish choice and this hellish life that the sinner encourages his protégés. That is, within the *Rapsody* the sinner's dramatic role is to act as Satan to his fallen world. Seen this way, Swift's sinner assumes his most frightening proportions and the very title Swift gave him—"an old experienc'd Sinner"—becomes ominous indeed. But, at the same time, seen this way, the sinner's career through the *Rapsody* does finally delineate the ultimate end of corruption in much the same way and just as positively as does Satan's career through Milton's *Paradise Lost*. Like Milton's Satan, Swift's sinner begins the *Rapsody* big with promise, offering to teach his disciples arts which are in God's gift only. But, again like Milton's Satan, the sinner is in constant decline. Proffering his own disciples ever less noble stations for ever more base reasons, he encourages his protégés first to be poets, then to be paid hack writers, then to be empty critics for vanity's sake.

Finally, then, like Satan's decline in *Paradise Lost* or the increasingly trivial temptations Satan offers Christ in *Paradise Regained*, the sinner's advice merely defines the ultimate limitation of corruption—its inability to destroy anything without simultaneously destroying itself. Appropriately, the sinner concludes his counsel by following his own bad advice and crawling panegyrically before a corrupt monarch. From this posture, in not too farfetched parody of Edward Young, the sinner offers up his last defiance of God. Allying himself with Thomas Woolston, who rejected Christ because Christ's miracles did not suit his reason, the sinner makes overt at last that absolute denial of God's immanence implicit in the lines with which Swift introduced him. "I'll give my monarch butter weight," he shouts,

> And Reason good; for many a Year
> [Christ] never intermeddl'd here;
> Nor, tho' his Priests be duly paid,
> Did ever we *desire* his Aid:
> We now can better do without him,
> Since *Woolston* gave us Arms to rout him. (489–94)

Of course, this utterly damning denial finishes the sinner. For, in the end, the truth of Swift's poem is that what is not of God cannot stand. Thus, immediately upon uttering this denial of God's sustaining and merciful immanence, the sinner's voice itself disappears into an eternal hiatus. The poem ends with only the words *"Caetera desiderantur"*—words which sound, in Swift's church Latin, very like a hiss and final groan.

Conclusion

ON THE TOPIC of the propriety of writing satire, it is very easy to quote Swift against himself. Thus, in *Thoughts on Religion* we find the following two admonitions to a wise silence: "Violent zeal of truth hath an hundred to one odds to be either petulancy, ambition, or pride"; and "There is a degree of corruption wherein some nations, bad as the world is, will proceed to an amendment; until which time particular men should be quiet."[1] In Swift's correspondence, however, we can hear these admonitions rebutted a thousand times. "Drown the World," Swift writes Pope in 1725, "I am not content with despising it, but I would anger it if I could with safety."[2] And referring primarily to *Gulliver's Travels*, he also writes that "the chief end I propose to myself in all my labors is to vex the world rather than divert it, and if I could compass that designe without hurting my own person or Fortune I would be the most Indefatigable writer you have ever seen."[3]

Easy as it is to do, though, it is pointless to amass many of these contradictory passages; they illustrate only what Swift himself well knew. From the beginning of his literary career he was conscious of the disparity between his often basely motivated fury at particular instances of human failure and his belief in a general providence. Yet though he recognized that to rail at man and to trust in God are usually oppugnant activities, he was tempera-

1. *Swift's Prose*, 9:261.
2. *Swift's Correspondence*, 3:117.
3. Ibid., p. 103.

mentally compelled to attempt both. Too much a part of this world to daff it aside, and too pious to despair of it, he had no real choice but to try to reform in it what he thought he could reform. To this task he brought what he had: anger and wit, pride and piety, envy and real concern. From this task, he tried to save himself.

To trace the ways Swift sought to temper his hubristic indignation with the world into a morally responsible reaction to it has been the chief effort of this book. Its chief argument has been that, in his verse at least, this attempt itself is Swift's most significant human lesson. For watching him struggle against the temptation to reduce the world to the shape of his own anger, envy, pride, and fear, we learn not only to scorn the particular follies and vices that move his fury, but also to recognize how complex the task of virtuous behavior really is. This lesson, more than any other, is the special mark of Swift's poetry.

Of course, Swift teaches this lesson very differently in his early verse and in the poems of his maturity. In his first poems Swift himself is genuinely baffled by the complexity of moral action. Helpless to do otherwise, he confounds his own peculiar vices with his general defense of virtue and only primitively recognizes that the resulting poems reflect his own mixed state much more powerfully than they achieve any conscious end. With maturity, however, he comes to recognize in his own mixed reactions to the world a central statement of human identity—a demonstration that, system-makers to the contrary, no moral situation can ever be simple for man. Having achieved this recognition, he is able to create a body of verse that transforms his own failures into lessons by exhibiting those failures along with the vices he attacks.

In maturity, Swift grows so proficient in writing such verse that he himself seems finally to transcend the moral dilemma that his verse dramatizes. Able simultaneously to revile what he hates and yet to place his abhorrence so that its folly is apparent, he achieves what we must feel to be a significant and a liberating victory over his own envy, anger, and pride. Further, by analogy, he is able to extend this victory so that it illuminates and transforms not only his moral failures but all the apparent limits of mortal life as well. The loss of place, causes, friendships, love, and life itself become in Swift's verse occasions not for a proud and removed stoicism but rather for that triumphant act of mind by which he finds his meaning in his suffering and offers that meaning to us through his art.

Yet highly as we must value the achievement of Swift's verse, we must not overstate that achievement lest we lose it in our very praise of it. For finally, like all art, Swift's poetry is necessarily both reactive and limited. It can transform present fury into lesson and present loss into wisdom, but it cannot finally change either the stuff of human experience or the life of the heart. That is why all Swift's battles must be fought again and again, and his liberty rewon each day from the envy, indignation, and pride that are the inevitable consequences of a moral involvement in the life of this world.

In *The Legion Club*, Swift himself tells us clearly enough what this process of successive struggles must mean over a long period of time. Of course, before it is anything else, *The Legion Club* is a masterpiece of libel. In it, Swift takes his contemporaries, members of the Irish Parliament, and transplants them as demons and madmen within a fantastic and allusive landscape that is part modern madhouse, part classical Hades, and part Christian hell.[4] Thus, Swift effects in the poem a marvelously imaginative vengeance on those whom he hates. Depriving them of their humanity and yet insisting on their actual existence, he traps his victims neatly and inextricably between their everyday identities on the one hand, and the grossly perverse enemies of God that he portrays them to be on the other.

This is masterful punishment, of course, but it is also venomous art. Swift knew it to be so, and so must we. Indeed, we miss half the force of the poem, and more than half of its significance, if in deference to Swift we fail to register its violent excessiveness. For by that very excessiveness Swift represents for us what his long battle with a wicked world has made of him. Cursing and sneering, spurning and lashing, he has become what he portrays himself to be in his poem—the maddest of those mad whom he excoriates.

To say this, however, is not to say that *The Legion Club*,

4. Peter J. Schakel has explored the allusions in *The Legion Club* thoroughly in his essay "Virgil and the Dean: Christian and Classical Allusion in the Legion Club," *SP* 70 (October 1973):427–38. Schakel, however, though he finds the poem's satire to be "venomous," thinks the poem less reflexive, more self-justifying than I do.

Swift's last great poem, is simply an unjust performance. Swift works hard in the poem, mostly through allusion, to assure us that the men whom he attacks really are wicked and thus comparable to those enemies of man and God whom Virgil placed in Hades and Christ drove from the Temple. In his portrait of himself, however, Swift works equally hard to demonstrate that though his attack is justifiable and even necessary, it is also finally self-corrupting. In effect, then, in *The Legion Club* Swift exhibits a terrible paradox: he shows us that when called on to participate in a world that moves horror, pity, indignation, and contempt, good men like himself must be undone if they respond to what they see, and be undone if they do not.

This is a tragic perception. But as Swift dramatizes it, it is not a despairing one. Rather, in his dramatization of this perception Swift captures the best glory of classical thought and the hope of Jerusalem. For by portraying himself as an exhausted old man, now tossed by mad energy and now filled with contempt, Swift exhibits that last, painful knowledge of himself which is the crowning achievement of natural man. And by concluding his poem with the hope that Satan may rise up against his own—"May their God, the Devil confound em"—he prays for precisely that division of Satan's house which he cannot accomplish but which he knows Christ has promised.

Index

Titles of Swift's works are entered separately. Pages of most extended discussion of an individual poem by Swift are given in boldface type.

Acts of the Apostles, in *To Mr. Congreve*, 47–49
Addison, Joseph: revision of *Baucis and Philemon*, 72–74; and *Vanbrug's House*, 76, 83
Alchemy: in *The Poet*, 40–42, 47; in *Verses wrote in a . . . Table-Book*, 58–59
Allen, Don Cameron, and Noah legend, 101*n*. *See also* Noah's Flood
Amphion, in *Vanbrug's House*, 72–95 passim
Ancients and Moderns, Battle of, in *Vanbrug's House*, 85–86
Apollo, character in *Stella's Birth-Day. A great Bottle of Wine*, 134–35
Arbuthnot, Dr.: S.'s compliments to, 164–65, 168, 179; and pun on name, 168
Architect, The, 83–85. *See also Vanbrug's House*
Athenian Society, 20–22
Augustine, Saint, and Noah's Flood, 101. *See also* Noah's Flood

Bacchus, character in *Stella's Birth-Day. A great Bottle of Wine*, 135

Ballad on the Game of Traffick, A, 65–69
Baucis and Philemon, 4, **72–75**, 81–83
Benevolism, 161–62. *See also* Cumberland, Richard
Berkeley, Lady Betty, and *To the Tune of the Cutpurse*, 65–72 passim
Berkeley, second Earl of, character in *The Humble Petition of Frances Harris*, 60–67 passim
Blenheim: and Vanbrugh's art, 91; mentioned, 76, 79, 84
Broughton, Panthea Reid. *See* Fischer, Panthea Reid
Bullitt, John M., 143*n*
Burke, Edmund, and modern architecture, 79–80
Butler, Samuel, 131

Cadenus and Vanessa, **110–20**; and S.'s view of sexual love, 5; and *Astrophel and Stella*, 121–22; and *To Stella, Visiting me*, 139; and *Stella's Birth-Day, 1726/27*, 146
Carnochan, W. B., 1*n*
Caroline, Queen: misunderstands *On Poetry*, 177–78, 182; praised by Young, 181

Cato (Uticensis): and Lucan, 37; and Swift, 37–38
Cibber, Colley, and S.'s imagined death, 158–68
Colmer, Robert G., and meditation on death, 157
Congreve, William: audience for *To Mr. Congreve*, 39, 49; subject of *To Mr. Congreve*, 44–46
Copernicus, Nicolaus, and *Ode to . . . Sancroft*, 31–32
I Corinthians, significance in *On Poetry*, 195
Cowley, Abraham: compared to Pindar, 10–11, 13; as Christian, 11; *Brutus* discussed, 11–14; mentioned, 2, 8, 15
Crashaw, Richard, and Stella's verse, 127
Cromwell, Oliver, and Cowley's *Brutus*, 12–14
Cumberland, Richard, and benevolism, 161–62, 164, 171
Cutts, John (Baron Cutts of Gowvan), 4

Dancourt, Florent Carton, and Vanbrugh, 76, 91 and *n*, 92
Da Padova, Andrea di Pieto, 78. *See also* Palladianism
Davis, Herbert, 7*n*
De Granada, Fray Luis, and meditation on death, 157
Delany, Patrick: and S.'s character, 1; on Bacchus, 135
Denham, Sir John, 2–3
Description of a City Shower, A, **95–109**, 110
Description of a Salamander, A, 4
Deucalion's Flood, 99–100. *See also* Noah's Flood; Ovid
Dingley, Rebecca, 123. *See also* Johnson, Esther
Doing Good, and *Verses on the Death*, 162–63
Donne, John: his verse compared to Stella's, 127; his meditations on death, 157–58, 165–66, 171
Dryden, John: and S. as poet, 19; on satire, 180; mentioned, 60
Dunton, John, and *Ode to the Athenian Society*, 20

Ecclesiastes, in *Verses on the Death*, 153

Ehrenpreis, Irvin, 7*n*; on S.'s *Shower*, 95–97; on Esther Johnson, 124
Epistle to a Lady, 2
Evans, Dr. Abel, 79. *See also* Vanbrugh, Sir John
Exodus, 10

Fall of Man, and *Ode to . . . Temple*, 23–26
Faulkner, George, 62, 100
Fischer, Panthea Reid. *See* Broughton, Panthea Reid
Flood, the. *See* Noah's Flood
Ford, Charles, 41
Frazer, Sir James George, and "Sawing the Old Woman," 133

Garrard, Samuel, and S.'s view of providence, 175
Gay, John: S.'s compliments to, 154, 163–65, 179; mentioned, 5–6
Genesis, and Fall of Man, 23–24
Gilbert, Jack G., 167*n*
Glanville, Joseph, and *Stella's Birth-Day, 1724/25*, 137
Glorious Revolution, the, and William Sancroft, 28–29
Grean, Stanley, 161*n*

Harris, Frances: as character in *The Humble Petition*, 60–65; and in *Ballad on . . . Traffick*, 67
Harris, Kathryn, 7*n*
Henley, Rev. John, and S.'s imagined death, 168
Hervey, John (Baron Hervey of Ickworth), and *On Poetry*, 177–78
History of Vanbrug's House, The, 83–85. *See also Vanbrug's House*
Hobbes, Thomas: and Lucan, 37*n*; and old experienced sinner, 190
Horace: and *Occasioned by Sir William Temple's . . . Recovery*, 51*n*; and *On Poetry*, 184–85, 187–90, 195
Horrell, Joseph, 7*n*, 111*n*
Howe, John Grubham, in *Ballad on . . . Traffick*, 67–68
Hudibras, 131
Humble Petition of Frances Harris, The, 4, **59–65**
Hume, Robert D., 153*n*, 164*n*

In Sickness, 156

James II, and William Sancroft, 28, 29

Janus, compared to virtue, 150

Job, and *To Stella, Visiting me*, 143 and *n*

Johnson, Bridget (mother of Esther J.), 123

Johnson, Esther: and Esther Vanhomrigh, 112, 146–47; recipient of S.'s poems, 122, 123; relationship with S., 123–27; as poet, 127–30; S.'s prayer for, 159; mentioned, 5

Johnson, Samuel, 19, 26

Jones, Gareth, 111*n*

Jonson, Ben: S.'s use of *Bartholomew Fayre*, 70–72; and *To Penshurst*, 93; mentioned, 185

Journal to Stella, 97

Jove: character in *Vanbrug's House*, 81; modified, 87; and faith, 89

Jude, and *Verses on the Death*, 172–73

Jung, Carl Gustav, and alchemy, 42 and *n*

Kuhn, Thomas S., and Ptolemaic cosmology, 31*n*

Lady Betty Berkeley finding in the Authors Room some Verses Unfinished, 65, **69–72**

La Rochefoucauld, François, duc de: and *Verses on the Death*, 152–54, 159, 169; S.'s opinion of, 160; and Christianity, 160–61

Legion Club, The, 5, 200–201

London, as Troy-Nouvant, 107

Louis XIV, in *Ode to the King*, 18

Lucan, amended by S., 37–38

Luke, in *Verses on the Death*, 170

Mack, Maynard, 154*n*

Marlborough, Duke of, and Vanbrugh, 84

Martz, Louis, and meditation on death, 156–57

Marvell, Andrew, *Upon Appleton House*, 93

Mayhew, George P., 56*n*, 177*n*

Mell, Donald C., 153*n*

Michelangelo, and Noah's Flood, 102

Milton, John: S.'s use of invocation to light, 35; and Noah's Flood, 98–109 passim; and Satan, 196–97

Montgomery, Robert L., 121*n*

Moore (James Moore Smythe), and S.'s imagined death, 158–68

Moor Park: emblem in early odes, 26–27, 47, 50; and Esther Johnson, 123–24

Murry, John Middleton, 7*n*, 153*n*

Muse, in S.'s early odes, 20–21, 27, 44–46, 53–54

Neoplatonic imagery, in *Stella's Birth-Day, 1726/27*, 149

Newton, Sir Isaac, and Fall of Man, 161

Noah's Flood: and *Ode to the Athenian Society*, 20; and S.'s *Shower*, 98–109 passim; and Christian commentary, 101–3, 109; and *Paradise Lost*, 102–4

Norwood, Gilbert, 9*n*

Oath of Allegiance (to William and Mary), and William Sancroft, 29

Occasioned by Sir William Temple's Late Illness and Recovery, 3, 39, **49–54**, 55, 56, 57

Ode to Dr. William Sancroft, 2, **28–38**, 39, 149

Ode to Sir William Temple, 19, **22–28**, 29, 38, 39

Ode to the Athenian Society, **19–22**, 26, 104–5

Ode to the King, 3, **15–19**, 21, 32, 54

O Hehir, Brendan, 96–97, 105

Ohlin, Peter, 111*n*

Old experienced sinner: narrator of *On Poetry*, 178; S.'s use of, 189; and Hobbes, 190, 194; S.'s exposure of, 191–97; perverter of Scripture, 195–96; as Satan, 196–97

On Mutual Subjection, 164–65, 182–83

On Poetry: A Rapsody, **177–97**. See also Old experienced sinner

On Stella's Birth-Day, 1718/19, 130–33

Ovid: and Cupid's arrows, 58; and *Baucis and Philemon*, 73–74; and S.'s *Shower*, 99–100; and *Cadenus and Vanessa*, 111*n*; and *Stella's Birth-Day, 1726/27*, 150

Padova, Andrea di Pieto da, 78. See also Palladianism

Palladianism, and *Vanbrug's House*, 78–79
Pallas: in *Cadenus and Vanessa*, 113–18; and *To Stella, Visiting me*, 138–39
Paulson, Ronald, 7*n*, 153*n*
Peter, Saint, 47–49
Pindar: odes, 8–10; compared to Cowley, 10–11, 13; compared to S., 15
Plutarch, 140–41
Poem as child, in *On Poetry*, 193
Poet, The, 39–43
Pope, Alexander: S.'s compliments to, 154, 163–65, 168; and La Rochefoucauld, 159–60; mentioned, 11, 179 and *n*, 198
Provoked Wife, The (Vanbrugh), 91
Psalms, and *Verses on the Death*, 171–76
Pulteney, William (Earl of Bath), 164

Rawson, C. J., 178*n*
Reichard, Hugo, 153*n*
Relapse, The (Vanbrugh), 91–92
Retrograde, and *Ode to . . . Sancroft*, 31–32
Reynolds, Richard, 62*n*
Rosenheim, Edward W., 38*n*
Rothstein, Eric, 73–74
Rowe, Nicholas, and meditation on death, 158

Saints, intercession of, 36
Sancroft, Dr. William, 28–38 passim
Savage, Roger, 96–97
Schakel, Peter J.: and *Verses wrote in a . . . Table-Book*, 56*n*; and *Cadenus and Vanessa*, 111*n*; and *Verses on the Death*, 153*n*; and S.'s impartial narrator, 169; and *The Legion Club*, 200*n*
Scouten, Arthur J., 153*n*, 164*n*
Shaftesbury, third Earl of, 161
Shakespeare, William, 21, 47, 185
Sheridan, Thomas, 1
Sidney, Sir Philip, *Astrophel and Stella*, 121–23
Slepian, Barry, 153*n*
Socrates: and piety, 139–40; "what is, is best," 179*n*
Stella. *See* Johnson, Esther

Stella's Birth-Day. A great Bottle of Wine, long buried, being that Day dug up, 133–35
Stella's Birth-Day, 1724/25, 134, 135–38
Stella's Birth-Day, 1726/27, 125, 138, 145–51
Swift, Thomas, 124

Tatler, The, 20, 105
Temple, Sir William: and *Athenian Mercury*, 20; subject in *Ode to . . . Temple*, 25–28; subject in *Occasioned by Sir William Temple's . . . Recovery*, 52–53; mentioned, 123, 124
Theobald, Lewis, and S.'s imagined death, 158, 168
Theriophily, 183
Thoughts on Religion: and sexual love, 116; and death, 156; and satire, 198
Tibullus, 111*n*
Tillotson, John, 36
To Dr. Swift on his birth-day, November 30, 1721 (Esther Johnson), 127–30
To Mr. Congreve, 39, 40, 43–49
To Stella, Visiting me in my Sickness, 126, 138–45
To the Tune of the Cutpurse, 65, 68, 69–72
Troy-Nouvant, 107
Tuveson, Ernest, 161*n*
Tyne, James L., 111*n*, 125*n*, 178*n*

Uphaus, Robert W., 7*n*, 125*n*, 153*n*

Vanbrugh, Sir John, as subject of *Vanbrug's House*, 72–95 passim
Vanbrug's House, 72–95; development, 72–77; first version, 72–82, 84; *The History of Vanbrug's House*, 83–85; final version, 85–95
Vanhomrigh, Esther: in *Cadenus and Vanessa*, 110–20 passim; relationship with S., 111–12; love for S., 116; and Esther Johnson, 146; mentioned, 121
Venus, in *Cadenus and Vanessa*, 112–13, 118–19
Verses on the Death of Dr. Swift,

152–56; and S.'s originality, 2; pane-
gyrist in, 169–70; mentioned, 5
*Verses wrote in a Lady's Ivory Table-
Book*, 56–59
Virgil: and S.'s *Shower*, 96–99, 105–6,
108; and *Cadenus and Vanessa*,
111*n*
*Virtues of Sid Hamet the Magician's
Rod, The*, 4
Vitruvius (Marcus Vitruvius Pollio),
and *Vanbrug's House*, 76, 78, 84

Waingrow, Marshall, and *Verses on
the Death*, 153*n*, 154–55, 160, 163
Waller, Edmund, 78*n*
Walpole, Sir Robert: and S.'s imagined
death, 168; Young's panegyric to,
181
Ward, David, 178*n*

Whitehall, and *Vanbrug's House*, 75,
80
Williams, Sir Harold: and Esther
Johnson's age, 131; and *On Poetry*,
192*n*
William III: subject of *Ode to the
King*, 15–19 passim, 20, 25, 33; and
William Sancroft, 29, 36
Wittkower, Rudolph, 78
Wood, William, 175
Woolston, Thomas: and S.'s imagined
death, 168; and *On Poetry*, 197
Wordsworth, William, 21, 42

Yeats, William Butler: and Esther
Johnson's verse, 127; mentioned,
108
Young, Edward: S.'s opinions of, 178–
82, 187; his gravity, 179*n*; his corruption, 194; as Tantalus, 196